Political Equilibrium

STUDIES IN PUBLIC CHOICE

Gordon Tullock, *Editor*
Virginia Polytechnic Institute and State University

Other volumes in the series:

James M. Buchanan and Richard E. Wagner, *Fiscal Responsibility in Constitutional Democracy*, 1978
Richard B. McKenzie, *The Political Economy of the Educational Process*, 1979
Richard D. Auster and Morris Silver, *The State as a Firm*, 1979
James B. Kau and Paul H. Rubin, *Congressmen, Constituents, and Contributors: The Determinants of Roll Call Voting in the House of Representatives*, 1982
Mary Jean Bowman, ed., *Collective Choice in Education*, 1982

This series, like the journal *Public Choice,* is devoted to an important aspect of the interaction between the disciplines of economics and political science: the application of economic methods of analysis to matters that have traditionally been regarded as political in nature. The objective of these publications is to further the growth of knowledge in this intersection of the social sciences.

Political Equilibrium

Edited by

Peter C. Ordeshook
Carnegie-Mellon University

Kenneth A. Shepsle
Washington University

Kluwer·Nijhoff Publishing

BOSTON/THE HAGUE/LONDON

DISTRIBUTORS FOR NORTH AMERICA:
Kluwer Boston, Inc.
190 Old Derby Street
Hingham, Massachusetts 02043, U.S.A.

DISTRIBUTORS OUTSIDE NORTH AMERICA:
Kluwer Academic Publishers Group
Distribution Centre
P.O. Box 322
3300 AH Dordrecht, The Netherlands

Library of Congress Cataloging in Publication Data

Main entry under title:
Political equilibrium.

  (Studies in public choice; #5)
  Based in part on the Conference on Political
Equilibrium in Honor of William H. Riker, held
in Washington, D.C., Aug. 1980.
  Includes bibliographical references.
  1. Political science—Methodology.
I. Ordeshook, Peter C., 1942- . II. Shepsle,
Kenneth A. III. Conference on Political Equilibrium
in Honor of William H. Riker (1980: Washington,
D.C.) IV. Series.
JA73.P64   320'.01'8   81-12364
ISBN 0-89838-073-1   AACR2

Part I of this volume originally appeared in the *American Political Science Review* 74 (June 1980): 432–58, and is used with permission.

The quote on the opening page of Chapter 7 is from *Gödel, Escher, Bach: An Eternal Golden Braid* by Douglas R. Hofstadter. Copyright © 1979 by Basic Books, Inc. Reprinted by permission of Basic Books, Inc., Publishers, New York.

CONTENTS

Editorial Acknowledgments   ix

Preface
Peter C. Ordeshook and *Kenneth A. Shepsle*   xi

I EQUILIBRIUM AND DISEQUILIBRIUM: THE CONCEPTUAL CONTROVERSY FRAMED

1   Implications from the Disequilibrium of Majority Rule for
    the Study of Institutions
    William H. Riker   3

2   Political Disequilibrium and Scientific Inquiry: A Comment
    on William H. Riker's "Implications from the Disequilibrium
    of Majority Rule for the Study of Institutions"
    Peter C. Ordeshook   25

3   An Altimeter for Mr. Escher's Stairway: A Comment on

William H. Riker's "Implications from the Disequilibrium
of Majority Rule for the Study of Institutions"
Douglas Rae   32

4   A Reply to Ordeshook and Rae
     William H. Riker   41

II ALTERNATIVE VIEWS OF POLITICAL EQUILIBRIUM

5   Equilibrium, Disequilibrium, and the General Possibility
     of a Science of Politics
     Morris P. Fiorina and *Kenneth A. Shepsle*   49

6   The Limitations of Equilibrium Analysis in Political Science
     John H. Aldrich and *David W. Rohde*   65

7   Instability and Development in the Political Economy
     Norman Schofield   96

8   On the Properties of Stable Decision Procedures
     John A. Ferejohn and *David M. Grether*   107

9   An Experimental Test of Solution Theories for Cooperative
     Games in Normal Form
     Richard D. McKelvey and *Peter C. Ordeshook*   118

III EQUILIBRIUM ANALYSIS IN PRACTICE

10   Political Inequality: An Economic Approach
     Peter H. Aranson   133

11   Sophisticated Voting under the Plurality Procedure
     Richard G. Niemi and *Arthur Q. Frank*   151

12   The Role of Imperfections of Health Insurance in Voter
     Support for Safety Regulation
     Melvin J. Hinich   173

13   The Entry Problem in a Political Race
         Steven J. Brams and *Philip D. Straffin, Jr.*   **181**

         References   **197**

         List of Contributors   **209**

EDITORIAL ACKNOWLEDGMENTS

Part I of this volume is reprinted from the *American Political Science Review* 74 (June 1980): 432–458. We gratefully acknowledge the permission to reprint from the journal and its authors.

Parts II and III derive from the Conference on Political Equilibrium in Honor of William H. Riker, coordinated by the editors of this volume and held concurrently with the annual meeting of the American Political Science Association in Washington, D.C., in August 1980. We are most appreciative of a small grant from the University of Rochester that partially covered expenses of the conference. Remaining expenses were absorbed by the participants represented in these pages whose generosity we acknowledge. Several additional participants at the conference provided criticism, ideas, and suggestions that benefited the papers. In their various capacities we acknowledge and thank Professors Theodore Bluhm, Richard Fenno, and Arthur Goldberg of the University of Rochester, Gerald Kramer of the California Institute of Technology, and David Koehler of American University. Professors Goldberg and Niemi of the University of Rochester, in addition, were especially helpful in providing logistical support and in negotiating the grant from the University of Rochester.

We are grateful to Carnegie-Mellon University and Washington University for the resources and support they provided. We are also pleased to acknowledge the help provided during the editorial and production stages by the staff of Kluwer·Nijhoff Publishing.

Finally, to William and Mary Elizabeth Riker, we extend our thanks for giving us the occasion to honor them.

PREFACE

Peter C. Ordeshook and
Kenneth A. Shepsle

If the inaugural date of modern economics is set at 1776 with the publication of Adam Smith's *The Wealth of Nations,* then the analytical tradition in the study of politics is not even a decade younger, commencing nine years later with the publication of the Marquis de Condorcet's *Essai sur l'application de l'analyse à la probabilité des décisions rendues à la pluralité des voix.* The parallel, however, stops there for, unlike Smith and other classical economists who laid an intellectual foundation upon which a century of cumulative scientific research proceeded, analytical political science suffered fits and starts. Condorcet, himself, acknowledges the earlier work (predating the *Essai* by some fourteen years) of Borda and, from time to time during the nineteenth century, their contributions were rediscovered by Dodgson, Nanson, and other political philosophers and arithmeticians. But, by century's end, there was nothing in political science to compare to the grand edifice of general equilibrium theory in neoclassical economics. Despite roots traversing two centuries, then, the analytical study of politics is a twentieth-century affair.

The initial inspiration and insight of Condorcet was seized upon just after World War II by Duncan Black, who wrote several papers on the equilibrium properties of majority rule in specific contexts (Black, 1948a,b). He expanded upon these themes in his now deservedly famous monograph, *The Theory of*

Committees and Elections, and the lesser-known essay with R.A. Newing, *Committee Decisions with Complementary Valuation.* His instinct, in light of Condorcet's long-ago discovery concerning the indeterminacy of majority rule, was to try to discover more specialized contexts in which Condorcet's paradox does not materialize—whence came his famous median voter theorem.

At about the same time, however, a source of "mischief" appeared in the form of Kenneth Arrow's *Social Choice and Individual Values.* Arrow took Condorcet in a direction precisely the opposite of Black, demonstrating that indeterminacy was not merely a property of special examples, but rather a generic property of majority rule and many other aggregation principles.

We have thus witnessed, in the last thirty years, a sort of multidimensional schizophrenia in the analytical study of politics. By far the bulk of research, under the rubric of social choice, seeks to broaden and enrich Arrow's research by establishing the perversity of alternative collective choice mechanisms. On the other hand, following Black, there is a growing body of research that focuses on specific contexts, in terms both of preference and of institutions, in which stability may exist. Yet a third avenue consists of testing the adequacy of equilibrium concepts and, under the rubric of "solution theory," extending those concepts. Overall, one may caricature these researches as "the search for conditions of equilibrium along with the development of the static and dynamic consequences of disequilibrium."

The rationale for this volume is twofold. The first is intellectual. Equilibrium, as we have noted, is the pivotal concept in analytical political science. Conditions under which Condorcet winners, cores, Nash equilibria and the like exist, or fail to exist, define political contexts in which political processes and strategic behavior are set in motion. The essays in Part I, reprinted from a recent symposium in the *American Political Science Review,* set the stage by framing the conceptual controversies that derive from a focus on equilibrium and disequilibrium. The essays in Part II examine critically equilibrium and disequilibrium theories, describing both their limitations and their possibilities. The Fiorina-Shepsle and Aldrich–Rohde papers question, through argument and example, the necessity and sufficiency of equilibriumlike properties for scientific progress in the study of politics. Schofield, responding directly to the symposium articles of Part I, suggests that the chaos and incoherence, seen by some to characterize political systems, are not unique to those systems; economics, contrary to the received wisdom of general equilibrium theory, are manipulable, incoherent, and chaotic, too. Ferejohn and Grether develop a social choice view of equilibrium by establishing the necessary properties of stable decision-making procedures. McKelvey and Ordeshook conclude Part II on a methodological and empirical note, subjecting several equilibrium concepts to experimental investigation and finding them wanting in various degrees. The papers in Part III provide a broad sampling of the ways equilibrium analyses are employed to study political processes, events, and concerns: political inequality and its consequences (Aranson), sophisticated behavior in plurality voting systems (Niemi and Frank), safety regulation (Hinich), and political candidacies (Brams and Straffin).

There is a second rationale for this volume. The contributors are friends, colleagues, or students (in some cases, all three) of the author of the first essay, William H. Riker. The bulk of the essays in Parts II and III have been drawn from a conference on political equilibrium held in his honor in August 1980. That conference and this volume are but a small token of our esteem and respect for a man who has not only inspired and influenced each of us, but who has also moved an entire academic discipline onto a more promising scientific trajectory. These essays fall short of the model he provides of the integration of careful analysis and rich substance. For that you must turn to Bill Riker's own contributions.

I EQUILIBRIUM AND DISEQUILIBRIUM:
The Conceptual Controversy Framed

1 IMPLICATIONS FROM THE DISEQUILIBRIUM OF MAJORITY RULE FOR THE STUDY OF INSTITUTIONS

William H. Riker

While contemporary political science (as, for example, in such subjects as political socialization, studies of public opinion, etc.) tends to emphasize the study of values and tastes (because of an assumption that political outcomes—like market outcomes—are determined by the amalgamation of individual preferences), the older tradition of political science emphasized the study of institutions. The line of research in political theory followed during the last generation has involved seeking an equilibrium of tastes; but it has revealed that such an equilibrium exists only rarely, if at all. The inference then is that prudence in research directs the science of politics toward the investigation of empirical regularities in institutions, which, though congealed tastes, are "unstable constants" amenable to scientific investigation.

Social scientists are now, and probably always have been, of divided opinion about the degree to which institutions as well as personal values, opinions, and tastes affect the content of social decisions. (I use the words "values," "opinions," and "tastes" interchangeably, not because they mean exactly the same thing, but because the processes by which they can influence decisions are identical.) It is clear that the values of at least some members of society do ineradicably influence these decisions. Even when it is claimed that God, or the law of nature, or the sovereign people, or the working class, or some other abstract nonhuman entity determines outcomes, it is still true that some members of society, say, priests, judges, parliamentmen, dictators, etc., must interpret what the abstraction directs. In the most extreme cases, the voice the people hear and the words spoken come immediately from the Delphic priestess, not from the god who is said to inspire her. That being so, we can never leave out the influence of some person's values and tastes on social decisions. Even if the priestess is unintelligible, the priestly interpreter tells the supplicants what to do.

On the other hand, we cannot leave out the force of institutions. The people whose values and tastes are influential live in a world of conventions about both language and values themselves. These conventions are in turn condensed into institutions, which are simply rules about behavior, especially about making decisions. Even the priestess in her frenzy probably behaves according to rules and, for certain, her interpreter is constrained by specifiable conventions. So interpersonal rules, that is, institutions, must affect social outcomes just as much as personal values.

Ambiguity arises, however, when we attempt to assess the relative significance of these two kinds of forces. Very probably, both are necessary and neither is alone a sufficient condition for outcomes. If so, a full statement of social causation must include them both. But, nevertheless, it is often believed to be convenient and practically useful to assume that one force (either the personal or the impersonal) is constant, while the other is variable and thus in some sense marginal and "more significant" than the other. With this assumption, if the institutions are constant, then one can predict outcomes from tastes, or, if tastes are constant, then one can predict outcomes from institutions. It is of course true that this easy predictability is an illusion—but it is an illusion by which many scholars are hoodwinked because in quiet times the institutions are constant and only tastes are in dispute, while in turbulent times the institutions are in flux and only human greed seems constant. One fundamental and unsolved problem of social science is to penetrate the illusion and to learn to take both values and institutions into account. In the last generation we have made some small progress in this direction, if only to acquire a bit of sophistication about the problem, and the purpose of this article is to chronicle this progress.

METHODOLOGICAL TRADITIONS IN POLITICAL SCIENCE

Political science draws almost equally on traditions that overemphasize institutions and traditions that overemphasize tastes, which is perhaps why political scientists seem so eclectic as compared to, say, sociologists (whose tradition is almost exclusively institutional) or to economists (whose recent tradition, at least, stresses tastes).

The emphasis on institutions is our classical heritage. Aristotle collected and described 150 constitutions because he believed that constitutions determined both social outcomes and individual character. Even Plato, who initially argued for the rule of men rather than the rule of law, nevertheless devoted most of the *Republic* to a description of the institutions necessary to produce the kind of people he wanted for rulers, thereby implying that the institutions were primary and the particular rulers merely intermediaries between the institutions and the outcome. The notion that the quality of men's character is controlled by the laws under which they live, a notion that comes to us from ancient Greece by way of Roman law and eighteenth-century philosophers like Montesquieu, is, consequently, very much a part of contemporary political science. For example, it is said, with astonishing variety, that both the welfare state and restraints on government make people free, productive, contented, and self-respecting; or, for another example, it is said that incompatible varieties of economic institutions such as capitalism and socialism make people better off both morally and economically. Doubtless, the most extreme and absurd of the modern versions of classical institutionalism is Marxism, a picture of society in which economic institutions determine not only individual character but also the whole course of human history.

The emphasis on taste and values, on the other hand, is our Christian heritage. Because Christianity based the social order on personal decisions about faith and love and because it rejected the Judaic system of rules and forms (which came close to classical institutionalism), Christian theologians—at least from the Middle Ages onward—insisted that the quality of social outcomes depended almost entirely on the moral quality of rulers: Christian kings make good decisions; pagan or irreligious kings do not. Even in this secular century, some writers directly in the Christian tradition have described society in exactly this way. For example, T.S. Eliot, responding to the Munich crisis with *The Idea of a Christian Society* (1940, p. 34), saw only a change in *beliefs* as a way out of the world crisis: A community of Christians in a Christian state governed by rulers who accept Christianity, "not simply as their own faith, . . . but as the system under which they are to govern." It would be hard to find a more complete conviction that social outcomes (and personal character) are determined by what people believe.

Owing, however, to the lack of interest in theology among twentieth-century intellectuals, the contemporary force associating individual values and social outcomes is wholly secular, though probably derived (as is, for example, extreme methodological individualism) from Christian modes of thought. In the ideology of democracy, which may well be a kind of secularized Christian theology, that form of government is often, though I believe quite inaccurately, defined as the rule of the people—by which it is meant that the people's values solely determine public decisions. For reasons that I have discussed at length elsewhere, this picture of democracy is internally inconsistent and cannot be sustained (Riker, 1978, 1980b). At most democracy involves a popular veto on rulers, not a popular rule. Nevertheless inconsistencies and inaccuracies do not deter most ideologues, so that it is probably the case that nowadays the most widely accepted interpretation of democracy is that it is a device to combine individual values into decisions of government. Furthermore, this understanding, which went by the name of Benthamite "radicalism" in nineteenth-century England and of "popular sovereignty" in nineteenth-century America, is today believed by huge numbers of people (incorrectly, of course) to describe what actually happens in democratic governments.

While this supposed political description is mere ideology, it is nevertheless an important part of some contemporary political science and contributes greatly to the scientific emphasis on tastes and values, an emphasis expressed, for example, in the great amount of research on public opinion (which concerns the nature of tastes and values), political socialization (which concerns the creation of tastes and values), and representation (which concerns the incorporation of tastes and values in public decisions).

Great as is the contribution of democratic ideology to an emphasis on tastes and values, there is an even greater contribution, I believe, from the example of microeconomics. The theory of price in a competitive market—one of the few well-tested and verified theories in all of social science—is a theory in which institutions (i.e., the market) are held constant, while tastes determine outcomes. The theory takes this form: Given an auction market for a continuously divisible commodity with several buyers and several sellers whose tastes are constant over the period of the auction, then the price of the commodity is jointly and completely determined in a particular, describable way by the sum of the buyers' desires to buy and the sum of the sellers' desires to sell. (These desires are, of course, tastes and values.) Furthermore, as long as tastes are constant the price so determined is a Pareto-optimal equilibrium in the sense that no *pair* of traders would agree to depart from it because any departure in favor of one trader would hurt another.

Since this theory admits prediction of an equilibrium and since the actual occurrences of numerous predicted equilibria have been verified, the prestige of this theory is higher, I believe, than that of any other theory in the social sciences. Indeed, it seems to me that this success alone (i.e., predictions from the theory of price) elevates the science of economics above all other social sciences in popular esteem among intellectuals, and renders economists believable even when they write of totally different subjects such as macroeconomics and social welfare, about both of which subjects their theories are as unverified as most others in social science. The scientific and intellectual success of price theorists in discovering equilibria has, of course, led many other social scientists to emulate them. We see, therefore, searches for equilibria of tastes in all branches of social science, not least of all political science.

THE SEARCH FOR GENERAL EQUILIBRIA

As I noted at the beginning of the previous section, political science draws eclectically both on traditions that overemphasize institutions and on traditions that overemphasize tastes. But, in the last 30 years or so, it seems to me that the traditions overemphasizing tastes have predominated. The study of constitutions, which characterized political science in the first half of the century, has latterly given way to the study of political culture, political behavior, and public opinion, all of which concern values and tastes. Simultaneously, with a kind of unspoken intellectual coordination, political theorists have analyzed the conditions for equilibria in abstract majority voting systems, which are in fact the conditions for an equilibrium of values. This development in political theory, which is described in this and subsequent sections, has by now revealed precisely what kind of equilibria can be expected, thereby allowing us to understand, with much more sophistication than was previously possible, the relation of values and institutions in structuring political outcomes.

The beginning of the search for conditions of equilibria is Duncan Black's rediscovery (in the mid-1940s) of the paradox of voting. Before that time scholars had indeed often discussed the equity and effect of voting systems, especially in disputes over proportional representation, methods of nomination, and forms of ballots. But, so far as I have been able to discover from a desultory survey, hardly anyone had recognized that the supposed defects might be based on individual tastes rather than structures of systems. If based on tastes, the defects are irremediable because, given an appropriate distribution of tastes, even a perfected system of voting might produce imperfect results. This is precisely the inference one draws from an analysis of the paradox and it is perhaps owing to an unspoken, even unrecognized, repugnance at this deduction that, when the paradox was initially discovered by Condorcet and rediscovered by Lewis Carroll, E.J. Nanson, and E.V. Huntington, it was nevertheless ignored (or perhaps repressed) by political scientists (see Black, 1958, pp. 156-238; Riker, 1961). Once Black brought the paradox irrepressibly to scholarly attention and showed that the disequilibria inherent in it depended not on the institutions of voting but on the distributions of taste, the search for conditions of equilibrium seemed an intellectual necessity.

To discuss this question, one needs an abstract society of these elements:

1. Alternatives: $\{a_1, a_2, \ldots, a_n\}$. If $n = 2$, equilibrium is certain because a_1

beats or ties a_2 or vice versa. Problems of equilibrium arise, however, when $n \geqslant 3$.

2. Voters: $\{1, 2, \ldots, m\}$. When $m = 1$, the problem is trivial, so it should be that $m \geqslant 2$.

3. Preference: Assuming that voters can compare alternatives and value some of them more than others, there are binary relations of preference, P_i (where $i = 1, 2, \ldots, m$), of indifference, I_i, and of the two combined, R_i, expressing a voter's estimate of the relative value of any pair of alternatives. (One writes "$a_j R_i a_k$" to mean "voter i prefers a_j to a_k or is indifferent between them.") Conventionally, R is assumed to be reflexive ($a_j R_i a_j$), connected (either $a_j R_i a_k$ or $a_k R_i a_j$), and transitive (if $a_h R_i a_j$ and $a_j R_i a_k$, then $a_h R_i a_k$), so that by R (or P or I) a voter orders any triplet of alternatives from best to worst: $a_h R_i a_j R_i a_k$ or $a_h a_j a_k$. [Notationally, $a_h P_i a_j I_i a_k$ is written: $a_h (a_j a_k)$.] Perhaps the attribution of the ability to order places unwarranted confidence in the fragile human ability to concentrate. By the assumption of the transitivity of R, however, we give voting on values a chance at equilibrium with the best of human participation. If, then, voting fails, it fails the easiest possible test.

4. Outcomes from voting: Given a society of m voters faced with n alternatives, there are $(n!)^m$ possible profiles of preference D, that is, possible ways the members of the group can individually order the alternatives. (That is, there are $n!$ possible orders of n alternatives and each of the m voters can select one of those orders.) The operation on a profile D of majority voting on pairs of alternatives yields an outcome relation M, where "$a_h M a_k$" means: "(the number of i such that $a_h P_i a_k$) $\geqslant$ (the number of i such that $a_k P_i a_h$)," assuming, of course, that no i such that $a_h I_i a_k$ participates in the voting. M may be, but need not be, a transitive relation so that M may yield either some one of the $n!$ orders of alternatives or intransitive cycles like $a_h M a_j M a_k M a_h$.

To consider the problems involved in the summation of preferences, observe the profiles, D^1 to D^4, where $n = m = 3$ (Diagram 1.1).

Diagram 1.1

D^1	D^2	D^3	D^4
1. $a_h a_j a_k$	1. $a_h a_j a_k$	1. $a_h a_j a_k$	1. $a_h a_k a_j$
2. $a_h a_k a_j$	2. $a_j a_h a_k$	2. $a_j a_k a_h$	2. $a_j a_h a_k$
3. $a_j a_k a_h$	3. $a_k a_h a_j$	3. $a_k a_h a_j$	3. $a_k a_j a_h$
$a_h M a_j M a_k$	$a_h M a_j M a_k$	$a_h M a_j M a_k M a_h$	$a_h M a_k M a_j M a_h$
		"forward cycle"	"backward cycle"

In profiles D^1 and D^2 there is a decisive winner by M in the sense that a_h beats each of $n-1$ other alternatives. But in profiles D^3 and D^4, which are examples of the paradox of voting, there is no decisive winner because in, say, D^3, a_h will win if the sequence of voting is a_j versus a_k and then a_j versus a_h, a_j will win if the sequence is a_k versus a_h and then a_j versus a_k, etc., or no alternative will win if a round robin is conducted. The absence of a decisive winner is particularly disconcerting because, after assuming that each voter can order his or her values, it turns out that the group of voters cannot order them. Indeed, the people are coherent but the group is incoherent.

It is precisely the absence of a decisive winner that constitutes disequilibrium, and the paradox of voting shows that disequilibrium can occur with majority voting, the relation M. Furthermore, the possibility of this kind of disequilibrium is present in *any* fair voting method, so it is not the institution of M, but the distribution of tastes, that is at fault (Arrow, 1963). One is consequently driven to ask what properties distinguish profiles with an equilibrium outcome (like D^1 and D^2) from profiles without one, like D^3 and D^4. (This question has usually been posed with respect to the relation M, so I will restrict my discussion to it. But, by reason of Arrow's theorem, we know that similar questions could be raised about any voting method, say, positional methods like plurality voting or approval voting.)

During the late 1960s, a systematic answer was developed, based on the observation that, for the 3! orders of a triplet of alternatives,

1. $a_h a_j a_k$
2. $a_h a_k a_j$
3. $a_j a_h a_k$
4. $a_j a_k a_h$
5. $a_k a_h a_j$
6. $a_k a_j a_h$,

numbers 1, 4, and 5 constitute D^3 and result in the forward cycle and numbers 2, 3, and 6 constitute D^4 and result in the backward cycle. Hence D^3 and D^4 exhaust the ways in which intransitive triples can occur. Any conditions on orderings by individuals such that either $a_h a_j a_k a_h$ or $a_h a_k a_j a_h$ are rendered impossible by M is thus a guarantee of equilibrium. One such condition is, for example, that, for any number of voters, some alternative in a triple is never in first place in a voter's order (as a_k is not in D^1) or some is never in last place (as a_h is not in D^2) or never in the middle place (as a_h is not in D^1)—this is the condition of "value restriction" (Sen, 1966). Or another condition is "extremal restriction," which is that, for any number of voters and for some order $a_j a_h a_k$ in D, if another order has a_k first, then this other order must have a_j last (as in D^2, $a_j a_h a_k$ is voter 2's order and $a_k a_h a_j$ is voter 3's) (Sen and Pattanaik, 1969). An exhaustive list of similar conditions is set forth in Fishburn (1973).

In addition to their completeness, the merit of these conditions on profiles is their clear revelation that equilibrium depends entirely on the accident of a noncyclical set of voters' preferences. The defect of these conditions is, on the other hand, their failure to indicate the likelihood that tastes might or might not be cyclical. Lacking that indication, they do not admit assessment of the practical significance of disequilibrium. Fortunately there exist less complete but intuitively more vivid geometric or topological conditions for equilibrium that do allow practical interpretation.

Historically, the first such condition, single-peakedness, was devised by Black even before Arrow's theorem was formulated (Black, 1948). If alternatives are arranged on a horizontal axis and the voters' ordinal valuation is measured on a vertical axis, then a voter's ordering may be represented as a curve on the positive quadrant connecting the voter's valuation of alternatives (see Figure 1.1). Such a preference curve is single-peaked if, as it flows from left to right, it is always rising, always falling, or rising to a peak or a plateau and then falling. By an appropriate arrangement of alternatives on the horizontal axis, any ordering of alternatives may be expressed as a single-peaked curve. If, however, three or more preference curves are drawn above a particular arrangement of alternatives on the horizontal axis, it may happen that all curves cannot be single-peaked. (See Figure 1.2, in which the reader may verify that, no matter how the three alternatives are ordered on the horizontal axis, at least one of the three curves from D^4 —a cyclical profile—must fail to be single-peaked. In the particular ordering of Figure 1.2, voter 3's curve fails; but, were the ordering on the horizontal axis to be, say, $a_h a_k a_j$, then voter 2's curve would fail.)

Black's discovery was that, if any ordering on the horizontal axis exists such that all voters' preference curves are single-peaked, then an equilibrium exists in

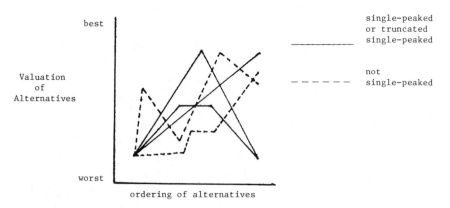

Figure 1.1. Preference Curves

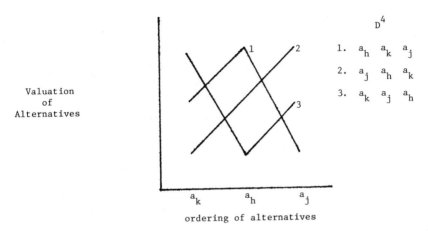

Figure 1.2. Nonsingle-Peakedness

the sense that one alternative can beat or tie $(n - 1)$ others. Moreover the winning alternative(s) can be specified: Identifying the alternative beneath the peak of voter i's curve as O_i (for "optimum for i") and numbering the optima so that O_1 is at the far left and O_m at the far right, then, if m is odd, $O_{(m + 1)/2}$ wins and, if m is even, $O_{m/2}$ and $O_{(m + 1)/2}$ tie. For proof, when m is odd, note that, if a curve is rising from a_h to a_j, then the voter prefers a_j to a_h and, conversely, when the curve is falling, the voter prefers a_h to a_j. Placing some a_k to the left of $O_{(m + 1)/2}$ against $O_{(m + 1)/2}$ in a vote, note that $O_{(m +1)/2}$ wins because over half the curves are rising between a_k and $O_{(m + 1)/2}$, specifically all those curves with optima numbered $O_{(m + 1)/2}$ to O_m (which is a majority itself) and all curves with optima lying between a_k and $O_{(m + 1)/2}$. Similarly, placing some $a_{k'}$ to the right of $O_{(m + 1)/2}$ against it, note that $O_{(m + 1)/2}$ wins because over half the curves are falling between $O_{(m + 1)/2}$ and $d_{k'}$, specifically all those from O_1 to $O_{(m + 1)/2}$ (a bare majority) and those with optima between $O_{(m + 1)/2}$ and $a_{k'}$. A similar argument establishes that $O_{m/s}$ and $O_{(m + 1)/2}$ tie when n is even.

It should be noted that this equilibrium at the median optimum is characterized by a balancing of opposites, a feature found in all other geometrically defined equilibria of voting. There is an equal number of voters on either side of the median, which is why it is the equilibrium. Suppose one subtracts (or adds) two voters whose optima are on opposite sides of the median; then the equality is unaffected and the equilibrium is characterized in some fundamental way by a pairing of opposites.

As a condition of equilibrium, single-peakedness (like the previously mentioned conditions, all of which were, however, discovered later) guarantees that neither $a_h M a_j M a_k M a_h$ nor $a_h M a_k M a_j M a_h$ occurs. It has the additional merit, moreover, of revealing a rationale for the existence of equilibria: That all curves are single-peaked means that all voters judge the alternatives consistently with respect to one issue, namely, that measured by the dimension on the horizontal axis. They may, of course, disagree about the best position on the issue, but they do agree that this single issue is the relevant basis for judgment.

This is why this condition has an intuitively obvious application to political campaigns, as in Downs's proposition that party platforms in a two-party system converge to the values of the median voter (1957, pp. 114-125). While Downs derived this argument from an economic model of the spatial location of firms, still his argument for equilibrium at the median voter's optimum assumes single-peakedness and is indeed invalid without it. This application suggests just how restrictive the condition is in practice because it seldom appears to be satisfied in the real world (Robertson, 1976). Despite the frequent journalistic use of dichotomies, e.g., "left–right," "Catholic-Protestant," "Fleming-Walloon," etc.—all of which are extremes on one issue dimension—still, scholarly efforts to describe real politics on one dimension seem always to break down. Indeed, once Downs set forth his model, it seemed so inadequate that other theorists soon developed an n-dimensional analog (Davis and Hinich, 1966; Davis, Hinich, and Ordeshook, 1970).

Given the intuition that the one-dimensional model is inadequate for description, the appropriate next step is to search for equilibria in two-dimensional and ultimately in n-dimensional issue spaces. Black and Newing (1951) started

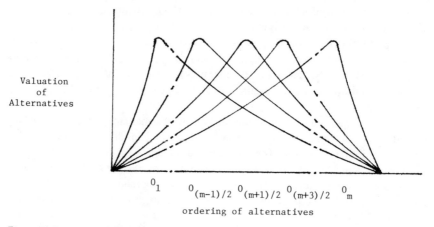

Figure 1.3. Voters' Optima

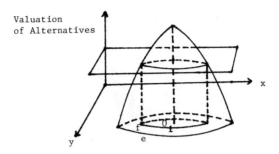

Figure 1.4. Single-Humped Valuation of Alternatives in Two Dimensions (x, y)

the search with three voters in a two-dimensional model in which the peaks of Figures 1.1, 1.2, and 1.3 have become the humps of Figure 1.4. The vertical axis in that figure is, like the vertical axes in previous figures, for the ordinal measure of valuations. The two horizontal axes are issue dimensions or bases of judgment that define a plane (rather than a line) on which alternatives are located. Voter i's optimum (O_i) lies in that plane directly beneath the highest point of the hump. Curves e and f, which are reflections into the $x_1 x_2$ plane of two levels of preference, are indifference curves in the sense that voter i prefers all alternatives in the open space between e and f to any alternative on e but i is indifferent among all alternatives on, say, e.

To search for an equilibrium we need look only at the indifference curves in the xy plane, as in Figure 1.5. Between two voters, with optima at O_1 and O_2, is a "contract curve" which connects points of tangencies of the voters' indifference curves. All the points on which voters 1 and 2 might agree lie on the contract curve. To see why, consider point a_k which lies, for each voter, on the outer of the two sets of indifference curves displayed. By definition, all points in the open shaded space are preferred by *both* voters to a_k. By successive reduction of the shaded area, one arrives at some point on the contract curve. When there are three voters, however, agreement is less easy to arrive at. Observe in Figure 1.6 that, while voters 1 and 2 might agree by majority vote on a_k, still a_j M a_k by voters 2 and 3. Nevertheless a_h M a_j (by 1 and 3) and a_k M a_h (by 1 and 2), so a cycle exists and there is no equilibrium.

There is, however, some chance for equilibria in this situation: If O_3 were to lie on the contract curve between O_1 and O_2, say, at a_k, then $O_3 = a_k$ would be a median between O_1 and O_2 and hence preferred by some pair (either 1 and 3 or 2 and 3) to *any* other point in the plane. In general, if one voter's optimum lies on a contract curve between two others, then there is an equilibrium outcome. Note that, as in the one-dimensional case, there is a balance between op-

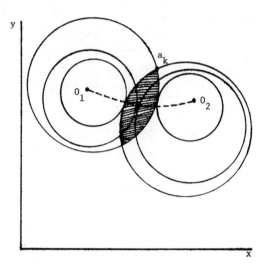

Figure 1.5. Indifference Curves

posites, because a_k would remain the equilibrium if O_1 and O_2 were removed or if additional pairs of optima were added, one of each pair on the $O_1 O_2$ contract curve between a_k and O_1 and the other between a_k and O_2. This discovery was generalized by Charles Plott (1967). For the expanded situation we need some new notation. Since we now assume an infinite number of alternatives and continuously differentiable utility (as a measure on individual preference), we can no longer use n for the number of alternatives. Rather we use it to identify dimensions by which voters judge alternatives, $1, 2, \ldots, n$ dimensions. Then $U^i = U^i(x_1, x_2, \ldots, x_n)$ is the utility to the ith voter of some point a in n-dimensional space. Let there be a status quo alternative, $\bar{a}$, that is, the alternative currently in force, and let some a_j, which is a "small" distance d from $\bar{a}$, be placed against $\bar{a}$ in a majority vote. If $a_j P_i \bar{a}$, voter i obtains an increase in utility from a_j over $\bar{a}$. Let ΔU^i be the measure in utility of a vector in n-space from $\bar{a}$ toward some (unspecified) other point. Specifying the other point as a_j, one can say that, if $\Delta U^i a_j > 0$, then voter i prefers a_j, that, if $\Delta U^i a_j < 0$, voter i prefers $\bar{a}$, and if $\Delta U^i a_j = 0$, voter i is indifferent between a_j and $\bar{a}$. If there is some set of voters of size $(m + 1)/2$ such that the gradient vectors, of utility for each voter, i, in the set are $\Delta U^i a_j \leqslant 0$, then a majority prefers $\bar{a}$ to a_j and $\bar{a}$ is a Condorcet winner or equilibrium.

A set of sufficient conditions for $\bar{a}$ to be in equilibrium are, for m odd:

1. that indifferent voters do not vote on a motion;
2. that there is at least one voter, i, for whom $\bar{a}$ provides the maximum utility;

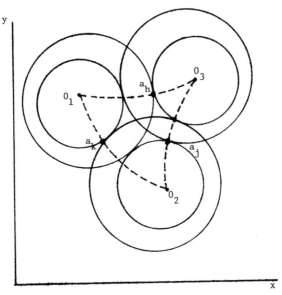

Figure 1.6. Contract Curves for Three Voters

3. that the $m-1$ remaining voters—an even number—can be divided into pairs, i and i', the interests of voters i and i' are diametrically opposed in direction and amounts of utility.

It is intuitively evident (and proved in Plott [1967]) that for m voters for which conditions 1, 2, and 3 hold, the voters would not wish to move from $\bar{a}$. One voter prefers $\bar{a}$ to anything else and for any a_j different from $\bar{a}$ one voter in each pair would prefer a_j to $\bar{a}$ and the other in the pair would prefer $\bar{a}$ to a_j. In Figure 1.7, where the maxima for voters 1, 2, 3, 4, 5 are at points numbered 1, 2, 3, 4, 5, $\bar{a}$ would beat a_j with a majority of 2, 3, and 5 or $\bar{a}$ would beat a' with a majority of 2, 4, and 5. Furthermore, any point $a' \neq \bar{a}$ can be beaten by some other point a_j, as in Figure 1.7 a_j beats a' with 2, 4, and 5.

The interesting feature of Plott's conditions for equilibrium are that the likelihood of satisfying them in the real world is extremely remote. Even if they were, by some amazing chance, to be satisfied, it would still be true that even a slight change in *one* voter's preferences would disrupt the equilibrium, because it would upset the necessary pairing of opposites. For all practical purposes, therefore, we can say that, given $m > 2$ voters and $n \geq 2$ dimensions of judgment with continuous alternatives, equilibrium of tastes is nonexistent.

This conclusion has been extended further by translating it into the language of game theory. When a majority prefers a_h to a_j, one says a_h *dominates* a_j and

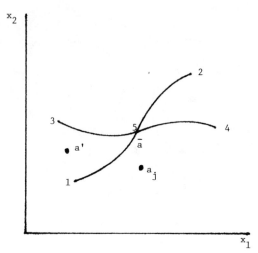

Figure 1.7. Equilibrium for $m = 5$ Voters in $n = 2$ Space

one defines a *core* as the set of undominated points, which is the same as the definition of Condorcet winners. Schloss (1973) has shown that the Plott equilibrium defines a core, given that the differentiability feature is removed; and Rubinstein (1979) has shown that, generically, cores of voting games, in which only continuous preferences are assumed, are empty.

Just how devastating is the absence of equilibria has been impressively demonstrated by Richard McKelvey, whose work has been aimed at showing that, when equilibrium breaks down, it breaks down completely (McKelvey, 1976, 1978). It has been frequently supposed that, although it is extremely unlikely that an alternative can beat $n - 1$ others, still all members of a relatively small set of k alternatives (themselves in cycle) can probably all beat the remaining $n - k$ others. If this were so, then some alternative in this "top cycle" might reasonably be regarded as a satisfactory winner and disequilibrium would simply mean the absence of a clear choice among several generally preferred outcomes. McKelvey has shown, however, that given continuous utilities, the top cycle can be expected to include all possible alternatives in an n-dimensional space. In a fashion similar to Plott's, McKelvey showed with an extremely general topological model, that the conditions for an equilibrium were:

1. that the indifference contour for some voter i (not restricted as to convexity or any of the usual economic assumptions) must coincide with the frontier of the set of points that can beat some point a_h;
2. that all other voters' indifference contours can be paired up in the sense

that, if some points a_j and a_k are on voter i''s indifference frontier, then they must also be on at least one other voter i'''s indifference frontier.

These are, of course, very general formulations of the same kind of symmetry conditions that have been required all along, by Black, by Black and Newing, and by Plott. And they tell us about the same thing, namely, that conditions for equilibria are so restrictive as to render equilibria virtually nonexistent. Furthermore, even in the unlikely event that they should be satisfied, any single individual who is paired with another to generate equilibrium can break it up by dissembling about his or her true preferences. Hence, not only are equilibria rare, they are also extremely fragile.

An important feature of McKelvey's condition is that, if they are not met, then the top cycle includes all points in the policy space. This fact means that there is some way by which *any* point can beat the status quo. Suppose $\overline{a}$ is the status quo; then, if it is desired to replace $\overline{a}$ with a', there is some sequence of majority rule decisions (and often many such sequences) such that a' beats a_h, a_h beats a_j, . . . , a_k beats $\overline{a}$. Hence, any official or participant who can control the agenda can bring about the adoption of his or her desired alternative a'. But, of course, there is also a path by which $\overline{a}$ may then beat a'. So a second participant may foil the first.

A result similar to McKelvey's has been arrived at from a quite different topological model by Schofield (1978). His analysis begins with the observation that, for any point x in a multidimensional issue space, some indifference curve for each participant passes through x. Given these indifference curves, one can find the set of points, $P_C(x)$, which is the set of points in the neighborhood of x that are preferred to x by some winning coalition, C_k, $k = 1, 2, ...$ If, for the set W of all winning coalitions, $P_W(x)$ is such that there are some points y in the neighborhood of x that cannot be included in $P_W(x)$ by some path $(y \, M_{C_i} z, . . . , w \, M_{C_k} x$, when C_i and C_k are any specific-winning coalitions), that is, if there are some points y that x can defeat no matter what, then there may be an equilibrium at x. If, however, all points in some arbitrary neighborhood of x can by some sequence of majority coalitions defeat x, then equilibrium at x is impossible. Furthermore, if for any particular set of individual ideal points and indifference curves, there is even just one point x for which equilibrium is impossible, then the system as a whole is cyclical. Effectively, this means that unless the individual preferences are highly similar—so that *all* winning coalitions are similar—social choices are certain to be cyclical. While this condition does not in itself indicate the likelihood of cyclical outcomes, Schofield has also shown that, if the issue space has at least as many dimensions as one more than the number of persons necessary for a minimal winning coalition, then the system is, for certain, cyclical. In legislatures most members probably have on every decision a dimension concerning the effect of the several alternatives on their chances of reelection, and in electorates on all political platforms containing issues of a distributive nature ("who gets what") each participant is concerned, *inter alia*, with what he or she gets. Hence for these types of voting situations, there are at least as many dimensions as voters and disequilibrium is, therefore, certain.

In comparison with McKelvey's statement of the condition for a global cycle from $\overline{a}$ to $\overline{a}$, Schofield's theorem is a condition for a local cycle in an open neighborhood of $\overline{a}$. Practically, the difference is that McKelvey's condition guarantees instability by admitting what may seem like farfetched alternatives. (For example, the free soil issue that broke up the great Jeffersonian-Jacksonian agrarian coalition seemed to Democratic politicians, southerner and dough-face alike, to be an absurd irrelevancy because it was an issue more or less proscribed by the constitutional settlement. Nevertheless it broke up a seemingly overwhelming and persistent majority. This is the kind of event that we are assured is possible by McKelvey's theorem.) Schofield's theorem, while not excluding global cycles, assures us that local cycles can occur based presumably on only "slight" changes in the alternatives. (This is the kind of change we see in ordinary American politics where parties that appear extremely close ideologically turn each other out of office.) Hence, for most practical politics disequilibrium is assured.

THE SIGNIFICANCE OF DISEQUILIBRIUM

I now return to the philosophical question I raised in the beginning by asking what is the relevance for politics of the rarity and fragility of majority rule equilibria. And I start off by observing that the discoveries about majority rule probably apply to all methods of summing individual preferences. We know from Arrow's theorem that cycles cannot be avoided by any fair system, but we do not know from that fact much about the likelihood or fragility of a cyclical outcome for other methods of summation. We do know, however, that other methods of voting (e.g., positional methods like plurality voting and approval voting and point counting or electoral methods like proportional representation which are intended to make minorities win) are subject to disequilibria, manipulation, agenda control, etc., in much the same way as majority rule. It seems fairly safe to conjecture, therefore, that equilibria in other voting systems are as rare and fragile as in majority rule. And this rarity and fragility are doubtless as much features of systems based upon coopted committees as of those based on popular election. Turning to nonvoting methods of summation (e.g., statements of the sense of the meeting by a speaker or the selection of alternatives by a dictator), we know that the single summarizer necessarily imposes his or her own order on the outcome. Inasmuch as equilibrium is thus achieved by suppressing alternatives that might beat the single summarizer's own choice, such an equilibrium is not the product of summation, but of force. The rebellious discontent of those whose preferred alternatives are suppressed is simply evidence that the equilibrium achieved by a dictator or single summarizer is spurious. It seems to me, therefore, that what we have learned about equilibria under majority rule applies equally well to any political society whether it uses the institutions of majority rule or some other kind of voting or merely dictatorship.

And what we have learned is simply this: Disequilibrium, or the potential that the status quo be upset, is the characteristic feature of politics.

In the nineteenth century, economics was often called the "dismal science" largely because the equilibria predicted from price theory were not palatable to those who called it dismal. In what seems to me a deeper sense, however, politics is *the* dismal science because we have learned from it that there are no fundamental equilibria to predict. In the absence of such equilibria we cannot know much about the future at all, whether it is likely to be palatable or unpalatable, and in that sense our future is subject to the tricks and accidents of the way in which questions are posed and alternatives are offered and eliminated.

Yet there are some features of social decisions that we do understand and, in the short run at least, those do grant us some prevision. Although there are not likely to be equilibria based entirely on tastes, still there are outcomes of social decision processes, those outcomes do embody some people's values, and the outcomes themselves are not wholly random and unexpected. What prevents purely random embodiments of tastes is the fact that decisions are customarily made within the framework of known rules, which are what we commonly call institutions. Since institutions certainly affect the content of decisions, we can see something of the future by specifying just what these effects are and how they are produced. Thus, despite the recent enthusiasm for studying tastes (e.g., public opinion, political culture, and the like), what we learn from recent political theory is that the particular structure of an institution is at least as likely to be predictive of socially enforced values as are the preferences of the citizen body. So the sum of the recent discoveries is to reemphasize some of the classical heritage of political science. It is important to study constitutions simply because, if there are repetitive equilibria in social decisions, these equilibria derive at least as much from institutions as from tastes and values.

The outcome, then, of the search for equilibria of tastes is the discovery that, failing such equilibria, there must be some institutional element in the regularities (or actual equilibria) we observe. We are forced back, therefore, to the eclectic stance that political scientists have typically taken. Outcomes are, of course, partially based on tastes because some persons' (not necessarily a majority of people's) tastes are embodied in outcomes. But the ways the tastes and values are brought forward for consideration, eliminated, and finally selected are controlled by the institutions. And institutions may have systematic biases in them so that they regularly produce one kind of outcome rather than another. In this sense, therefore, both institutions and tastes contribute to outcomes. To offer an example, in electoral systems it not infrequently happens that the same party or coalition of parties wins election after election. Conceivably, this stability may be caused by the fact that tastes are constant, but more often it is caused by the fact that exactly those issues likely to upset the stability of tastes are kept out of the electoral process by structures like constitutions and political parties. (An excellent example of this process is the exclusion of the issues of slavery and free soil from American national politics from the 1780s to the 1840s. The hegemony during that period of the Jefferson-Jackson Democracy, which did provide a long-term equilibrium, could exist only by suppressing the slavery issue. Once it was raised, dividing rural slaveholders from rural yeomen, the Democracy and the nation were disrupted.) What results, therefore, is an outcome based both on tastes and on the way in which some tastes are admitted to and some not admitted to the decision process.

Consequently, we cannot study simply tastes and values, but must study institutions as well. Nevertheless, as we return to the study of institutions after a generation of preoccupation with values and preferences, we do so with a deeper appreciation of the appropriate scientific program and of our opportunities and limitations as scientists. The scientific program is to explain by the application of covering laws to particular situations how institutions generate equilibrium by systematically excluding or including certain tastes or values. As for our opportunities and limitations, we have already learned from the developments chronicled here that we cannot expect to find equilibria of preferences, but we may be able to find equilibria generated from a given subset of preferences by particular institutions.

In the earlier tradition of studying constitutions, it was customary to look for the centers of power in a constitutional structure — to look, that is, for who could control which portions of the political process. This is, of course, an interesting practical question for the world, because it concerns the distribution of "power." But while such distributions are a fascinating subject for ideologues and inside dopesters, they are not of much scientific interest because the idea of power is itself an inexact and probably meaningless notion (Riker, 1965b). What is instead scientifically interesting is the interaction among the several participants in a system to discover the particular kinds of outcomes that are both feasible and likely, given a particular institutional arrangement.

This is the kind of study of institutions that has developed more or less unconsciously among specialists on the U.S. Congress, who are among the first

political scientists to study a single institution in intensive detail. Having identified the several centers of authority in the conventional kind of constitutional
analysis, they have gone on to generalize about how these centers interact in the
selection of values to be incorporated into legislation. So sophisticated has this
kind of inquiry become that Kenneth Shepsle, a scientist trained in both fields,
has attempted to integrate it formally with the study of equilibria of preferences. Thereby he has managed to lay down an outline of what the new kind of
study of institutions might typically look like (Shepsle, 1979a). Shepsle dis-
tinguishes two ways in which rules and structures may impose conditions that
affect the outcome of the decision-making process in a legislature, or indeed in
many other kinds of decision-making bodies. One is decentralization: to divide
the body into subsets which act on some issues for the whole body: e.g., committees or parties in legislatures, departments in colleges or firms or bureaucra-
cies, etc. The other is the creation of jurisdictions: to divide up for separate
consideration the dimensions of decision so that, in a policy space with m dimensions, it may be required that each dimension, $x_1, \ldots, x_m$, be considered by
itself. Sometimes these two kinds of rules are combined, as when a congressional
committee is given control over one feature, and only one feature, of a bill.
Shepsle defines a structure-induced equilibrium as one in which, taking tastes
as given, a particular arrangement of subsets of decision makers and particular
assignment of jurisdictions allow for the passage of a motion that cannot be defeated by any other alternative. (Of course, an equilibrium of tastes, where,
regardless of institutions, a motion can beat any other, implies an equilibrium of
structure. But the converse does not hold: a structural equilibrium does not
imply an equilibrium of preferences. In that sense, the notion of a structural
equilibrium is narrower in meaning than an equilibrium of values or tastes.)
Shepsle's main theorem is that structural equilibria exist in a committee system,
provided the members' preferences can be represented by quasi-concave, continuous utility functions and the committee system operates in an m-dimensional
space in such a way that each dimension is under the jurisdiction of a particular
committee. (Particular assignments of jurisdiction are assumed to be protected
by a germaneness rule that permits amendments in committee only on the appropriate dimension.)

The secret of this theorem is that, when social choices are made dimension
by dimension, then, if an equilibrium condition (say, single-peakedness) is satisfied on one of the dimensions, some degree of stability is imposed on the whole
system. Since equilibrium conditions often do exist when choice is on only one
dimension, especially if the decision-making body shares cultural standards, it
follows that structural equilibrium is much easier to obtain than a pure equilibrium of tastes.

But, asks Shepsle, how robust is a structural equilibrium? The answer is that, insofar as a constitutional system supplies an outcome that is not the same as outcomes that might have been obtained from simple majority rule in the system without committees, jurisdictions, etc., the losers are likely to want to change the committees and jurisdictions in the hope of winning on another day. In the end, therefore, institutions are no more than rules and rules are themselves the product of social decisions. Consequently, the rules are also not in equilibrium. One can expect that losers on a series of decisions under a particular set of rules will attempt (often successfully) to change institutions and hence the kind of decisions produced under them. In that sense rules or institutions are just more alternatives in the policy space and the status quo of one set of rules can be supplanted with another set of rules. Thus the only difference between values and institutions is that the revelation of institutional disequilibria is probably a longer process than the revelation of disequilibria of taste.

Our new sophistication about institutions, induced by our long foray into the search for equilibria of tastes, is that institutions are probably best seen as congealed tastes. We ought, I think, to be thoroughly aware that the distinction between constitutional questions and policy questions is at most one of degree of longevity. If institutions are congealed tastes and if tastes lack equilibria, then also do institutions, except for short-run events.

It is true that we can get a lot of mileage out of relatively stable institutions. If elections are zero-sum or constant-sum, then all the restrictions embodied in game theory notions of solutions of zero- or constant-sum games and all the restrictions embodied in sociological laws like the size principle are more or less permanently imposed on outcomes. Only the abolition of zero-sum or constant-sum methods of election is likely to eliminate these restrictions. Similarly, while it is easy enough to change some prisoners' dilemmas to situations with Pareto-optimal outcomes (as for example the so-called "tragedy of the commons" was solved by the enclosure of common lands into private property), still there are other apparently intractable prisoners' dilemmas (such as arms races and the extinction of species of creatures like passenger pigeons and perhaps whales). In the former cases there are governmental organizations inclusive enough to change the institutions of the dilemma. But the latter sort of institutions are likely to last for a very long time.

Nevertheless, if the non-Pareto-optimal feature of an institution is sufficiently distasteful to most participants, it is possible to reconstruct institutions. Private property in land was extended to the commons to prevent the destruction of soil, and it is not impossible to imagine private property in whales. If institutions do generate an outcome in which everyone loses, it is reasonable to expect some new and less distasteful institutions—which is to say that even the most fundamental institutions lack equilibria, although it may take generations to alter them.

The sum of our new sophistication is, therefore, that political outcomes truly are unpredictable in the long run. We may have a few pretty well-verified generalizations to guide us (for example, the size principle or Duverger's law), but for the most part we live in a world that is uncertain because it lacks equilibria.

CONCLUSION

And this conclusion sets the problem of political science: In the long run, outcomes are the consequence not only of institutions and tastes, but also of the political skill and artistry of those who manipulate agenda, formulate and reformulate questions, generate "false" issues, etc., in order to exploit the disequilibrium of tastes for their own advantage. And just what combination of institutions, tastes, and artistry will appear in any given political system is, it seems to me, as unpredictable as poetry. But given the short-term structural and cultural constants, there is some stability, some predictability of outcomes, and the function of the science of politics is to identify these "unstable constants."

APPENDIX

This paper was originally presented at the meeting of the International Political Science Association, Moscow, 1979. For that occasion the concluding remarks were as follows:

Given the location of the platform for the presentation of this paper, I should conclude with the observation that political science can exist only in an open society, that is, a society with unfettered freedom of speech. Insofar as the science involves a study of values and tastes, scientists can be accurate in their predictions only if they are able to ignore official doctrine (as, for example, in Marxism) about the preferences and interests of groups and classes. Official doctrine may be right or wrong, but whether it is or is not right is a subject not for official decree but rather for empirical investigation, which is possible only in an open society. Moreover, insofar as the science of politics involves the study of institutions, scientists must be able to examine critically the way governmental institutions operate at the highest as well as lowest levels of government. Only thus can they study the way institutions systematically bias the selection among preferences. Of course, this means that governmental secrecy, if it exists, prohibits scientific investigation of political structures.

Which of the two—official doctrine about preferences or governmental secrecy—is the more inhibiting for scientific inquiry probably varies from place to place. But I believe secrecy is more often a barrier. The scientist can often guess fairly well about tastes and preferences, but the way institutions work is extremely difficult to guess about. Consequently, if I am correct in believing that the study of tastes is not enough and that one must study institutions as well, then it follows that the new emphasis on institutions as a necessary part of the science of politics probably precludes this science in any society governed secretly.

Finally, there is another way in which the conclusions of this paper imply that political science can exist only in an open society. One important conclusion, indeed the most important conclusion, of the line of reasoning set forth in this paper is that, in the long run, nearly anything can happen in politics. Naturally this conclusion is a sharp contradiction of all philosophies of history (such as Marxism) that necessitate a belief in the existence of a determined course for the future. This belief is precisely what the discoveries recounted in this paper deny. So, if these discoveries are true—and mathematically they appear to be irrefutable—then a science of politics is incompatible with Marxism.

2 POLITICAL DISEQUILIBRIUM AND SCIENTIFIC INQUIRY:
A Comment on William H. Riker's "Implications from the Disequilibrium of Majority Rule for the Study of Institutions"

Peter C. Ordeshook

> *Politics is* the *dismal science because we have learned from it that there are no equilibria to predict. In the absence of equilibria we cannot know much about the future at all, whether it is likely to be palatable or unpalatable, and in that sense our future is subject to the tricks and accidents of the way questions are posed and the way alternatives are offered and eliminated.*
>
> —William H. Riker (1980a, p. 443)

And thus, in two sentences, I am told that I cannot attain that goal toward which my research is directed: a scientific understanding of political processes. More importantly, Riker's conclusions call into question the objectives and methodologies of most students of politics. While not all of us abide by the same paradigm, or use a similar professional argot, most of us do share, knowingly or unknowingly, a common goal: to search for political equilibria. For most of us believe that empirical regularities exist to be discovered and explained or that

25

events are not principally determined by the idiosyncratic and unpredictable personalities of a few decision makers. Therefore, we can take comfort in the fact that Riker misconstrues the nature of equilibrium and that an appropriate understanding of this concept diminishes the overriding relevance and impact he imputes to his conclusions.

Behind Riker's argument stands a particular concept of equilibrium. Capable of being stated in many ways and even of being disguised, this concept nevertheless appears in two basic forms. First, for situations in which people act alone without explicitly coordinating their actions with others (noncooperatively, in game-theory terms), an equilibrium corresponds to an outcome in which, *ex post*, no one person has any incentive to change his or her decisions unilaterally and to do something else. Second, for situations in which people can act in concert, with various subsets of people coordinating their actions to form "coalitions," an equilibrium corresponds to an outcome in which no coalition has the incentive or the means for unilaterally insuring an improvement in the welfare of all of its members. In game-theory terms such an equilibrium is called a core and corresponds in simple voting games to a Condorcet winner.

Scholars have long known that equilibria of either kind need not exist. Moreover, two decades of research and countless professional papers clogged with impossibility theorems point out that such equilibria are the exception rather than the rule and that "disequilibrium" cannot be precluded unless a variety of special circumstances prevail. We have also learned that, in the abstract at least, without equilibrium, an agenda setter—for example, one who can decide the order of voting—commands an extraordinary opportunity to dictate outcomes.

These are the conclusions that Riker laments. Believing that political processes do not share the straightforward stability found in abstract representations of economic markets, he infers that political scientists are disadvantaged in their "science" in contrast to economists, whose paradigm Riker has borrowed. But this claim seems less than compelling.

First, the presumed stability of markets is an abstract fiction that most economists recognize as a *theoretical* impossibility. Second, traditional definitions of equilibria may provide inadequate predictions and explanations. Third, the presence of an equilibrium in a static model does not guarantee its presence in more robust dynamic conceptualizations. Finally, disequilibrium of the traditional sort does not preclude explanation and science.

The presumed stability of markets resides principally in our abstract description of them and not necessarily in reality. That description is largely static and thereby precludes the "disequilibrium" occasioned by changing tastes and technologies. Neither economists nor anyone else knows much about tastes, how they are formed, and the laws governing their change. And, while abstract descriptions of markets might predict how the introduction of new technologies affects prices and consumption, these descriptions cannot anticipate that technology. Indeed, we can think of the firm that finds a less costly production method as a "market agenda setter"—as one who determines the set of alternatives from which we must choose—and as such possesses a powerful influence over final prices, levels of production, and future incentives for new invention.

A market's stability is also a fiction of the mathematical abstraction used to represent it. For instance, consider a market with one seller and two buyers. The usual representations of markets assign a zero marginal value to a coalition of the two buyers and the equilibrium of the core predicts that the single seller, being a monopolist, will extract all the added value from any exchange. But once the buyers learn the consequences of this situation, it seems reasonable to suppose that these buyers will form a "cartel" and negotiate as a team and on more even terms with the monopolist. Termed by some as "the problems of theory absorption," it is thus argued that the core's stability can be self-defeating in markets. A new "equilibrium" prevails, but one that is not terribly informative, for it includes all possible efficient outcomes. The monopolist's problem now is to try to disrupt the cartel or to bargain with the cartel for as advantageous an outcome on the Pareto frontier as possible. We cannot predict which situation will prevail—whether the game will involve three persons (two buyers and one seller) or two persons (a cartel and a seller)—and thus we remain uncertain about the eventual outcome.

Attempting to circumvent the theoretical problems occasioned by such possibilities, economists commonly assume that there are a great many buyers and sellers, that none individually can affect price or industry output, and that their numbers effectively preclude cartels. But, cartels do form—unions, trade, professional and farm associations, or trusts—and are designed to subvert the process of perfect competition. Cartel strategies vary, but a common one is lobbying for centralized government intervention. Such intervention, in turn, comes in many forms, including industry subsidies, benefit-in-kind transfer payments, and regulation to exclude competition.

Understanding such intervention, its genesis and its impact, is a central objective of political science. Hence, the problems Riker sees for our discipline are also common to economics. That is, because market processes sometimes resemble and are necessarily linked to government activity, an understanding of how markets function and the outcomes they produce seems impossible without also understanding political processes. If the methodologies and theoretical perspectives borrowed from economics are inadequate to comprehend political phenomena because of the absence of political equilibria, then those methodologies and perspectives must remain equally inadequate for comprehending market phenomena as well.

This cartel example also shows that the existence of equilibria does not guarantee that we can satisfactorily predict outcomes. Once the two buyers form a cartel and negotiate as one, the situation corresponds to a two-person (seller, cartel) bargaining situation in which the game-theory equilibrium termed the core consists of *all* Pareto-optimal outcomes that satisfy the security levels of the individual players. Such a prediction, however, does not usually limit the number of anticipated outcomes to any reasonable degree. And, while a variety of ad hoc normative arguments and other "solutions" that seek to narrow this prediction further have been proposed for such situations, none is generally accepted.

Nonuniqueness of equilibria can bring other problems. If an equilibrium is not unique, then it may be difficult to assert that people will arrive at any such outcome. The simplest example of such a possibility is a two-person game in which each person, in ignorance of what the other does, must choose an integer between 0 and 10. If they choose integers that sum to ten, they each win, in dollars, an amount equal to the numbers they chose respectively; but, if they choose numbers that do not sum to ten, they each lose, say $25. This game has 10 equilibrium outcomes $[(1,9), (2,8), \ldots, (9,1)]$ out of 100, but played noncooperatively, there is no guarantee that such an outcome will prevail.

Other situations may have unique and well-defined equilibria, but their properties may be sufficiently onerous that we are convinced they will be avoided. The best example is the prisoners' dilemma in which two persons seem inevitably led to an outcome they unanimously prefer to avoid. While its original form corresponds to a situation in which two prisoners are locked in separate cells with a choice between confessing and not confessing, this simple game is used also to represent more complex and common situations of market failure owing to the existence of public goods and externalities. For example, choosing between polluting the environment or voluntary installation of antipollution devices can correspond to a prisoners' dilemma in which everyone unilaterally chooses to pollute despite unanimous agreement that installing antipollution devices is preferred.

But, if the corresponding outcomes are sufficiently onerous and inescapable, the players will soon change the game. In the case of environmental pollution, the game is moved to a higher level with government intervention to alter people's incentives—to break the dilemma—and to induce a preferred outcome. In fact, aside from issues of redistribution and equity, much of the traditional and accepted justifications for the state's existence reside in the desire to avoid those prisoners' dilemma situations that perfectly competitive markets are presumed to engender.

Governments, though, engender new kinds of dilemmas. With a government's usual powers to expropriate wealth, interest groups form to lobby for particularized private benefits. Economic efficiency becomes the new undersupplied public good, and, while all groups might agree jointly not to use the coercive powers of government for their particularized ends, none has any incentive unilaterally to choose another course. There is now, in fact, a growing belief that governments, in the grip of this dilemma, have grown too large and unwieldy, and that new constitutional rules such as spending limits are required to control the prisoners' dilemmas among interest groups and constituencies that governments engender.

All of these prisoners' dilemma situations, when modeled statically, have exactly the kind of unique and well-defined equilibria that Riker would prefer. But when they are viewed with any historical perspective, they portray the disequilibrium that corresponds to the tension between laissez-faire and collectivist philosophies.

To this point, these comments do not detract from Riker's concerns, and might even be interpreted to support his argument. The central point here, however, is that even if equilibria of the traditional sort exist, either in reality or in our abstractions, there remains no guarantee about the predictive and explanatory productivity of scientific inquiry; traditional definitions of equilibria may be inadequate for reasons other than existence. Yet what bothers Riker is that equilibria seem uncommon in even static theories. We cannot disagree. The theorems that demonstrate this proposition are incontrovertible. But the implications Riker draws about the presence of disequilibrium and the scientific tasks that lie before us need not follow.

First, equilibria and predictability are not synonymous. For instance, consider a simple majority voting situation in which there are 100 possible outcomes denoted O_1 through O_{100}. Suppose O_1 defeats O_2, O_2 defeats O_3, and O_3 defeats O_1 (that is, O_1, O_2, and O_3 cycle); but individually these first three outcomes defeat all that remain. This system has no Condorcet winner nor is the social order under majority rule transitive. Nevertheless, we can predict with confidence that outcomes O_4 through O_{100} will not be chosen.

Admittedly, this kind of situation does not fuel Riker's concern. Predicting "O_1, O_2, or O_3" is to say simply that the final outcome will be in the *top cycle set*, the set of outcomes that can be reached by some finite agenda from any other outcome. What troubles Riker is that for many situations, the top cycle set may include all possibilities. Riker refers particularly to McKelvey's result that, for a broad class of spatial games, if a majority equilibrium does not exist, then under majority and other such rules, the social preference ordering is wholly intransitive: one can cycle endlessly throughout the entire alternative space. Thus, an agenda setter, confronted with a naive committee, legislature, or electorate can manipulate them to any possible outcome. Herein is the source of Riker's conclusion that outcomes are determined by the act of persuasion and the inventiveness and artfulness of our political leaders.

However, notice the important shift in Riker's perspective, a shift from evaluating the properties of traditional kinds of equilibria—Nash equilibria, Condorcet winners and cores—to the properties of an alternative definition of a solution—the top cycle set. Riker's argument rests on the properties of but one solution hypothesis, a hypothesis that is by no means the sole candidate for resolving voting games without a core, Condorcet winner or Nash equilibrium.

Actually, Riker's argument is curious, given his research experience. Much of that experience is devoted to experimental work establishing the predictive value of a particular game-theory solution hypothesis, the Von Neumann–Morgenstern set (V-set). Briefly, the V-set is a hypothesis about what outcomes will prevail when a game (for example, a voting situation) does not have a core (majority dominant point) or when the top cycle set is large. Thus, for the three-person game in which any two people can decide how $10 is to be divided among themselves, the top cycle consists of all possible divisions, whereas the V-set predicts that two people will divide the money equally. Riker marshals considerable experimental support for this prediction.

The V-set has been largely discredited as an appropriate solution hypothesis principally because it does not exist or predicts poorly in a large class of voting games. Nonetheless, the perspective implicit in the development of the V-set is important: while personalities and abilities may dictate which particular outcome prevails, the range of possibilities can be narrowed down to some relatively small subset of the top cycle set.

A variety of alternatives to the V-set have been proposed and are now receiving close experimental and theoretical scrutiny. These include the Bargaining Set, the Competitive Solution, the Kernel, and the Defensible Set. Each alternative abides by the common belief that the absence of equilibria of the traditional sort does not preclude prediction and scientific explanation. And, while no wholly satisfactory or generally accepted solution hypothesis now exists, we should not suppose, as Riker implicitly does, that it *cannot* exist.

The scientific task before us, then, appears no different from the one Von Neumann and Morgenstern confronted: generalizing and redefining the meaning of the word "equilibrium." Twenty years of research compel us to conclude that traditional definitions of equilibria are unsatisfactory, or at least that they are not sufficiently general. Several such generalizations, such as the top cycle set, have been attempted but none possesses the full range of desired properties. The inadequacies of these generalizations, however, are only now beginning to be appreciated, and as the need for more general definitions becomes apparent we can suppose that considerably more effort will be directed at this scientific task. Disregarding his pessimism about the productivity of abstract theory, Riker's essay nonetheless highlights the necessity for further fundamental theorizing in the areas of decision theory, game theory, and the rational choice paradigm.

In summary, Riker incorrectly equates the possibility and fruitfulness of scientific inquiry with some notions of equilibria that are themselves subject to refinement and scientific advancement. Thus, reflecting on his argument and on the near countable infinity of impossibility theorems and negative results that form its basis, I arrive at a conclusion that contrasts sharply with his. I do not view these results as proving something unsavory or even disturbing about democratic processes in particular and political processes in general. Rather, they tell us that such processes do not operate in trivial, straightforward ways; that theorizing about them requires developing new concepts and that the optimism of the past over the ease with which the economists' paradigm could be transplanted into politics must give way to the realization that political scientists themselves must contribute to the development of that paradigm.

3 AN ALTIMETER FOR MR. ESCHER'S STAIRWAY:
A Comment on William H. Riker's "Implications from the Disequilibrium of Majority Rule for the Study of Institutions"

Douglas Rae

The real world of values is inconsistent; that is to say, it is made up of antagonistic elements. To grant them full recognition simultaneously is impossible, yet each demands total acceptance. This is not a matter of logical contradictions, because values are not theoretical theses. It is a contradiction which lies at the heart of human behavior.

—Leszek Kolakowski (1968, p. 216)

Politics is the dismal science because we have learned from it that there are no equilibria to predict. In the absence of equilibria we cannot know much about the future at all, whether it is likely to be palatable or unpalatable, and in that sense our future is subject to the tricks and accidents of the way . . . alternatives are offered and eliminated.

—William H. Riker (1980a, p. 443)

William Riker's article explains a central thesis of social choice theory with its author's characteristic vigor. The initial notion, first put forward some 195 years ago in Condorcet's *Essai* (1785) is this: Given three or more alternatives (say, laws or candidates) and three or more voters, majorities may march in circles even while individuals do not. The contemporary literature presents an essentially two-sided extension of Condorcet's little discovery: (i) that the Condorcet paradox can be avoided only at cost of violating some other reasonable-sounding axioms for social choice (viz., Arrow's theorem), and (ii) that under majority rule itself, cyclic majorities will be common, often large, generally without a single alternative immune to the process of cyclic dominance. This second range of findings, built up by Kramer, Plott, Fishburn, Bell, McKelvey, Schofield, and many others, tells us that the Condorcet paradox is no fluke, and therefore is not the dismissible "phantom" which Gordon Tullock used to make it out to be. It must be integrated with, not banished from, our understanding of political theory. This is what Riker tells us, and I agree. The question is to see why we should *care* about transitive consistency in liberal democratic (or any other) political theory.

WHY TRANSITIVE CONSISTENCY?

To the untutored eye, the underlying idea is not prepossessing. Why should we care about the possibility—even the overwhelming likelihood—that majorities may go marching around in circles? What, in other words, justifies transitivity itself: If x is better than y, and y is better than z, *why should x* be better than z?

Surely there are some aspects of life in which transitive consistency would be rejected by persons not certifiably irrational. Imagine, for example, the following announcement to a crowded stadium:

Cal Tech defeated Carnegie-Mellon on September 12, Carnegie-Mellon defeated Harvard on September 19, Harvard defeated Minnesota on September 21, and Minnesota defeated Texas on September 28: Therefore Cal Tech has been declared the winner of today's game with Texas, which will not be played lest a violation of transitive consistency occur.

One would need *guns* to justify this reasoning.

Or consider Leo Strauss's case against rational consistency in the thought of Max Weber (1950, p. 47):

I must act rationally: I must be honest with myself, I must be consistent in my adherence to my fundamental objectives, and I must rationally choose the means required by my ends. But why? What difference can this still make after we have been reduced to a condition in which the maxims of the heartless voluptuary as well as those of the sentimental philistine have to be regarded as no less defensible than those of the idealist, of the gentleman, or of the saint? We cannot take seriously this belated insistence on responsibility and sanity, this inconsistent concern with consistency, this irrational praise of rationality.

What this suggests for the present case is that the formal vacuity of transitive consistency—aimed at ciphers like "x" or "a_j"—may miss what is rationally defensible (even what is consistent)[1] by placing all laws, all leaders, all policies under its blind exaction, and doing so blindly.

Coming back within the horizon of Riker's analysis, please hear Robert Dahl asserting the *irrationality* of the demand for transitivity within a democratic framework (1956, p. 42, italics added):

> Because Arrow . . . assumes "transitivity of collective choice" as a criterion of rational social action, it is worth noting that under almost any theory of democratic politics . . . the *requirement of transitivity would be irrational* in a great many types of collective choices. By "transitivity" we mean, on the analogy of inequalities in mathematics, that if an individual prefers x to y and y to z he must also prefer x to z—at least, if he is to behave rationally. But whatever the case may be with individual choices—and even here the requirement is somewhat tendentious—clearly it would lead to *irrational* results in a democracy to require transition choices. For example, along 101 individuals assume that
>
> > 1 individual prefers x to y, and y to z;
> > 50 individuals prefer z to x, and x to y;
> > 50 individuals prefer y to z, and z to x.
>
> Then 51 prefer x to y, 51 prefer y to z. If we assume transitivity in collective choice, it would follow that a majority of at least 51 prefers x to z also. But in fact, 100 individuals prefer z to x. And *the requirement of transitivity would produce the anomalous result that the preferences of the singular eccentric would be translated into public policy despite the fact that 100 individuals prefer the opposite policy.*

Now Riker and his colleagues supply a kind of answer to this heterodoxy, namely, that intransitivity makes majority rule not simply inconsistent but also *unmajoritarian*. Indeed, the final conclusion of his essay is that "in the long run, outcomes are the consequence of the political skills and artistry of those who manipulate the agenda, formulate and reformulate questions, generate 'false' issues, etc., in order to exploit the disequilibrium of tastes for their own advantage" (1980a, p. 445).[2] In short, majorities become the means of minority rule.

But then Dahl (or, better, a Marxist critic) can remind us that the undemocratic forces which *really* limit majoritarianism come before preferences form, if ever they do form, and are at most complicated by the disequilibrating effects of intransitivity. This is not to dismiss Riker's point, or to imply that transitivity is meaningless, but it does suggest that its importance lies elsewhere, in a larger argument of which it is only part.

TWO LIBERAL VALUES

The central concern of all liberal thought is the promotion of *rights* for persons. Yet, at least since Condorcet's era, liberal thinkers have given two utterly different accounts for the *value* of rights. Neither view is singular or simple, but both are coherent enough to serve our small purpose. The first view, held by figures as different as Paine and Kant, treats rights as valuable in themselves, no matter what their consequences may turn out to be. It is not that rights tend to promote some further good, but that rights are right. A second view, taken by Bentham, Mill, Pareto, Hayek, and many others, claims that rights have good consequences—for the discovery of truth (Mill), or for economic efficiency (Pareto), or for framing felicitous laws (Bentham). This second view then goes on to imbed these good consequences in a *utilitarian* theory of value, so that we are asked to think that rights promote the maximization of utility in society, and are to be respected for this reason.

This two-sided theory of value perpetually threatens to come apart when either (i) rights fail to promote utility, or (ii) the efficient promotion of utility entails a violation of rights. It is not, therefore, entirely surprising that the most revered works of liberalism have included those which forge an analytical link between rights and utility, so that we may rule out embarrassments (i) and (ii) as defined above.

While Mill's *On Liberty* (1849) presents a complex and deeply problematic instance of such joinery, the most spectacular attainment of this sort is not a single work but a tradition and discipline, neoclassical economics. No one book can be said to contain the core of neoclassicism, although my own vote for the single most essential work would go to Pareto's *Manual of Political Economy* (1971). For present purposes, we need not explore the neoclassicists very extensively, but need only consider two conceptions—property rights and Pareto-style efficiency—as they are related to one another in economic theory. Here in the simplest terms are the essentials:

1. *Property rights* mean the authority to dictate the use of what one owns, and to sell it as one chooses, free from constraint or coercion by others.
2. The *Pareto principle* tells us (a) that one social state x is Pareto-superior to another social state y if and only if some persons prefer x to y and none prefers y to x, and (b) a social state x is Pareto-optimal if no other state y fulfills criterion (a) in respect to it.

The innocuous-seeming Pareto principle is the version of utilitarianism that these economists accept, and upon which their rights–utility synthesis is based. Its main feature is that no cardinal, interpersonal comparisons of utility, like those imagined by Bentham, are required. This last, the stricture against "interpersonal comparisons," is a methodological point pregnant with philosophical and ideological significance (Rae, 1975).

Neoclassical economics is to be sure a complex doctrine, and it is currently perhaps less simple and more problematic than at any time in our century. I therefore neglect a great deal in saying so little, but only a little needs saying for our immediate purpose. It is this: Property rights are the sine qua non of the Pareto principle. These rights promote utility in Pareto's sense at two distinct levels. They provide, first, an epistemology of utility by revealing preferences through behavior. The utility of a transaction for a given person need not be measured by politicians or scientists, for it is measured by the agents themselves: If I give you alpha in exchange for beta, then my utility is increased; if you accept alpha for beta, yours is also increased. Because we have property rights, and are thus thought to be free of coercion and compulsion, this indication of increased utility is, the doctrine assumes, to be taken as valid. At a second level, property rights provide the practical rubric for actually effecting such gains of utility. Every market transaction actually consummated is, in theory, the implementation of precept (2a), for the post-transaction outcome is preferred by both traders to the pretransaction outcome. If and when transactions occur, Pareto-superior arrangements displace Pareto-inferior ones. We thus can think of the market as a system of innumerable little liberal polities, each lasting only as long as its partners find mutual gain from trade, each evanescing at the merest rejection of a price or lot of goods. Each such polity is created by right of property, and each may be terminated by the same right. Utility is promoted thanks to the existence of these rights, and we know it to be a promotion of utility because of these rights. The two faces of liberal value are in this way welded together as means to end, end to means, inseparable faces of the liberal market itself.[3]

It would, therefore, be merely a cruel illusion if the market went round and round in circles, never approaching the state of optimality posited by precept (2b). If the market began with distribution x, then passed by a vast series of transactions through distributions y and z, what an awful embarrassment it would be to discover that we had traded our way back where we began, to x. What a monstrous failure and fraud would the precept of Pareto-superiority now seem, for it suggests that society is getting to better and better places—superior ones with more and more social utility—and yet we have come back to where we began. If this cyclic, disequilibrating process occurred because people changed their tastes, that would be tolerable. But if it happened for any other reason, and optimality was never approached, that would make markets like one of

Escher's stairways leading always up yet always coming back down to its own foundation.[4] Most of all, it would spoil the reconciliation of rights and utility. *The idea beneath all this is our friend transitivity, and its importance is to underwrite the rights-utility bond.*[5] Transitivity works as an altimeter that assures that the stairway leads always up, to loftier preference levels, to greater utility. It thus assures that the rights–utility bond is self-consistent. A longer article would pause to criticize and observe the nuances of this point, a point somewhat less straightforward than it may seem. But for now, our job is simply to see how *badly* majority rule in government compares with the market scheme as it is *imagined* in this simple digest of neoclassical thought.

The same two-sided account of value appears again when we turn to the liberal state and majoritarianism. Here is a classic rights-in-themselves argument from Tom Paine's *Dissertation on First Principles of Government* (1953, p. 165):

> The right of voting for representatives is the primary right by which other rights are protected. To take away this is to reduce a man to slavery, for slavery consists in being subject to the will of another, and he that has not a vote is . . . in this case. The proposal, therefore, to disfranchise any class of men is as criminal as the proposal to take away property.

Rights may be seen as protecting other rights, but rights are themselves what must be valued. This stands in stark contrast to the theory of constitutional order, of collective choice, proposed by Buchanan and Tullock, Downs, Riker, and the public choice school generally. Here, utilitarian tradesmen take center stage, as in this metaphor:

> An acceptable theory of collective choice can perhaps do something similar in pointing the way toward those rules for choicemaking, the constitution, under which the activities of political tradesmen can similarly be reconciled with the interests of all members of the social group. (Buchanan and Tullock, 1962, p. 23)

The idea is that the value of constitutional arrangements, including voting rights, are reducible to their consequences as measured in utility. Now it would be a fine and useful theory which could link the rights-qua-rights and the rights-utility views of voting.

ESCHER'S STAIRWAY

Let us therefore imagine that Riker and all his associates right back to Condorcet are flatly wrong, and indeed that we can forge a link between a further pair of ideas:

$1'$. *Voting rights* mean the authority to express one's judgment of state policy and to have those judgments counted under the principle of majority rule.

$2'$. *Majoritarian analog of Pareto principle* tells us: (a) that every political outcome x preferred by more rather than fewer voters to its alternative y is majority-superior, and (b) political outcome x is majority-optimal if no other outcome y fulfills criterion (a) in respect to it.

Now this ill-shaped principle $(2')$ is tailored to fit majority voting rights just as the Pareto principle x fits property rights. It succeeds in the small fact that $(2a')$ follows majority rule $(1')$ as neatly as $(2a)$ follows market exchange (1). That is, however, only a small blessing. For $(2a')$ has no definite relation to the principle of utility maximization, and is in this way unsuited to the tasks accomplished by (2). For, if the minority loses more utility than the majority gains, then majority-preference may actually diminish total utility. This is a first, and important, fissure in our little welding job. Dahl puts it very nicely $(1956, p. 90)$:

> By making "most preferred" equivalent to "preferred by the most" we deliberately bypass a crucial problem: What if the minority prefers its alternative much more passionately than the majority prefers a contrary alternative? Does the majority principle still make sense?

If one relies upon a link between voting rights and utilitarianism, the answer is either a firm "no" or an equivocal "maybe"—which is quite enough to cause us to wonder whether majority rule is not an Escher staircase, and whether we do not need an altimeter which assures our upward progress.[6]

We turn now to $(2b')$, which defines a "majority-optimum" as a policy against which no further policy wins a majority.[7] This is exactly what Riker and his associates tell us cannot be expected, for the operation of $(2a')$ would lead to the discovery of an outcome meeting $(2b')$ only if transitive consistency governed its behavior. Only then could each binary application of majority rule be a knowable step up in utility space, and only then could we make the rights-utility link which is so characteristically important in liberal thought. Only then would we possess an altimeter so as to treat a staircase in confident knowledge that none of Mr. Escher's tricks would take us back where we began. What we have learned from the work discussed in Riker's article is that this altimeter—transitive consistency—will not give us the sequence of increasing altitude readings that we need.

I think that is reason enough to grant the importance of these results, but I do not think it provides a reason to think we have arrived at a resting point in the theory of constitutions. I think it tells us that utilitarianism, including its

Pareto version, is simply one among many criteria of choice which men and women may apply *within* a democratic order. Though John Plamenatz (1973, esp. p. 184) was evidently unwilling to explore the literature Riker considers, he was driving thought in a similar direction when he wrote that

> democracy is a matter of rights and obligations. . . . Whoever seeks to explain it, no matter how much his purpose is merely to explain and not also to justify, cannot avoid a kind of exercise which is more properly called philosophy than science. . . . Democracy can neither be explained nor justified as a political system that maximized the satisfaction of wants (or the achievement of goals) better than other systems do. (1973, p. 181; see also Hart, 1979)

An understanding of majority rule, of democracy, of liberalism which does without utilitarianism, and which does more than merely assert that rights are right, must travel in a more mysterious space, must walk up odder stairs, and must employ a more intricate altimeter than transitive consistency.

NOTES

1. We might thus find ourselves consistently choosing what is absurdly inconsistent, if it were observed that x was preferable to y, and y preferred to z, therefore x preferred to z, where

x = giving everyone an income above the national average;
y = giving everyone an income equal to the national average;
z = giving no one an income on which he or she will starve.

In brief, the consistent selection of an inconsistent policy.

2. Notice, incidentally, that Riker assumes that political manipulators care mainly about policies, while in fact the incentives they face may induce them to care very little indeed about actual policy outcomes. See, for instance, Mayhew (1976).

3. In this connection, I cannot resist noting that Riker is quite wrong to brand Marx "absurd." Here is Marx on the sort of thinking we are summarizing here, which he mocks as

> a very Eden of the innate rights of man. There alone rule Freedom, Equality, Property, and Bentham. Freedom, because both buyer and seller of a commodity . . . are constrained only by their own free will. . . . Equality, because each enters into relation with the other . . . and they exchange equivalent for equivalent. Property, because each disposes only of what is his own. And Bentham, because each looks only to himself. . . . Each looks to himself only, and no one troubles himself about the rest, and just because they do so, do they all, in accordance with the pre-established harmony of things, or under the auspices of an all-shrewd providence, work together to their mutual advantage, for the common weal and in the interest of all. (1906, Vol. 1, p. 194)

4. For a discussion of Escher in a broad and speculative essay of great merit, see Hofstadter (1979).

5. It must be admitted that the Pareto principle itself would violate transitivity if the judgments it deems undecidable were declared indifferent.

6. It may actually be conjectured that this point partly *explains* the intransitivity of majority rule. Imagine a cardinal, interpersonal criterion of utility and hypothesize *any* decision rule which never chooses less total utility over more total utility: Could such a scheme ever violate transitivity? It could not, and could not do so for the same reason that a grocer's scale cannot. Majority rule is not such a scheme and thus does assure transitivity.

7. Criterion (2b') corresponds to the solution proposed in Condorcet's *Essai* (1785), viz., of points to what is now called a "Condorcet winner" (which, we now know, may not exist).

4 A REPLY TO ORDESHOOK AND RAE

William H. Riker

Both my critics agree that, under majority rule, individual values are likely to be in social disequilibrium—barring such rare events as unanimity on a complete ordering of all possible alternatives, etc. From this admitted potentiality of disequilibrium, two kinds of inferences can be drawn:

1. In the realm of political philosophy, the inference that social decisions under majority rule cannot usually be defended as logically coherent or as the work of some anthropomorphized entity like the "society" or "the people." Given that a winning platform or motion or candidate exists, the fact of disequilibrium means that, at the time of the choice of the winner, there existed potentially a platform or motion or candidate that could beat the winner. Furthermore, potentially another alternative could beat the potential victor over the actual winner, and so forth around a cycle. This fact in turn means that the products of majority rule are probably seldom defensible as consistent or as the "true" choice of the voting body. Indeed, with a slightly different turn of events, some other alternative could have been the choice of a (differently composed) majority, though not necessarily a more coherent choice than the alternative actually chosen.

2. In the realm of political theory (i.e., description as distinct from prescription), the inference that social decisions cannot be predicted simply from a knowledge of individual orderings of values. Given a set of individual tastes, what comes out of majority rule is a function not only of the tastes of persons, but also of the political institutions surrounding the process of voting, of the skill with which individuals manipulate the selection of alternatives and the statement of issues, and indeed even of the intelligence and character of the voters. Consequently, the prediction of social outcomes is rendered difficult.

THE PHILOSOPHICAL PROBLEM

My article now under discussion was limited entirely to the inference in the realm of political theory or description and had nothing to do with political philosophy and the defense or criticism of democracy. Indeed, insofar as something remotely like majority rule exists in all societies with even the most muffled forms of consent, my discussion was intended to deal with a quite general description of politics. It is, therefore, quite a surprise to find Douglas Rae (1980) discussing my article as if it dealt with the inference in the realm of political philosophy. While I believe that the latter inference is worth considerable attention, and I have in fact discussed it at length in a paper delivered at the 1978 meeting of the American Political Science Association (where it was commented on by Rae) and in *Liberalism against Populism* (1980b), I did not discuss it here because I sought to focus attention on the theoretical question. Since, however, Rae has raised the philosophical question, I feel constrained to make a few remarks about it.

I point out first that, whatever may be the need of classical economic liberalism to reconcile rights and efficiency, liberal democracy has never faced that problem because it has never been concerned with social utility as set forth in Rae's principle (2b'). (It is only populists from Rousseau to contemporary social democrats who anthropomorphize a majority which is to have its utility maximized.) Rather, liberal democracy (as explicated by, for example, Madison) is aimed solely at protecting rights, and in that sense I can quite agree with the remark of Plamenatz, quoted by Rae, that democracy has nothing in particular to do with satisfying wants. Indeed, I have utterly failed to make my position clear to Rae if he believes it is utilitarian. My position is indeed based on methodological individualism and on the assumption that individual persons choose rationally, but nevertheless it is not utilitarian, and I can find as much amusement as Rae did in his well-known quotation from Marx on the utilitarians, who from Bentham and Mill to Rawls and Nader have consistently subordinated humane values to some arbitrary and imposed virtues they prefer. (Just for the record and in response to Rae's note 3 [p. 39], I called Marx "absurd," in the precise sense of "plainly irrational," not because he satirized utilitarianism—in words, as he said, to give the bourgeoisie cause to remember his carbuncles—but because he reduced the complexity of politics to a few economic institutions, thereby reducing human beings to atoms maneuvered by economic forces, one-dimensional people in a one-dimensional world. One of the great virtues of the literature here reviewed is that it rescues the humanity of mankind from the slough of technological determinism in which Marx tried, misanthropically, to submerge it.)

My more significant failure in conveying my position to Rae is revealed in his belief that my concern is that majority rule is not likely to be consistent. While it is certainly the case, as he agrees, that disequilibrium implies inconsistency, the main problem for democracy is not inconsistency but the manipulability of majority rule outcomes. Given manipulability, it is likely that outcomes will never have any meaning, that they will always involve strange bedfellows, and that, even if one sacrifices consistency (as I am perfectly willing to do), there is simply no possible way to interject meaning into majority rule decision, that is, no "more intricate altimeter" can exist. It does not follow, however, that democracy is without value. Rather, it has a different kind of value: the protection of rights by means of popular vetoes over officials, as explained originally by Madison and latterly in my *Liberalism against Populism* (1980b). A democracy of that kind is, however, wholly incompatible with imposed moral standards, so that people like C.B. MacPherson or John Rawls cannot possibly be democrats in the one sense of the word that remains after the revelations of the literature I have surveyed.

THE THEORETICAL PROBLEM

Turning now to the inference from disequilibrium in the realm of political theory, which was entirely the subject of my survey of literature and which is indeed the subject that Peter Ordeshook (1980) addresses, I think this format of criticism and response is useful because it allows for a clarification of issues.

Unfortunately, Ordeshook has misread my emphasis. For example, he seems to think that I am attempting to import economic models or economic notions of equilibrium into politics. Yet it is precisely that importation I am objecting to. My whole argument is directed toward a renewal of political scientists' interests in the study of institutions. This study has to some degree been neglected, I argue, because of the influence of the economic model which, as I observed, overemphasizes tastes. Consequently, I agree for the most part with Ordeshook's conclusion, which, however, he believes differs from mine, that "the optimism of the past over the ease with which the economists' paradigm could be transplanted into politics must give way to the realization that political scientists themselves must contribute to the development of that paradigm." My only disagreement with this conclusion is that it does not go far enough: The paradigm political scientists ought to develop is uniquely political and it is not their duty simply to develop "that paradigm" from economics.

There are a number of other details in Ordeshook's remarks that indicate that he believes our opinions differ, when in fact we have extremely similar views. Let me make it clear that simply because I have pointed out that the form of issues (often an individual contribution) influences outcomes in the same way as institutions and individual values, it does not follow that I have denied the possibility of a science of politics. That an equilibrium of individual values is extremely unlikely means that one cannot predict political outcomes simply from a knowledge of those values. It does not mean that there is no science of politics. Indeed, the whole purpose of my article is to point out precisely what that science consists of. I do not deny but celebrate the possibility of a scientific understanding of political *processes*. What I deny is, for the present, the possibility of a general scientific prediction of outcomes. As I emphasized throughout my review, it is exactly empirical regularities of process, which I called "unstable constants" and which are the interesting features of institutions, that we ought to be studying, now that we know for certain that particular outcomes of interlocking tastes are not themselves predictable.

As Ordeshook points out, this is one kind of empirical work that both he and I have done in studying particular solution concepts for games. These solution concepts exist in terms of a set of rules—which are institutions. The fact that a particular set of rules, such as the kind of communication allowed, the method of voting, the kind of exchanges allowed, etc., influences the kinds of outcomes in the same way as do the tastes of the participants is a scientific discovery of great value, though one ought not to confuse it—as Ordeshook does—with general theory. It is even more valuable when one can state in just what ways the institutions (rules) do in themselves influence outcomes. Hence the comparative study of what combination of tastes and rules lead to outcomes described by such solution concepts as the V-set, the bargaining set, the competitive solution and others which Ordeshook lists is one of the kinds of scientific investigation that I regard as both possible and important. Precisely like Ordeshook, I think that it is the absence of what he calls equilibria of the "traditional" sort and what I call equilibria of tastes—and what probably should be called "general" equilibria—that leads us to investigate these processes. It was because I believe that these things are what make up the unique subject matter of political science (as distinct from, for example, economics) that I wrote this review of political theory. Far from wishing to transplant economic theory to politics (as, so I infer from the fourth paragraph and then the last sentence of his comment, Ordeshook seems to think I wish), I wrote and write to emancipate political theorists from their fascination with the economists' equilibria of tastes and to urge them to study political institutions.

It may seem from these remarks that I regard my position and Ordeshook's as identical even though he does not. But in fact there are important differences between us:

For one thing, "redefining" the notion of equilibrium, as Ordeshook proposes, into what he mistakenly believes will be general, is not likely to improve the science because we now know that general equilibrium is impossible. If equilibria of tastes are indeed rare and fragile, then redefining "equilibrium" will not produce equilibrium. To believe so is like believing one can cure cancer by redefining it as a state of health. Ordeshook's main criticism of my article is that I have "misconstrued" equilibrium. I think he is the one who misconstrues. By assuming he can redefine equilibrium into existence, he is attempting to substitute a word for the thing. But redefinition will get us nowhere. A more sensible route, I think, is to specify special equilibria for particular institutions, as, for example, Ordeshook and McKelvey have themselves done with the competitive solution—for which the particular institutional feature is the absence of side-payments. If every set of institutional arrangements has a different kind of solution (or "structural equilibrium," in Shepsle's words), we may often have problems deciding which game is going on in the real world, but at least we will be working toward the understanding of institutions that I think we can increasingly achieve.

Incidentally, Ordeshook calls my use of "equilibrium" the "traditional" usage and also says it is "peculiar." How did he get himself into this contradiction, which consumes and vitiates most of his essay? The answer is, I believe, that he has systematically confused the structural or institutional equilibria of game solutions—which, though abstract, are still special cases—with the general equilibrium of tastes.

For another thing, I think Ordeshook and I disagree rather sharply about how fast the science of politics is progressing. For the active theorist and investigator, each step forward toward the identification of an empirical regularity is a triumph. But identification of such regularities in theory and the laboratory is a long way from encompassing the political reality of the larger world (see my article, 1977). I suppose this disagreement is largely a matter of temperament. His position might be described as enthusiasm while mine is a more cautious optimism.

The really important difference between us, however, lies in our notions of what kind of science the study of politics is. A science can describe either process or outcome or both. The mature physical sciences, and even microeconomics, for example, do both. Some sciences in their beginnings (for example, the study of evolution prior to recombinant DNA) emphasize process at the expense of outcomes. Other sciences, perhaps descriptive geology (before plate tectonics), emphasize outcomes at the expense of process. I think political science is now in the stage of emphasizing process very much like biology in the first part of this century. Ordeshook believes our science is much more mature and can handle both process and outcomes. Only time and future developments will show which one of us is right about the state we are in now, although assuming there is progress no one in the future will care very much about this dispute — which will then be ancient history.

II ALTERNATIVE VIEWS OF POLITICAL EQUILIBRIUM

5 EQUILIBRIUM, DISEQUILIBRIUM, AND THE GENERAL POSSIBILITY OF A SCIENCE OF POLITICS

Morris P. Fiorina and Kenneth A. Shepsle

Perhaps it overstates matters to say that there is a crisis in formal political theory, but it is apparent that much mischief has been caused by a series of theorems that depict the chaotic features of majority-rule voting systems. These theorems, proved elegantly in recent papers by Cohen (1979), McKelvey (1976, 1979) and Schofield (1978), establish that the cyclicity of the majority preference relation is both generic and pervasive. To paraphrase the title of a recent paper by Bell (1978), when majority rule breaks down, it breaks down completely; and it "almost always" breaks down.

Although these results are of relatively recent vintage, and their implications are only now being traced, signs of intellectual indigestion are already observable. Certainly, there is no clear consensus on the import or significance of these results. At one extreme, some scholars continue business as usual. The new results simply constitute a political fact of life—a fact that may be artfully employed to further an interest. Thus, Plott and Levine (1978) and McKelvey (1977, 1978), posing as latter-day Machiavellis, profess to offer advice to the

The authors acknowledge comments on an earlier draft, ranging from constructive hostility to benign neglect, from Randall Calvert, John Ferejohn, Robert Parks, Charles Plott, Robert Salisbury, and Barry Weingast.

prince of a majority-rule committee – the chairman – as to how he might manipulate the sequence of committee votes in order to arrive at a final committee decision identical to his ideal point.

At the other extreme, some scholars fear that the new disequilibrium results are inimical not only to current ideas about politics, but to the scientific enterprise itself. These scholars conclude that, as a consequence of majority cycles, there are no political regularities ("Anything can happen"), or that what appear to be regularities are inexplicable as equilibria in some model of politics. This latter view is advanced and discussed in a recent symposium on disequilibrium and majority rule (see Riker, 1980a; Ordeshook, 1980; and Rae, 1980).

The Cohen-McKelvey-Schofield theorems are profound and, as noted above, are only now being digested by students of the science of politics. These results provide some basis for questioning the utility of equilibrium concepts and provide the occasion for us, in this paper, to explore the importance of equilibrium (and its absence) for a science of politics. We begin, in the first section, by reviewing the reasons why equilibrium concepts, in *all* the social sciences, are not what they are sometimes believed to be. Even when equilibria exist, they are often imprecise, unrelated to observable regularities, or dependent upon unjustified (if not perverse) individual behavior. In the second section, we advance a possibly controversial position – that instances of disequilibrium, as in the Cohen-McKelvey-Schofield results, are not nearly so serious or debilitating for a science of politics as sometimes feared. We argue that the distinctions between equilibrium and disequilibrium are typically overdrawn, and that the existence of equilibrium in one model as opposed to another, or indeed in one discipline as opposed to another, is largely a matter of scholarly choice. In the concluding section, we offer a not particularly original suggestion that political theorists avoid the choices made in both economic theory and in recent efforts in formal political theory, and instead follow a third path when formulating models to explain observed political regularities.

DO EQUILIBRIUM RESULTS PROVIDE THE BASIS FOR A
SCIENCE OF POLITICS?

We have neither the competence nor the inclination to engage in an abstract discussion of the philosophy of science. Our viewpoint in this paper is that of practitioners who feel confident that at least some part of their research activity is "scientific" in nature. To us, science is a method for comprehending the world, not as a collection of unique events, but in terms of *regularities* that may be observed in the world. Such regularities include the repeated occurrence of particular *outcomes* – the regular formation of minimal winning coalitions, for example. They include the existence of *trends* — by a variety of measures modern governments have steadily grown, for example. And such regularities include the existence of *patterns* — the identification of an elections-economic cycle is an example. Regularities are preconditions of scientific analysis, grist for science's mill.

Traditionally, the scientific method has aimed at formulating theories that would account for observed regularities. And a generally accepted condition for a theory to be judged scientific is that its implications be clear and specific. It is this condition that excludes "the will of God" or, according to many, psychoanalysis, from the class of scientific theories. The implications of a scientific theory must be sufficiently clear and precise that competent scholars can agree upon real-world data that could in principle be inconsistent with the theoretical implications. The question we pose is whether existing social science equilibrium theories generate such clear and precise implications.

Certainly, if the concept of equilibrium present in social science equilibrium theories were akin to the concept of a black hole in space, social science theories would have clear and precise implications. Such equilibria would have irresistible attracting power, and once attracted, nothing would escape them. Unfortunately, there are myriad equilibrium concepts in social science theories, and few put one in mind of black holes, even gray holes for that matter. Some of the problems with social science equilibria are well known and the subject of scholarly concern. Others are obvious but by general agreement not discussed — the soft underbelly of social science. In this section, we shall briefly review the state of social science equilibrium theory as a means of reminding our colleagues of how fragile most equilibrium theories are.

We begin by noting the manner in which equilibrium concepts differ from black holes, lacking either their drawing power or their capacity to retain. Consider the set A of alternatives, the *majority dominance relation* $>: A \times A \to A$, and an alternative $x^* \in A$ with the following property:

x^* satisfies the condition that

$x^* > y$ for every $y \in A - \{x^*\}$.

We can assert, though not without qualification, that if black hole equilibrium concepts are to be found in social science, then x^* must be included among them. Surely it retains in the sense that, once arrived at, it is never departed from. Thus, if a *majority trajectory* $(x_1, x_2, \ldots)$, where x_{i+1} differs from x_i only if $x_{i+1} > x_i$, ever reaches x^* it remains there, since x^* is undominated, viz., $(x_1, x_2, \ldots, x_i, x_{i+1}, \ldots, x^*, x^*, \ldots, x^*)$. Its attraction characteristics, however, must be couched in a more contingent fashion. In particular, the attraction of x^* depends not only on the majority dominance relation $>$, but on the rules for comparison as well. Even if an $x^* \in A$ exists, it may never be "reachable" from some specific initial status quo if it is excluded from comparison by features of the agenda-construction process. It may be said, however, that if there are no agenda obstacles, so that every majority trajectory must pass ultimately through x^*, then, by stipulation, x^* is an attractor or sink.

This distinguished point, along with the added stipulation, identifies a scientific ideal for the class of equilibrium notions in the context $(>,A)$. But, on the strength of the Cohen–McKelvey–Schofield theorems, it is not very interesting in the following sense: If $\{(>,A)\}$ is the family of contexts consisting of a set of alternatives and a majority-dominance relation, and μ is an appropriate measure on subsets of this family, then the subset consisting of contexts in which x^* exists is of measure zero. For our purposes, then, equilibrium concepts must have strong attraction and retention properties, but we cannot require x^* as stipulated for then we risk (with near certainty—hardly a risk!) coming up empty-handed.

It is well known that most current equilibrium ideas in political science and economics fall far short of the black hole desiderata in that they entail relaxing either the strong attraction property or the strong retention property that black holes possess. Consider first the *core* $C \subseteq A$, consisting of undominated outcomes: $C = \{x \in A \mid y > x \text{ for no } y \in A\}$. When x^* exists, it is an element of C, but the requirements for membership in C are not so stringent. C consists of the set of strong retainers. If a majority rule trajectory moves into C, it will not depart; indeed, it will not leave the particular element of C at which it arrives. Yet, the following example from Ferejohn, Fiorina, and Packel (1980) illustrates the well-known weakness of the core's attraction properties. Let there be four voters (1–4) and five alternatives (x_1–x_5) described by the schedule of preferences in Table 5.1. $>$ is the strict majority preference relation according to which $x > y$ if and only if x obtains three or more votes against y. According to $>$, x_1, x_2, x_3, and x_4 cycle. None strictly majority-dominates x_5—hence $C = \{x_5\}$. However, x_5 strictly majority-dominates none of the remaining alternatives. Thus, if the

Table 5.1. Schedule of Preferences

1	2	3	4
x_1	x_2	x_3	x_4
x_2	x_3	x_4	x_1
x_5	x_5	x_5	x_5
x_3	x_4	x_1	x_2
x_4	x_1	x_2	x_3

institutional matrix into which $(>,A)$ is embedded designates some $x \in A$ as the initial status quo, then only if x_5 receives this designation will it ever be observed as the group choice.

Lest the reader think this critique of the core (even when it exists) is limited to politics in general and majority rule in particular, it should be observed that the core of a private economy is plagued by similar defects. Weintraub (1979, p. 35), describing the grand edifice of general equilibrium theory elaborated by Arrow, Debreu, and McKenzie, concedes that "a particularly curious dynamic process was needed to ensure any robustness of [the core]." Noting, moreover, the state of flux in which stability theory, the study of dynamic adjustment, currently resides, he quotes one of its more eminent students, Frank Hahn, to the effect that the theory of dynamic adjustment to a general equilibrium consists of a "collection of sufficient conditions, anecdotes really."[1] So it seems, then, that even when an equilibrium with strong retention properties exists, its accessibility depends upon the institutional matrix in which it is embedded; and our theories, thus far, of this larger context are only "anecdotes really." The core, in sum, is not only plagued by familiar existence problems; additionally, it may not be a very attractive equilibrium (pun intended!).

Other cooperative equilibrium concepts fare no better. Whereas the core is retentive but not necessarily attractive, the *stable set, bargaining set*, and *competitive solution* (to select some of the more prominent alternatives to the core) tend to be attractive but not retentive. We restrict our remarks to the von Neumann-Morgenstern stable set, though they apply to the others as well. The stable set, or V-solution, is a collection of alternatives no one of which is dominated by any other and any nonmember of which is dominated by some member. Thus, for the 4-voter, 5-alternative example of Ferejohn, Fiorina, and Packel given above, there are two (nondiscriminatory) V-solutions:

$$V_1 = \{x_1, x_3, x_5\}$$
$$V_2 = \{x_2, x_4, x_5\}.$$

The V-Solution may not exist, as Lucas (1969) showed, but the more typical difficulty is one of nonuniqueness. In the particular example above, it turns out that every alternative is a member of some V-solution, so that the process is tautologically characterized by a V-solution concept of equilibrium. (No evidence could be adduced from this example for the proposition that non-V-solution forces were at work.) More to our point, however, is that either of the V-solutions in the example is attractive but not retentive. The process is always at a V-solution, as noted above, and always heading for the other, unless the process hits the core x_5 (which, if it exists, is always part of every V-solution). Indeed, in our example, unless it begins at x_5, the process will bounce between V_1 and V_2, reflecting the cycle among x_1, x_2, x_3, x_4 and the nondominating property of x_5.

These remarks extend to any collection of alternatives cum equilibrium. They attract but they do not retain. Indeed they may not even attract if local cycles are present. In the earlier example, if we add x_6, x_7, x_8, which cycle among themselves but individually are dominated by $x_1, \ldots, x_5$, it is possible to observe the process caught in a local cycle $x_6 \rightarrow x_7 \rightarrow x_8 \rightarrow x_6$—with neither V_1 nor V_2 ever being reached. Thus we arrive at equilibrium concepts that "sometimes" attract and do not retain, hardly a firm basis on which to predict, explain, or control.

Frustration with the V-solution convinced John Nash (1951) that noncooperative, unilateral behavior was both more basic and offered more promise for the formulation of fruitful equilibrium notions. But are noncooperative equilibria any more successful in attracting and retaining than their cooperative counterparts? A *Nash equilibrium* consists of a collection of individual choices or strategies from which no individual, acting independently, has any incentive to depart by altering his choice unilaterally. The cooperative generalization of this equilibrium is the core, in which no coalition of players has an incentive to change its individual choices jointly. Like the core, and subject to the proviso of noncooperation, the Nash equilibrium retains but does not necessarily attract. If a social process arrives at a Nash equilibrium, then it will not depart since unilateral behavior—the only kind allowed in this context—will not support any change. But do individuals have any incentive to play their Nash strategies? Not necessarily.

First, and perhaps of only minor importance, is the problem of *imperfect Nash equilibrium*. Imperfect equilibria, in Harsanyi's (1978, pp. 50–51) words, "assume highly *irrational behavior* [emphasis included] on the part of some players, yet they fully satisfy the mathematical definition of an equilibrium point." He illustrates this idea with a two-person example in which, in the extensive form, player 1 chooses a or b and, if he chooses the latter, player 2 then selects between x and y. The game tree is shown in Figure 5.1. There are two Nash equilibria, easily identified in the normal form:

		2	
		x	y
1	a	1,3	1,3
	b	0,0	2,2

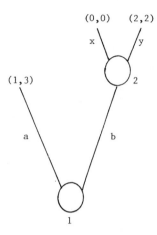

Figure 5.1. Imperfect Nash Equilibrium

Both (a, x) and (b, y) satisfy the mathematical definition of a Nash equilibrium; yet (a, x) is imperfect. As a glance at the extensive form provides, it depends on player 1 choosing irrationally[2] inasmuch as he can reasonably assume player 2's self-interest will lead him (player 2) to select y if 1 selects b. And, since 1 prefers (b, y) to (a, x), the latter does not attract. The bottom line, then, is that some Nash equilibria are inaccessible by rational choice unless a social process should find itself in that state, *ex ante*.

A related, but more serious, criticism addresses the incentive problem directly. To make this point, we consider the quintessential noncooperative circumstance – the two-person zero-sum game. We offer the following partition of this class of games and speculate that the reader will find the Nash equilibrium established by von Neumann's minimax theorem an increasingly *less* persuasive equilibrium concept as he or she descends the list:

1. Both players possess dominant strategies.
2. Exactly one of the players has a dominant strategy.
3. There are no dominant strategies, but there is a pure strategy equilibrium point, and
    i. one player believes the other will play a security level maximizing strategy, or
    ii. one player believes the other believes the first will play a security level maximizing strategy, or
    iii. there are higher-level conjectures about beliefs as in (ii).

4. There are no dominant strategies, there is a pure strategy equilibrium point, but (i)–(iii) in (3) do not hold.
5. There are no pure strategy equilibrium points.

Class (1) situations are hardly games at all since each player has a maximal element of his choice set unaffected by the choice of the other player; the resulting equilibrium is both attractive and retentive. Class (2) games differ only slightly. They require the same modicum of intelligence in players as do class (1) games regarding dominant strategies, viz., select them when they exist. In addition, they require in players a capacity to recognize when the other player has one. Again, the attraction and retention power of this equilibrium point is strong, though perhaps weaker than its predecessor class. For class (3) the attraction is weaker still since it is contingent on fairly specific beliefs of one player about the choices or about the beliefs of his opposite number. By class (4) there is only a flicker of attraction left and the persuasiveness of the Nash equilibrium is probably strong only in situations involving incredibly cautious players. In class (5) there is neither attraction nor retention (except in a very weak form) since, if one player believes the other is playing his "optimal" mixed strategy, he (the former) is nevertheless free to choose any of his pure or mixed strategies; all have the same expected value.

Noncooperative equilibria, we believe, suffer defects similar to those we discussed in the cooperative realm. Their persuasiveness, especially regarding their attracting power, depends upon highly contingent circumstances of play. And the only way to determine whether these circumstances are reasonable to assume or are likely to transpire is to *look at the world*. There may be no accounting for tastes, as the old Latin expression tells us, but the necessity of some accounting, of an empirical sort, regarding attitudes, aversions, beliefs, or whatever becomes apparent – a point to which we return in our concluding section.

We are not yet finished with our critique of equilibrium concepts since we have not discussed some areas of discretion available to actors that are normally stipulated to be exogenous in many equilibrium theories. To begin this discussion we note that economists generally regard theirs as a science of voluntary exchange in which the "hold harmless" rule applies. Accordingly, the choices by individuals to buy and sell, produce and consume, spend, save, and invest are regarded as voluntary acts that reflect individual assessments of their well-being. *Ex ante*, the individual believes his circumstances will have improved, *ex post*, if he buys or sells or . . . compared to what they would be if he did not.

Politics on the other hand is, in Riker's (1980a) view, a considerably more dismal affair since it transcends the voluntary and is not constrained by the "hold harmless" rule. There are winners and losers, and losers lose not only in the sense of bearing opportunity costs, but often in the sense of being denied property rights, freedom, or even their lives. Under these circumstances (and we are not convinced it is *that* much different in economics) losers have strong incentives to alter undesirable equilibria. And this possibility is clearly feasible if the equilibrium in question is nonretentive. Somewhat surprisingly, even if an equilibrium is "well-behaved" in terms of attraction and retention, the theoretical framework in which this obtains often has held constant a number of behavioral dimensions that, in fact, are variables.

In economics, the notion of voluntary acquiescence or participation in economic activity is reflected in the ability of an individual to pick up his marbles and go home. If the terms of trade are unfavorable, he need not participate. In politics, this same option is (sometimes) available, though it is normally not accorded great import, in the form of *emigration*. To "avoid harm," an individual may resign from a club, withdraw from a school, organization, or private society, or move to a different political jurisdiction. And emigration, broadly construed, is one of the more extreme measures by which individuals may destroy an otherwise prevailing equilibrium. It may be argued, of course, that if emigration is an available choice, then the so-called equilibrium is not really an equilibrium at all.[3] And this is precisely our point. Nevertheless, how many equilibrium theories begin "Consider a set $N = \{1, \ldots, n\}$ of players . . ."? The context of most equilibrium theories is one in which the set of actors is fixed so that a political outcome or decision must be endured by all.

Even if we stipulate that N is fixed, however, there still may be the means by which to upset an equilibrium. They include generating new alternatives or destroying existing alternatives (that is, not requiring the set A to be fixed and immutable), altering the dimensions of choice (fixing A but changing the basis for evaluating its elements), changing the rules of choice (allowing the dominance relation $>$ defined on $A \times A$ to change or be determined endogenously), or moving the decision to some new arena of choice. Each of these strategies for upsetting some prevailing equilibrium is commonly observed in everyday political life. This suggests that even the prospect of an undesirable equilibrium at one level provides the incentives for losers under that equilibrium to agitate for some form of change in the institutional fabric. In sum, even under the most convincing of our equilibrium concepts there exist features of any political or economic situation that are subject to strategic exploitation. No law of logic requires that losers accept their status as losers, and empirical observation tells us that some do not.

This brings us to a related point, the final one we shall raise about the fragility of social science equilibrium. Most of our concepts are highly static—even examples of dynamic equilibria presuppose a considerable amount of constancy. We take as given the set of actors, the set of alternatives, and the distribution of preferences. But just as losers have incentives to attempt to alter such initial conditions, so, too, may exogenous influences change those conditions. Even if it were in strong general equilibrium, we daresay that the U.S. economy would be perturbed dramatically by the sudden invention of cars that run on water. Or to take an example from the political realm, even if the early nineteenth-century Democracy were a reflection of a majority-rule equilibrium (who knows?), how can we predict the kind of evangelical protestant revivalism that swept the Midwest in the antebellum period and made the slavery issue so much more potent in the 1850s than it had been a generation earlier? Or to take a more short-term example, how could we have predicted the swings in popular preference that led to a heavy economic emphasis in mass voting behavior in the late spring of 1980 after a heavy foreign affairs emphasis in the winter and early spring? Even the chimerical x^* introduced at the beginning of this section is woefully dependent on the absence of such changes.

Thus, for any number of reasons, we conclude that social science equilibrium concepts, *examined in an abstract context*, fall short of providing the kind of predictability desirable in scientific theories.

DO DISEQUILIBRIUM RESULTS DASH HOPES FOR A SCIENCE OF POLITICS?

Having argued that social science equilibrium theories often fail to provide the predictability desirable in a scientific study of politics, we shall now argue the obverse, namely, that the absence of such equilibria does not preclude the desired predictability. Our argument hinges on the simple distinction between "equilibrium" in the world and equilibrium in our models. Conflation of the two is an understandable occupational hazard, but that does not excuse the confusion.

Models provide *partial* descriptions of phenomena. A model that gave a complete description would be identical to the phenomenon of interest and therefore of little use to us. Thus, all models involve a restricted focus, a choice to examine or emphasize some aspect(s) of a phenomenon but to ignore or deemphasize others. This much is old hat. But the obvious implication is often overlooked: Because models provide only partial descriptions, several can be applied to the same phenomenon and the resulting inferences may differ, even conflict. Ordeshook (1980) provides a simple example. Several plausible models applied to a simple market of one seller and two buyers produce several rather different predictions. A classical economic model predicts that the seller captures all the added value from exchange, while a fully cooperative game-theoretic model predicts all the Pareto-optimal allocations.

Even more interesting in our view are situations in which a disequilibrium inference from one model stands opposed to an equilibrium inference from another. In *The Theory of Political Coalitions*, for example, William Riker questioned the advisability of modeling political situations as games and of searching for possibly nonexistent or infinitely large V-solutions (1962, pp. 36-39). His suggestion was to look at a different aspect of political situations, namely, the coalitions that support the winning outcomes rather than the outcomes themselves. Riker believed that disequilibrium at the level of outcomes was compatible with equilibrium at the level of coalitions:

> It may be, of course, that the reasonable outcomes in an *n*-person model or an *n*-person real situation are in fact so numerous and diverse that systematic analysis and prediction is impossible. But it may also be that game theorists have not asked the questions most useful to social scientists and that by exclusive emphasis on the attempt to delimit admissible imputations they have overlooked the possibility of delimiting coalition-structures directly. (1962, pp. 38-39)

Another example comes from the article by Ferejohn, Fiorina, and Packel (1980). After noticing that the nihilistic McKelvey et al. result did not appear to describe the dynamics of experimental processes in which cycling and instability had free room to operate (Fiorina and Plott, 1978), these authors proposed a Markov model that provides a limiting probability distribution over the feasible outcomes of a majority decision process. Again, this work involves a shift in focus from past studies of majority decision making. Rather than examine the question of existence of stable outcomes, it attempts to examine in a systematic way the relative "difficulty" of moving from one (typically unstable) point to another, and the constraints such relative difficulties might place on the majority decision process.

As a third example, consider several recent papers by Kramer (1977, 1978). Instead of considering an election as a discrete decision in which the McKelvey result is known to apply, Kramer embeds each electoral decision in a time sequence of elections. This approach yields inferences other than "Anything is possible." To wit, the model implies that any particular outcome is part of a "trajectory" that leads to the minimax set, which in this case is likely to constitute only a small part of the feasible set.

As a final example of the simultaneous existence of disequilibrium and equilibrium inferences, consider Shepsle's (1979a,b) work on structure-induced equilibrium (the product of both tastes and institutional arrangements). Shepsle establishes conditions under which structure-induced equilibria exist while the set of preference-induced equilibria is empty. This work follows in the spirit of Duncan Black, who in his early paper on the unity of political and economic science observes that "equilibrium in Politics is 'the resultant of tastes and obstacles'; and these are the words Pareto used of equilibrium in Economics"

(1950, p. 118). "Obstacles" is Black's nomenclature for the forms of committee procedure that, in his view, combine with the preference scales of committee members to determine formal decisions. It seemed obvious to Black that political equilibria were inextricably linked to institutional arrangements that constrain political processes, just as economic equilibria are linked to often implicit institutional arrangements that constrain economic forces.

In discussing the preceding examples, our purpose is not to assert that coalition models, stochastic models, dynamical models, or institutionally rich models are sure-fire means of exorcising the spectre conjured up by McKelvey and friends. Rather, our purpose is to establish that the existence of equilibria has as much to do with the *choices* made by the scholar as with the characteristics of the phenomenon he or she is studying. We describe and comprehend empirical phenomena through the lenses of particular models. And the particular lenses we use are, partially at least, a matter of *choice*.

Continuing with this argument, it seems to us that our colleagues in economics have deliberately chosen a research program different from that embraced by the younger generation of positive political theorists. As members of interdisciplinary "shops" we have both attended numerous economic theory seminars. In reflecting on these, it seems to us that they generally proceed under the constraint that only equilibrium-preserving extensions of models are of interest (i.e., publishable). The typical budding theorist adds to or generalizes an existing model and makes his or her personal contribution by showing that with the given addition or generalization an equilibrium continues to exist. When questioned as to why the modification or generalization was not done in some other way, theorists typically respond that the suggested alternative entailed either intractable problems or that no results could be established under the suggested alternative, i.e., in either case the alternative was "uninteresting."

In contrast, McKelvey, Schofield, and other political theorists have followed a path blazed by "Arrow's Mathematical Politics" (note the choice of terminology by an economic theorist, Paul Samuelson) through the "impossibility" terrain of social choice theory. Positive political theory did not always follow this path. In the early development of spatial models, the emphasis was on equilibrium results. The basic model was extended to different voter distributions, abstention was introduced, and sequential elections were considered, but always the symmetry conditions that would produce equilibrium were imposed. Why this research program was abandoned is not clear; perhaps those involved became convinced that reasonably interesting equilibrium models of political situations constituted a set of measure zero. But it is not obvious that the situation is any different in economics.

In fact, it is not outrageous to speculate about alternative scenarios. Political theorists might have decided early on that unidimensionality was a basic assumption of all political models, akin to the regularity conditions imposed on the consumption and production sets by economists. Alternatively economists might have followed up Scarf's (1960) examples of instability that led Nikaido (1968, p. 337) to observe that "global stability is so special a dynamic property that contrary to the Walrasian view, one can hardly expect it to be shared by all competitive economies. . . . [I]nstability seems to be a universal phenomenon in competitive economies, rather than an exceptional one, whereas global stability is expected to prevail only in very well-behaved systems." Perhaps some of the differences between economic and political theory arise less from the greater instability of political phenomena than from the attraction of stability-loving personalities to economics in contrast to the gravitation of chaos-loving personalities to political science.

If equilibrium is necessary for scientific prediction and explanation, and lack of equilibrium is fatal for those activities, it would seem that economics is scientific because its practitioners have chosen to be scientists whereas political science is not because its practitioners have chosen not to be. In that case, the route to science is clear: we can choose to be scientists. This answer is facile, however. It is our belief that the common element in the choices of both the economic and political theorists is that their theoretical choices arise from considerations mostly unrelated to and uninformed by the real world. Some attention to the latter provides the grounds for a "third way" to a science of politics, an old way too often overlooked by economic and political theorists.

CONCLUSION AND MODEST PROPOSAL

Our tentative conclusions are several. First, most social science equilibrium concepts are, at best, distant cousins to what we have termed black hole equilibria. Specifically, they rarely are so conspicuous, so centripetal, or so retentive as their ideal in the physical sciences. And even when they are both attractive and retentive, they are embedded in a larger net of institutional and social relationships that themselves are not immutable. Outcomes, whether equilibria or not, distribute gains and losses. Losers may not be able to replace a prevailing outcome with one more to their liking, but surely they may agitate for change in the broader institutional matrix and, when successful, destroy an earlier outcome, whether an equilibrium or not. In consequence, the link between equilibrium and scientific predictability is both weak and tenuous.

The same may be said about the link between disequilibrium and unpredictability. Disequilibrium, unpredictability, and chaos are certainly possible at some levels of political description. Indeed, they are generic and all-encompassing at the level of outcomes, if the theorems of Cohen, McKelvey, and Schofield serve as plausible descriptions of majority rule. But notice the qualifications. First, we might observe in a committee's *decisions* over time no apparent pattern as it moves hither and yon through Euclid's space. Yet we might also observe that the decisive coalition each time, though different in composition, always contained no more members than necessary. Alternatively, we might discover that the changing decisions of the committee were perfectly associated with the ideal point of the chairman, whose identity rotated among committee members over time. (More incriminating still, we might witness each chairman having a drink at the bar with Dr. McKelvey just prior to his committee's deliberations!) In each of these instances, disequilibrium, chaos, and unpredictability at one level are transformed into predictable regularities, explicable in terms of rationality and equilibrium, at some other level of conceptualization.

There is a second important qualification to the interpretation of a disequilibrium result like those of Cohen, McKelvey, and Schofield: it may not constitute a plausible description, even at the conceptual level at which the disequilibrium is established. Equilibria and disequilibria are properties of models. It remains to be demonstrated whether they are descriptive of empirical phenomena. One of the objectives of the Fiorina–Plott experiments was, in fact, to discover whether a host of ideas bearing on equilibrium and disequilibrium were empirically plausible under the best of experimental conditions; many failed their test.

While we have hardly "proved" our dual conclusions that equilibrium models in the social sciences (including economics) are less than wholly persuasive for, and disequilibrium results less than wholly inimical to, a science of social phenomena, we think these conclusions rest on a solid base and would be agreed to by reasonable men. Arguably more controversial are several related points. The first is that an equilibrium concept should be regarded as a conceptual invention – the property of a model, not of the world of phenomena. As a consequence, scholars have some degrees of freedom in choosing levels of analysis, models, and equilibrium concepts. And the usual philosophy-of-science criteria apply in this choice and in the evaluation of the resulting scientific product. In our view, a model without equilibrium constitutes no more of a scientific improvement in the state of knowledge than a wholly complete description of the phenomenon in question. Each suffers the debility of failing to inform. (Parenthetically, however, we admit that the discovery of disequilibrium serves the same constructive purposes as a "detour" sign; it cautions the traveler about trouble ahead and may even urge that an altogether different route be contemplated.) Each fails to isolate that which is regular and hence understandable. (So-called complete descriptions fail in that they do not discriminate regularities from idiosyncrasies and other attendant circumstances.)

So much for critical commentary. But what do we offer by way of positive recommendations? Our position is that scientific progress reflects (1) the scholarly *choice* of models that (2) possess equilibria that (3) correspond to observed regularities. This entails neither constructing equilibrium models *ex ante*, generalizing and refining subject to the constraint that equilibrium be preserved (the path traveled by most general equilibrium theorists in economics), nor retaining disequilibrium models only to be tongue-tied when asked to say something positive about the world of phenomena (the path recently traveled with seeming relish by some political theorists). To travel the first path is to say little that applies to the world of phenomena, and to travel the second is to say little, period. Instead, we recommend a third path, one termed "retroduction" by the philosopher Peirce.

As exposited by Goldberg (1968) retroduction emphasizes the construction of theories, but it similarly emphasizes the importance of empirical regularities in that process. Put simply, the retroductive process begins with an empirical regularity X and poses the question "How might the world be structured so that X is an anticipated feature of that world?" The answers (and there should be several) are models, all of which have in common the regularity X as a logical implication. We understand that most theoretical work resembles the retroductive process in that pure deduction seldom occurs; usually some desired result determines the choice of premises. What we are saying that is different is that the desired result should be based primarily on empirical regularity (at least on "stylized facts"), rather than on its strength, neatness, or other aesthetic criteria. Thus, regularity in the world should motivate scholars to construct the theoretical worlds in which that regularity exists. Construction of a world without regularities constitutes a failure, not an achievement, though as we have earlier noted, such failures may serve a useful purpose in identifying paths not worth pursuing and in suggesting enrichments by which to augment disequilibrium models in order to accommodate observed empirical regularities. Indeed, the central constructive feature of the Cohen-McKelvey-Schofield theorems is precisely that "other features," *not* the majority rule mechanism, are decisive in democratic institutions.

NOTES

1. Most mechanisms of dynamic adjustment in general equilibrium theory are highly artificial "stories" — artful fictions. The classic mechanism, of which there are several variations, is the *tâtonnement*, a process in which a mythical market auctioneer calls out a vector of prices, observes the plans rational economic agents intend to follow subject to those prices, computes excesses of supply and demand, and then announces a revised price vector according to some adjustment rule. The actual implementation of economic plans is permitted only after this price adjustment process converges to an equilibrium. Arrow and

Hahn (1971), after two chapters of discussion and results on dynamic adjustment in their treatise on general economic equilibrium, are quite frank in their appraisal of *tâtonnement*:

> Some of the difficulties we have encountered may be due to the abstraction of a tâtonnement; this will be discussed in the next chapter. Even if it had been possible to show that in a perfectly competitive economy a tâtonnement is always stable, it is not clear that such a result could have been given much weight in forming a judgment of the performance of the price mechanism in actual economies. The fiction of an auctioneer is quite serious, since without it we would have to face the paradoxical problem that a perfect competitor changes prices that he is supposed to take as given. In addition, the processes investigated in this chapter assume that, disequilibrium notwithstanding, there is only a single price for each good at any moment. It is also postulated that at each moment, the plans of agents are their equilibrium plans. Lastly, of course, there is no trade out of equilibrium. All of these postulates are damaging to the tâtonnement exercise. It may be that some of the theorems and some of the insights gained will have application when a more satisfactory theory of the price mechanism has been developed. *At the moment the main justification for the chapter is that there are results to report on the tâtonnement while there are no results to report on what most economists would agree to be more realistic constructions.* (Arrow and Hahn, 1971, pp. 321-322; emphasis added)

2. In some models it would not necessarily constitute irrationality for player 1 to believe his adversary may deliver on a self-damaging threat.

3. Assume for a moment that political science had developed theories built around a black hole equilibrium concept, and that past experience had shown such theories to be devilishly accurate predictors of future states of society. Then the very act of making a prediction could be the stimulus for a mass emigration to Canada and/or Mexico, or even a violent revolution in the United States. If sufficiently powerful (i.e., credible), a social science theory could provide human actors with the incentive to change the *ceteris paribus* conditions on which the theory's predictions depend.

6 THE LIMITATIONS OF EQUILIBRIUM ANALYSIS IN POLITICAL SCIENCE

John H. Aldrich and David W. Rohde

William Riker, in his essay on the scientific problems created by disequilibrium (1980a) and in his essay on the philosophical problems raised (forthcoming), has offered a serious challenge to positive political theorists. Our essay is intended to do two things. First, we argue that the prospects for a science of politics are, perhaps, not as dismal as a reading of Riker's essays suggest. We, at least, remain hopeful if not optimistic. Second, we offer our view of how we see this scientific accounting of political phenomena proceeding. We do so by presenting specific examples of various aspects of social choice via voting or similar methods of preference aggregation. We emphasize that we are concerned with the scientific endeavor, not the philosophical. Even if our optimism is realized scientifically, very serious ethical problems will remain.

The essential problem that Riker poses is this. Positive political theory rests on equilibrium analysis, based on the analogy of comparing political choice with microeconomics. From Black (1958), to Arrow (1963), to Plott (1967), to Gibbard (1973) and Satterthwaite (1975), to McKelvey (1976, 1979) and Schofield (1978), social choice theory has been dominated by the impossibility theorem demonstrating that equilibria fail to exist. This failure of general equilibria to exist seems most straightforward in voting and in other political means of collective decision making, and the latter references indicate just how serious are the implications of Arrow's theorem. What Riker calls a fundamental "equilibrium of tastes" is nonexistent in politics, and hence political outcomes are unpredictable in the long run. Riker then argues that political scientists should focus on the *process* of choice, rather than the *outcome* of choice. In particular, Riker calls for an emphasis on the structure of institutions and how that structure affects choice.

We agree with the basic points in Riker's analysis and, in effect, this essay is an amplification of his accounting. We agree with Ordeshook, however, that political science can study both process and outcome, where Riker believes that the current status of the discipline affords the possibility of studying only process. It is hoped that our examples demonstrate the point.

We believe that there are two elements of "process." First, there is the structure of the institutions governing the particular voting context. Second, there is process in the sense of dynamics or time-related aspects in virtually all voting contexts. The combination of preferences, institutions, and time dynamics is what makes the study of process and of outcome together possible, in our view. Our first illustration, for example, is of the series of primaries, etc., that constitute our current presidential nomination system. This system has a very different structure than other voting institutions. What makes the system decisive (i.e., select one nominee from many) is precisely the combination of the peculiar institutional arrangements with the voting "choice" occurring over extended periods of time (and also is due precisely to the absence of stable equilibrium). Our second example consists of a model of political party activists added to the usual spatial model. The goals of potential and actual activists are, we assume, long term, transcending the time frame of any specific spatial election. It is precisely this combination of long-term goals and of the structure of political parties that has the potential, at least, of providing some regularity (not equilibrium) to the McKelvey-Schofield chaos possible in the disequilibrium of spatial voting models. Our third example is an aspect of so-called electoral economic cycles. Here, we argue that it is precisely the nature of electoral institutions and the systematic timing of elections that makes ordinary questions of equilibrium analysis less useful than ordinarily assumed. Our final illustration raises a potentially serious problem with, to use Shepsle's term (1979a), "structure-induced equilibria." The example is of recent changes in the rules governing congressional choice. We argue that it was precisely the nature of the structurally induced equilibrium and its repeated realization over time that led liberal Democrats to seek—and made it possible for them to enact—institutional reforms. One difference between politics and economics is that those whose tastes are being amalgamated in political choice possess the potential to change institutional arrangements. It is at least easier for political than economic actors to do so (not the least reason being that economic institutions are often political creations). In effect, rules and outcomes are both endogenous to political systems. If you do not like the political outcomes, you may be able to change the rules.

What, then, of equilibrium analysis? By "equilibrium analysis" we mean the sets of equilibrium-type questions that seem to have dominated positive political theory to date. These include, to us, the search for the existence of equilibria (often a futile search) and their characterization in terms of uniqueness of stability, and of location. Existence, uniqueness, stability, and location cover virtually all the problems examined so far. We make two arguments: Equilibrium analysis is neither necessary nor sufficient for a science of politics. We pose each example in these terms: Is equilibrium analysis helpful in studying this aspect of voting and, if helpful, is it enough to ask? By answering "No" to one or both questions, we make our case. The choice is designed to be a clear, qualitative, deterministic distinction. The choice is realistically a matter of degree. We are not arguing that equilibrium analysis be banished. Far from it. This set of questions should remain central. In part, we are arguing that more questions be added to equilibrium analysis, especially characterizations of short- and medium-term dynamics around equilibria (i.e., we have yet to borrow all of equilibrium analysis from economics). In part, we are arguing that there may be systematic regularities even in the absence of equilibria (cf. our discussion of "structurally induced regularities" in the spatial voting model). And, in part, we are arguing that a science of political choice is possible in the absence of stable equilibria. The case, we believe, is made most strongly by actual examples, and it is to these we now turn.

MOMENTUM IN PRESIDENTIAL NOMINATION CAMPAIGNS: THE LACK OF NECESSITY OF EQUILIBRIUM

Our first task is to demonstrate that the existence of equilibrium is neither necessary nor sufficient for understanding the outcomes of political choice processes. We shall do so by examples. Here, we shall illustrate the lack of necessity, specifically by proposing a system that yields a determinant outcome only in the absence of stable equilibria. The example is that of resource and vote dynamics in presidential nomination campaigns as developed in Aldrich (1980a,b).

Briefly, suppose there are a set of m ($m \geqslant 2$) candidates seeking a party nomination by competing for delegates in a set of sequential primaries occurring on dates $t; t = 1,2,\ldots,n$. Let the difference between votes and/or delegates actually won by a candidate, say, i, on the primary or primaries on date t and the votes/delegates i was expected to have won be denoted DS_{it}. Let the amount of time variable resources (e.g., money) raised and expended by i at time t be denoted R_{it}. The following are the two central assumptions about campaign dynamics:

1. Investing more resources R_{it} rather than fewer yields a larger rather than smaller DS_{it} *ceteris paribus* (while a larger investment by an opponent yields a smaller rather than larger DS_{it}, *ceteris paribus*).
2. The larger DS_{it}, the more resources i can gather and expend between t and $t + 1$, *ceteris paribus*.

The particular specification of these assumptions was a set of m, first-order, linear difference equations of the form

$$DS_t = A(R_t) + C + E_t,$$ (6.1)

$$\Delta R_t = B(DS_t) + D + U_t,$$ (6.2)

where

$$DS_t = \begin{bmatrix} DS_{1t} \\ \vdots \\ DS_{mt} \end{bmatrix}, \quad A = \begin{bmatrix} a_{11} & \cdots & -a_{1m} \\ & & \\ -a_{m1} & \cdots & a_{mm} \end{bmatrix}, \quad R_t = \begin{bmatrix} R_{1t} \\ \vdots \\ R_{mt} \end{bmatrix}, \quad C = \begin{bmatrix} c_1 \\ \vdots \\ c_m \end{bmatrix},$$

$$E_t = \begin{bmatrix} e_{1t} \\ \vdots \\ e_{mt} \end{bmatrix},$$

$$\Delta R_t = \begin{bmatrix} \Delta R_{1t} \\ \vdots \\ \Delta R_{mt} \end{bmatrix}, \quad B = \begin{bmatrix} b_{11} & \cdots & -b_{1m} \\ & & \\ -b_{m1} & \cdots & b_{mm} \end{bmatrix}, \quad D = \begin{bmatrix} d_1 \\ \vdots \\ d_m \end{bmatrix}, \quad U_t = \begin{bmatrix} u_{1t} \\ \vdots \\ u_{mt} \end{bmatrix}.$$

the matrices C and D are matrices of constants, capturing "initial allocations," and E_t and U_t are independent stochastic terms (to be discussed below). The A and B matrices contain parameters specifying the first-order linearity assumption. All on-diagonal entries are positive, and all off-diagonal entries negative, consistent with the two assumptions listed above.

Detailed explanations of Equations (6.1) and (6.2) can be found in Aldrich (1980a,b). Briefly, they formalize the common observation that a candidate who does surprisingly well in a primary finds it possible to raise money, to obtain volunteer help, etc., while a candidate who fails to live up to expectations finds that such resources dry up. Further, the richer the resource base, the more effectively a candidate can contest later primaries.

For our purposes, the central result is the following:

THEOREM: Equations (6.1) and (6.2) define a dynamic system with no stable equilibria.

Proof: See Aldrich (1980b, Appendix).

The outcome space here is that of the delegate term and the resource term, both defined as equivalent to $\mathbb{R}^1$ for each candidate. This space has no locally or globally stable equilibria. There is one unstable equilibrium defined by the constants in Equations (6.1) and (6.2). The system could be at rest at this unstable equilibrium, but any perturbation (e.g., any one nonzero entry in E_t or U_t or both at any one t) will drive the system away from this equilibrium explosively. Thus, equilibrium analysis is particularly unhelpful in this case.

The point of the example is not to add yet another impossibility theorem to the list. Rather, the point is that this impossibility result is "good." What it says in particular is that if n is sufficiently large (i.e., there is a sufficiently large set of distinct primary election dates), the system will be decisive; precisely one candidate will win. Under most circumstances, if the system started at and remained at the unstable equilibrium, there would be no winner. With three or more candidates, none of whom is stronger than all others combined before the campaign begins, if the system stays in equilibrium, then the convention will open with no candidate having sufficient votes to win a first-ballot victory. As opposed to the McKelvey–Schofield implication of Arrow's theorem, then, this impossibility result implies that there will be a single element in the social choice set unless the system is in equilibrium. There are, of course, other substantive consequences of this result as detailed in Aldrich (1980a,b).

If we take the position that this system is decisive *because* it contains no stable equilibrium, then the scientific explanation (if not theory) of such a system requires the accounting of the starting positions of the various candidates and the nature of possible time paths. In general, starting positions may be unaccountable in any scientific sense (or, any accounting of a given initial allocation simply pushes back the process one step further, giving rise to another "starting position" question). Yet, at least in specific instances, it may be possible to do so, as in, for example, this nomination system.

Let us suppose that the campaign starts at the unstable equilibrium. If expectations are based on "reasonable information," the DS_{it} terms are expected to be zero, so that the system will indeed start in equilibrium. If so, the theorem implies that, ordinarily, there will be a victorious candidate by time n (if n is sufficiently large). The equations do not imply, however, which candidate will win. The question then is how to study the time paths. What is necessary, of course, is a perturbation from equilibrium. That is, the action must lie in the stochastic term. (In the jargon, the system is "open.") Given parametric values or estimates, one could then introduce a perturbation to investigate the number of periods it takes for the system to move sufficiently far from the unstable equilibrium to be considered decisive.

The openness of the system has a more important theoretical role. It can admit of candidate strategy. Suppose the candidate has a set of strategies that could affect the system. Some of these are more or less "usual" tactics, say, working somewhat harder, refocusing resources into different channels or in different proportions, modifying the issues the candidate emphasizes, etc. Some are more unusual (e.g., Reagan selecting Schweiker as running mate), perhaps "risky." For example, in a two-candidate campaign, a strategy might have a probability of 0.1 of shifting the time path one unit in the candidate's favor, 0.9 of moving it a half unit in the other candidate's favor. The expected value of this strategy is unfavorable (on average hurting the candidate by moving the path 0.350 units away). Clearly, at the unstable equilibrium the candidate would reject it. If the system is diverging from equilibrium away from a candidate, however, he might try it if there is no other strategy that would bring the campaign back to unstable equilibrium or "turn it around" in his favor. That is to say, we would expect candidates to adopt different types of strategies at different points in the process, becoming perhaps more "risk acceptant" (or what we might call the "politics of desperation"). In short, it is possible to imagine systematic study of a problem in public choice in the absence of stable equilibria.

NOMINATIONS CONTINUED: EQUILIBRIA DEPEND ON HOW YOU LOOK FOR THEM

One could take essentially the same process and find multiple equilibria. The lack of stable equilibria result depended, *inter alia,* on equating R_{it}, etc., with $\mathbb{R}^1$. As a result, "resources" can assume any real number, including positive and negative infinity. One could imagine (rather more easily, in fact) bounds on resources and delegates variables. Or, one could specify (as in Aldrich, 1980a,b) that the key concept is the probability of candidates being nominated. At any time t, that is, there is a vector of length m specifying the probability of $i, i = 1, \ldots , m$, being nominated. The reinterpretation of the theorem, above, then, is that there are $m + 1$ equilibrium values to the vector. The first m such are the "degenerate" probability distributions of 1 in the ith position, 0 elsewhere, while the last such vector is the unstable equilibrium vector induced from the constants in Equations (6.1) and (6.2). Also, the first m vectors are stable equilibria. The outcome space, therefore, is the m-fold cartesian product of the unit line. As such, this space is partitioned into stable equilibrium points, their neighborhoods, and the unstable equilibrium.

In one sense, viewing the problem this way is the exact opposite of the problem of the last section. We have gone from a problem with no equilibrium (or an equilibrium describing the outcome with probability trivially different from zero) to a problem with equilibrium analysis describing the outcome with probability one. In another sense, however, the problem is exactly the same. We know no more or less than before by knowing that the outcome space is partitioned by equilibria and their neighborhoods. All of the questions remain, and they remain in the same form. That is, the accounting of the outcome still depends on "starting points," time paths, perturbations (random or purposeful), etc.

Another example of "Equilibria depend on how you look at (and for) them" occurs in voting games. There are very many equilibria to the voting game in the sense of Nash, or there are virtually none in the sense of Plott (1967), Sloss (1973), Cohen (1979), McKelvey (1976, 1979), or Schofield (1978). The nomination example is, perhaps, extreme (where equilibria are no help at all), but the general point is made; to wit: the normal kinds of questions asked in equilibrium analysis may be unnecessary and/or unhelpful. In the case of voting games, Nash equilibria are unhelpful. In more usual cases of multiple (stable) equilibria, such analysis may be useful, but it is insufficient.

A SPATIAL MODEL WITH POLITICAL PARTIES: HOW TO
PICK ONE EQUILIBRIUM FROM MANY—OR FROM NONE

It is taken for granted that the nature of political decision making rules out the existence of a global equilibrium in all but the rarest instances, and this holds most prominently for voting mechanisms. At best, we may hope for the existence of several locally stable equilibria. If even two stable equilibria exist, the central problem is to explain which one (if either) will be the actual choice of society. We believe that this problem can be addressed only by study of the process of choice and the particular institutions constituting the choice mechanism. We shall illustrate both points in this section by considering an adaptation of the usual spatial model.

We shall first propose a conception of political parties, defined simply as a set of activists, and examine its effects in a unidimensional spatial model. We then shall consider an example of a two-dimensional spatial model in which there is no voting equilibrium and the McKelvey-Schofield results apply. There will be equilibrium position for the parties, however. If we assume that party activists have control over nominations and impose some restrictions on candidate mobility, then we can predict some regularity for candidate positions and, thus, spatial voting. The party equilibrium positions need not be unique. We shall illustrate this case in another two-dimensional space. We shall introduce the second point, that of process, to account for the particular equilibrium positions that are realized. We shall propose an instance for which the process leads to abrupt changes in party equilibrium positions that provides a possible characterization of what are called "critical realignments" in the empirical-voting literature. Detailed analysis of the one- and two-dimensional cases may be found in Aldrich (1980c) and (1980d), respectively.

The first problem, then, is to define the notion of party. We do so in the context of a typical spatial model. In the unidimensional case, let X denote the dimension ($X = \mathbb{R}^1$). Let the set of citizens, of which i is one of its infinite number of members, have strictly quadratic loss functions defined over this dimension, say $L_i(X)$. Each i has an ideal point, say X_i $[L_i(X_i) = 0]$, and $f(X_i)$ denotes the density function of ideal points. Assume that $f(X_i)$ is unimodal. [If the mode is at, say, $X = 0$, then $f(X_i)$ is strictly unimodal if $f'(x) > 0$ for $x < 0$ and $f'(x) < 0$ for $x > 0$.]

We assume that a political party consists of a set of activists (let Θ and Ψ denote the two parties). We conceptualize these activists as continuing members of the party; they are the party regulars, whether party or public officeholders, the "rank and file" members, regular financial donors, or those who volunteer their time and effort. By "regular" or "continuing" we mean that the decision of a citizen to be and to continue to be a Democratic or Republican activist is not election or candidate specific (although extensions address this question). Rather, the decision to become a partisan is based on the characteristics of those already active in the party. Moreover, the relevant characteristics are the policy preferences of current activists. In short, one joins a party based on the policy preferences of those already in the party.

To be more specific, we assume that a citizen i examines the policy preferences of those who make up the two parties and decides to contribute to one party or the other through the same sort of calculus citizens use to choose between two candidates. The citizen compares the policy position of a typical activist in each party to his own loss function and joins only the closer party, if either, but fails to join either party if he is "indifferent" between or "alienated" from the two parties. The most obvious measure of the policy preference of the "typical activist" is the mean policy position of current activists, say $\overline{\Theta}$ and $\overline{\Psi}$, both of which are points in X, the policy continuum. Then, each itizen has a loss function for the parties, $L_i(X_i, \overline{\Theta}, \overline{\Psi})$. The decision to join acti ely or not is then based on the relative losses associated with the average par y positions. Let c^2 denote the maximum loss a citizen will tolerate and still consider being active in a party. Then, a citizen who associates a loss greater han c^2 (or

c units in the policy space) with the closer party is "alienated" and joins either party with zero probability. Further, if i does not associate c^2 more loss with one party than the other, that citizen is "indifferent" and joins either party with zero probability. (The following results do not depend on there being the same c^2 for indifference as for alienation.) Finally, if i is neither alienated nor indifferent, i is active in the closer party with a nonzero probability that strictly increases as the distance from i's ideal point to that party's average policy position decreases. In sum, i joins a party only if it is close enough on average to i's own ideal policy position and only if it is sufficiently distinctive on policy from the other party. The probability of joining the party, then, increases as the mean policy preferences of current party activists are closer and closer to the citizen's ideal point.

People join a party if it is populated with "people like me" and the other party is not. However, if some people become active in a party, that will cause its mean policy position to shift, which might encourage still others to join while some drop out. (And, indeed, some might become active or drop out of the other party, as well.) Thus, there is a dynamic to the parties as sets of activists. The question, of course, is whether there are equilibrium positions for the two parties, say $(\overline{\Theta}^*, \overline{\Psi}^*)$.

In unidimensional spaces, it turns out that stable equilibrium positions exist ordinarily. In some cases, multiple stable equilibrium positions exist, and in all cases the number and location of such equilibria are influenced strongly by the distribution of ideal points. But consider the following theorem:

THEOREM: If X is unidimensional, if $f(X_i)$ is strictly unimodal, and if the citizen decision calculus is as outlined above, then

1. there is a global, stable pair of equilibrium positions for the two parties $(\overline{\Theta}^*, \overline{\Psi}^*)$ and
2. the two parties are moderately divergent and located on either side of the mode of $f(X_i)$.

Proof: See Aldrich (1980c).

If $f(X_i)$ is symmetric, the two party memberships will be symmetric, but note that symmetry is not assumed here.

One interpretation of the above theorem is that it derives what Aranson and Ordeshook (1972) assumed in their study of sequential spatial elections. In their model, they assumed there were two sets of party activists, each of which was relatively cohesive in policy preference and was divergent from both the other party and the policy center in the electorate. Candidates had to appeal to the activists to win their party's nomination and then to the general electorate. If candidates could adopt only one spatial position for both "elections," Aranson and Ordeshook argued that the optimal location for a candidate was some policy position between the median activist and the median voter in the general election. This result has a very strong ring of plausibility, and there is evidence such as that provided by Page (1978) consistent with it. The result depends, however, on the existence of two cohesive and distinctive parties. The above theorem provides one justification.

To this point, we have offered an institutional structure that seems consistent with the description of policy preferences of activists and that can keep the two candidates from being able to converge fully to the existent voting equilibrium. That there is a global voting equilibrium depends, *inter alia*, on X being unidimensional. If X is equivalent to even $\mathbb{R}^2$, voting equilibria are so rare as to be nonexistent for all practical purposes. Kramer (1977) and McKelvey and Ordeshook (1976) provide some bases for expecting less than the full realization of the chaos possible via the McKelvey-Schofield result. If political activists are crucial ingredients in nomination campaigns (and thus constrain candidates in their general election campaigns), and if there is an equilibrium for party activists, then the stability of parties will help stabilize spatial elections, and thus provide another basis for avoiding chaos.

Consider, for example, the two-dimensional space illustrated in Figure 6.1. There, $f(X_i)$ is strictly unimodal, with indifference contours enclosing convex sets and with a greater dispersion of ideal points along one dimension (say X_1) than the other (X_2). While $f(X_i)$ is unimodal, it is *not* symmetric. As a result, the symmetry conditions of Plott (1967) or of the typical Davis-Hinich-Ordeshook result (1970) do not apply. For candidates, then, there are no equilibrium positions. Suppose, however, that we generalize the decision rules for party activism in the obvious ways. For example, suppose the loss functions for all i are strictly quadratic with a "weighting matrix" (the A matrix) of the identity matrix. (E.g., if all i have the same quadratic loss function, the figure could represent a suitable transformation of the more general loss function; the key is to relate the marginal density of $f(X_i)$ to the marginal loss of citizens.) The c^2 term, then, defines a circle of radius c centered at the citizen's ideal point. If Θ is more than c units from the ideal point, i is alienated from Θ. Indifference contours of the probability of activism in, say, Θ are strictly unimodal about $\overline{\Theta}$ and will be circular for just alienation, and other terms may be generalized similarly. Then, the following proposition about party positions holds:

Proposition: If X is two-dimensional, if $f(X_i)$ is strictly unimodal and satisfies the conditions outlined above and exemplified in Figure 6.1, if X_2 is the dimension with greater concentration of ideal points, and if citizens become active in a party based on the calculus outlined above, then

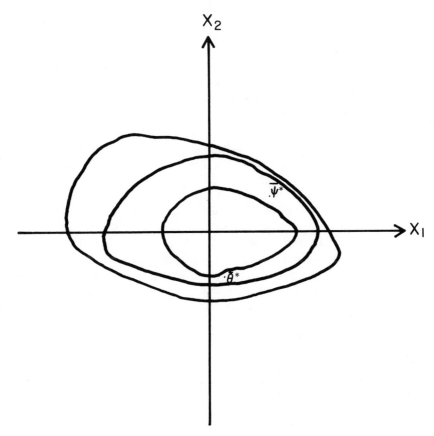

Figure 6.1. A Policy Space with Unimodal $f(X_i)$ and Unique Party Equilibrium Positions

    a. there is a global stable equilibrium pair of party positions $(\overline{\Theta}*, \overline{\Psi}*)$ and

    b. the two parties will be moderately divergent on dimension X_2 (and less divergent, possibly even convergent, on X_1) and located on either side of the mode of $f(X_i)$ on X_2.

Proof: See Aldrich (1980d).

    Thus, in this example at least, there are stable positions for the two parties— indeed, exactly one pair of such positions for the mean preference of party activists that parties align along X_2, not on X_1. If party activists are crucial for nominations and thus constrain candidates for the general election, then the "institution" of party activists and their party preferences provides a structure that should be expected to induce some regularity to the positions candidates will adopt. We conjecture, at least, that activists who choose nominees by considering policy and electability will choose nominees someplace between their center and the "center" of the general electorate; i.e., moderate but systematically divergent candidates (who diverge along Page's "party cleavage" lines) should be the general rule.

That the party equilibrium positions are unique is a feature of the specific example. Even if $f(X_i)$ is unimodal (and all other assumptions remain constant), there might be multiple, but locally stable, equilibrium positions. For example, in the two-dimensional, unimodal case illustrated in Figure 6.2, there are two possible stable equilibrium positions. While the exact locations of the party means depend upon specific parametric values, the pairs $(\overline{\Theta}_1^*, \overline{\Psi}_1^*)$ and $(\overline{\Theta}_2^*, \overline{\Psi}_2^*)$ are both possible equilibrium pairs (for demonstration, see Aldrich, 1980d). Clearly, these two pairs of positions are quite different, and we would expect the sequential nomination–election process to produce quite different candidates. Thus, while parties may induce regularity into a nonequilibrium voting model, the sort of regularity induced will depend on the particular equilibrium for parties that actually occurs. It is here that the "history" or process of elections over time becomes relevant.

The literature on U.S. presidential election history (as seen by political scientists) has been dominated by the idea of "party systems" (cf. Chambers and Burnham, 1975). The basic argument is that there are periods of "normal elections" in which a type of balance is struck between the two parties. Within one such period, there are durable and identifiable voting patterns, coalition bases of parties at the mass and elite levels, and consistent cleavages between the parties on policy. These periods are punctuated by "critical elections" (from Key, 1955) or "realignments." These relatively short periods are those in which voting patterns, party coalitions, and policy cleavages between the parties alter fundamentally and the competitive balance between the parties is liable to shift. The typical story runs something like this. The cause of the realignments has been periods of crisis (the Civil War, the Depression, etc.). At these times a new dimension of evaluation dominates. That is, a new issue or cluster of related issues is transcendent. Its salience to all participants vastly outweighs any other source of potential division. The usual interpretation is that the electoral arena, *inter alia*, is unidimensional. Parties (whether new or old in name) divide over this dimension not unlike that of the theorem for unidimensional spaces presented above. Either one party is advantaged [as could easily happen in the above theorem with asymmetric $f(X_i)$] or the two parties could be very closely matched (as in the period from the end of reconstruction to 1896). As this new party system ages, the transcendent dimension loses its dominance (to entirely

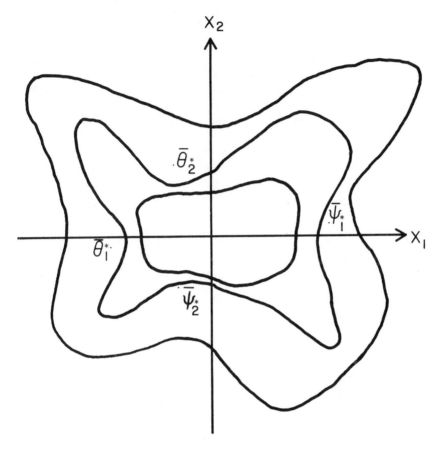

Figure 6.2. A Policy Space with Unimodal $f(X_i)$ and Multiple Party Equilibrium
Positions

new issues or even to old dimensions). The party system will remain in something like equilibrium, however, until some new dimension arises that "cuts"
in new directions. The apparent equilibrium will be broken, however, only when
this new dimension also becomes of major, even transcendent salience. Then,
especially according to Sundquist (1973), but echoed by most others, new activists take charge of old parties (as in the New Deal, for example) or form entirely new ones (as the Republican party was formed in the 1850s). At this
point, a new party balance is struck, there is a new party alignment, and a new
period of normalcy is initiated.

This scenario is at least consistent with the following variation on the above one- and two-dimensional spatial models. The unidimensional theorem can be used to describe the new issue–new alignment case. Indeed the theorem, since it assumes unimodality of $f(X_i)$, presents the most difficult case to achieve party divergence. If, for example, $f(X_i)$ is bimodal, equilibrium positions exist and are even more divergent (see Aldrich, 1980c). As a new dimension arises to begin to "challenge" the dominance of the old, we get something like the following dynamic. In Figure 6.3, the length of the dimension is meant to illustrate the

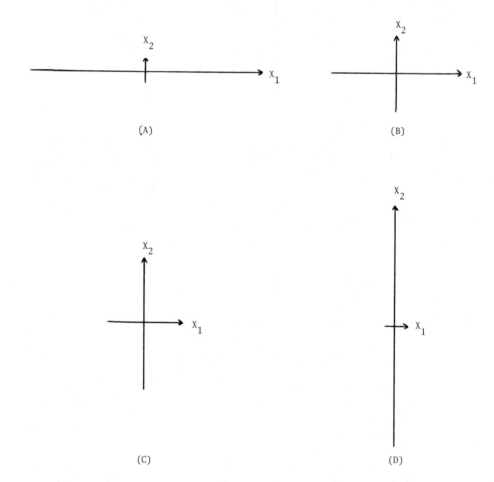

Figure 6.3. The Evolution of Dimensions in Electoral Realignments (Length of axes indicates relative salience of two dimensions in electorate.)

salience of the dimension. Thus, in Figure 6.3A, X_1 is the dominant dimension; it gradually loses its dominance to X_2 as we move from Figure 6.3B to 6.3C. In Figure 6.3D, X_2 is dominant in salience. This evolution is representative, we think, of the usual story line as told by political scientists.

If Figure 6.3 is, indeed, an accurate accounting, what then of political parties? The basic argument, of course, is that the location of the party activists on policy provide the central definition of the "party system" and its partisan policy cleavages. The two bidimensional examples discussed above provide slightly different variants of the same story. At some point in the "evolution" of the two dimensions in Figure 6.3 there will be an abrupt and "radical" redefinition of the policy preferences of the party activists. The status quo, unidimensional equilibrium along X_1 describes the party positions through much of the "evolution." At some time, however, the two parties will realign to be divided over X_2 rather than X_1.

Consider the first example with "unimodality" defined by indifference contours of $f(X_i)$ enclosing convex sets. In this case, the equilibrium positions remain along X_1 for some time because of its greater saliency. Even if ideal points are somewhat more concentrated along X_2 (thus "attracting" activists), the lower salience and consequent greater indifference over this dimension keep the parties in the original equilibrium positions. At some point, as X_2 becomes increasingly salient in comparison to X_1, the parties will be taken over by activists who are relatively extreme on X_2 and, as the figure is drawn, moderate on X_1. *Both* parties "move" in this example, for indifference links the location of the two parties. The exact time of the realignment is a function of salience and of the relative concentration of the electorate on the two dimensions. But, the point is that there is exactly one equilibrium pair of party positions, but one that shifts from division on X_1 to division on X_2 at some time in the evolution from Figure 6.3A to 6.3D. Note that $f(X_i)$ and/or loss functions might determine which party goes where in the realignment, but which party is "liberal" and which "conservative" *may* be unpredictable.

The second case is a bit more interesting due to the existence, in at least some portion of the evolution, of multiple potential equilibria. The example was constructed to have, essentially, barriers separating the potential equilibria — barriers consisting of portions of the policy space with relatively few potential activists. In the extreme cases, where one dimension is very much more salient than the other, the consequent indifference associated with the latter dimension implies that there is only one possible equilibrium pair of positions. At these points, the analysis follows that of the first case. In between these extremes, however, things are a bit more interesting. It may be the case, for example, that there are four equilibrium points. While the parties will start with one pair of positions, it may be that any other pairs would be in equilibrium. That is, only one party might move (until the extreme case is reached), and it might move to either "vacant" potential equilibrium, or both parties might move (depending on the relation of $f(X_i)$ to the loss functions, it might also be the case that only joint movement is possible). We do know, however, that, eventually, both parties will realign. In the middle of the evolution, there is potential for one or both parties to realign, simply because there are multiple equilibria. The entrepreneurial activities Sundquist describes (1973) may be necessary for accounting for the shift. But, we can make some positive statements about even this process. The described evolution of salience will mean that the new potential equilibria will be relatively unattractive to entrepreneurs early (there being relatively few potential activists there), but it will provide for increasing incentives as its relative salience increases. At some point, of course, entrepreneurial activity becomes unnecessary, as the realignment occurs "naturally."

It should be emphasized again that the assumption of unimodality yields this process in perhaps the most nonobvious circumstances. The multimodal cases give rise to this process more obviously. It should also be emphasized that these "tipping" processes, in which activists in a party change rapidly, are predicated on the dimensional evolutionary "story line" and the (near) orthogonality between dimensions. Slower or less radical changes in the composition of party activists are much more common (and are probably more common empirically).

We hope that the major purposes of this example are clear. The pure voting disequilibrium of the usual spatial model (with multiple dimensions) has long been disquieting to positive theorists. Finding disequilibrium so often, however, might be due in part to failure to build in the full institutional structure of real electoral systems. We have not proved that there are structurally induced equilibria. We have shown that our definition of party does imply an equilibrium for parties in at least some cases. It is at least reasonable to presume that this sort of equilibrium will impose some patterning or regularity (but *not* necessarily equilibria) on voting. What we have for voting, then, is a sort of structurally induced regularity. In terms of the process and dealing with multiple equilibria, we believe we have shown that the process itself has provided a basis for making some scientific statements about behavior in the face of multiple equilibria. (We should add that political scientists have proposed plausible-sounding rationales for the "evolution of dimensionality" story line; cf. Beck, 1974.) What we are arguing, therefore, is not that we abandon equilibrium analysis, but that it is insufficient. Not only might institutional structure and dynamic processes (which are at least partially exogenous) provide crucial ingredients of scientific explanation; in addition, the possibility of nonequilibrium regularity raises questions of an order wholly different from those found in equilibrium analysis.

ELECTORAL-ECONOMIC CYCLES: INSUFFICIENCY OF
EQUILIBRIUM ANALYSIS CONTINUED

One important case of insufficiency of equilibrium analysis remains. It is fairly easy to argue that equilibrium analysis is insufficient if there are several stable (or, even easier, unstable) equilibria. If, however, there is one global, stable equilibrium to which the system converges, then it might be maintained that equilibrium analysis is sufficient. Here, we try to make a counterargument.

Recently, political scientists have discovered that government has played a not inconsequential role in national economic policy—at least since the time of Keynes; that elected officials care about elections; that the public cares about the status of the economy in such areas as inflation, unemployment, income, etc.; and that they arguably might hold these elected officials responsible for the status of the economy. If the public does care and does hold elected politicians accountable, and if politicians do desire reelection, then (so the argument goes) we should expect to find that politicians target the economy to be at a desirable status at or near the day of accounting. Everything else being equal, then, we might expect government policy, as it affects key economic indicators, to be responsive to the preferences of citizens.

Models of so-called political–business cycles, originally developed by economists (Nordhaus, 1975; MacRae, 1977), examined the mix of unemployment and inflation to investigate whether incumbents manipulate (at least) a short-run Phillips curve for electoral advantage (while Hibbs, 1977, 1979, argues that there may be a long-term difference between parties of the left and right on this mix). The central question of plausibility rests on the electorate; are they "myopic" (evaluating economic performance over short intervals) or "rational" (i.e., using a longer time frame)? If myopic, short-term economic management is feasible, and an electoral–economic cycle of this sort might be observed.

Tufte (1978) made a similar argument, adding a special emphasis on real disposable income. He argued in particular that incumbents would make a special effort to see that real, disposable income would increase just prior to attempts at reelection. This argument has two major advantages over cycles in inflation-unemployment. First, inflation and unemployment targets are the subject of ideological divisions between the parties. Increased real disposable income is more likely to be consensual; few desire to see their income decline. Second, the incumbent has quick and reliable instruments to affect income, notably by manipulation of transfer payments (thus, the immediate instrument is "purely" fiscal). Moreover, the recipients of these transfer payments, while they are far from a random subset of the population, include groups in the population that few object to assisting; the elderly, the sick, the veteran, etc. Perhaps most to the point, the data support the electoral connection of transfer payments more clearly than they support electoral cycles in other economic indicators (Tufte, 1978; Kolb, 1980).

Here, we shall assume that a global, stable equilibrium exists in the macro-economy (especially — or at least — in terms of real, disposable income), and that governments do manipulate it through — at least — transfer payments prior to the election for electoral purposes. The question, then, is whether the most interesting and/or important questions are addressed by equilibrium analysis, per se, or whether these questions must be supplemented.

Any electoral-economic cycle model combines three separate models: one of candidates' electoral behavior, one of citizens' electoral behavior, and a model of the relevant macroeconomic variables. We treat these in turn, starting with the briefest, that of candidates.

Most rational choice and political-economic models of elections assume that candidates seek to win elections. More specifically, they are assumed to be plurality maximizers in most cases. We so assume here, but note that this rules out any preferences that candidates might have over policy (e.g., a desire for economic stabilization and/or growth). We shall speak of "incumbent" and "challenger," and by "incumbent" we shall mean the nominee of the incumbent's party. For economic performance measures, we assume that the incumbent (or his/her party's nominee) is held accountable, whether for good or ill, whether of the same party as the president (for, say, congressional elections) or not, and will thus attempt to achieve electorally advantageous economic performance.

Let us divide citizens into two groups, those in families who will receive transfer payments and those who will not. In general, we assume that all citizens possess well-defined utility functions by which they evaluate all candidates for whom they could vote. Citizens vote for the more preferred party nominee of each office, except when they abstain due to indifference (and/or, perhaps, alienation). Utility functions are assumed to have many arguments, one of which is real disposable income (also known as income; we ignore monetary illusion to follow Tufte's arguments about real income). Income, as other dimensions of evaluation, may enter utility functions in many forms (in absolute level, rate of change, or change over the entire period of incumbency; in retrospective comparisons, projective forecasts, or referendum on the incumbents; etc.). All we assume is that the incumbent is evaluated higher if the citizen's real, disposable income is higher, while the citizen evaluates the incumbent lower if income is lower, *ceteris paribus*. (This assumption is compatible with, but not limited to, "myopic" voting.)

Now, recipients of transfer payments will have higher real, disposable income by virtue of the increased transfer. All recipients, therefore, evaluate the incumbent higher than before the transfer. One of four cases must hold. In consequence of the higher utility associated with the incumbent (a) there is no change in intended voting behavior, (b) a supporter of the challenger becomes indifferent, (c) one intending to abstain from indifference (or alienation) now decides to vote for the incumbent, or (d) a supporter of the challenger switches to become a voter for the incumbent. As long as the last three categories are not empty, then the incumbent's plurality among recipients is increased due to increased transfer payments. The plurality never decreases.

What we assume about nonrecipients is that any change in their intended behavior that is attributable to increased transfer payments never leads to an aggregate decrease in the plurality of votes cast for the incumbent sufficient to offset any gains in plurality from recipients. (I.e., the total plurality is increased, or at least not decreased by an increase in transfer payments.) This assumption, which we believe to be fairly weak, can be justified in several ways. First, many nonrecipients may be unaware of increased transfer payments, or at least any costs associated with them. (E.g., Tufte shows that increased social security collections were deferred until after the election in 1972.) Second, their being the larger set of citizens, increased taxes or other costs (if any are realized or understood by election day) will be smaller for the individual than the payments to recipients. These dispersed costs, therefore, may be expected to change nonrecipients' utility for incumbents much less. Third, especially since recipients are concentrated among the relatively disadvantaged and costs are dispersed, many nonrecipients may favor increased transfer payments in principle, even if they are fully aware of costs involved (they may also calculate some expected gain, based on the probability of their receiving higher benefits later if they should go on social security or whatever). At any rate, any loss (and there may actually be a plurality gain) the incumbent receives from nonrecipients is assumed to be more than made up from the gain in votes from recipients. Consequently, increasing transfer payments increases (or does not decrease) the plurality of votes cast for incumbents. Seeking to maximize plurality, incumbents, therefore, increase transfer payments at a propitious moment—as close to election day as possible. (Actually, our assumptions about voters need not be true; candidates must only believe them true.)

We can now turn our attention to real, disposable income, and the effects on equilibria, if any, of an increase in transfer payments. As noted, we focus on income because Tufte does and because some of his most convincing evidence is about the electoral effects of increased income. We focus on transfer payments as an instrument to increase income for several reasons. First, there is evidence that they increase (in nominal dollars at least) at or near elections. Tufte, of course, devotes considerable space to this demonstration (Kolb, 1980, finds evidence of an electoral cycle in Germany *only* in transfer payments). Moreover, and important for this argument, Tufte argues that there is a *two-year cycle.* Second, they are quick and reliable policy instruments (and, being fiscal, in the hands of elected officials). They directly affect income, increases can be timed virtually to the day, as Tufte shows, and, as he also shows, incumbents can claim credit directly (e.g., social security increases being announced on the check itself). Finally, they are targeted fairly directly to the disadvantaged. Thus, incumbents can appear (justifiably) to be helping groups hard to knock. Moreover, such groups tend to be at the periphery of active participants. Thus, money is not "wasted" disproportionately on the hard-core, committed partisan. Turnout, however, needs to be stimulated, perhaps more than an increase in social security or veterans' benefits can accomplish. At the same time, these groups are the most in need of increased income, so that it can be expected to increase their utility disproportionately.

For the purposes of our illustration, we assume that there is, always, a single (global), stable equilibrium in the relevant portion of the macroeconomy. Every two years, we assume, transfer payments increase — and, in most cases, this is a permanent increase. We adopt a very simple specification of a three-sector (closed) economy. Some notation follows (assuming all dollars are real): Let

Y = income;
Y^d = disposable income;
C = consumption expenditure in the private sector;
I = gross private domestic investment;
G = governmental purchases of goods and services;
r = interest rate;
T = taxes;
u = tax rate;
R = transfer payments;
M = money supply;
P = price level;
S = private savings;
B = government bonds.

Some usual definitions for a closed economy are

$$Y = C + S + T,$$

$$Y^d = Y - T,$$

$$GNP = C + I + G.$$

At the assumed equilibrium, real income is equal to GNP:

$$Y = C + I + G.$$

The theory of income, then, involves the theory of consumption, investment, and government purchases. Ordinarily, G is taken to be exogenously determined. (As Nixon said, "We are all Keynesians.") The simplest formulation of consumption and investment is

$$C = C(Y^d), \quad 0 < C' < 1,$$

$$I = I(r), \quad\quad I' < 0.$$

Somewhat richer models of consumption have it dependent on disposable income, the interest rate and real wealth of the private sector (say, V) and of investment have it dependent on the interest rate, income (not just disposable income), and the existing capital stock (say, K):

$$C = C(Y^d, r, V), \quad 0 < C_1 < 1; \; C_2 \gtreqless 0; \; C_3 > 0,$$

$$I = I(r, Y, K), \quad I_1 < 0; \; I_2 > 0; \; I_3 < 0,$$

where C_i = derivative of C with respect to argument i. We shall assume the simple version of C and the more complex version of I but hold K constant.

Then, the IS curve gives equilibrium values for the pair (Y, r) for the simplest case:

$$Y = C(Y - T) + I(r) + G.$$

This curve is, then, downward sloping (with (Y, r) being the space). The unique equilibrium value is solved for as the intersection of the IS curve with the LM equilibrium curve. That is, the money market is taken as the second one, in addition to the above output market. Treating the money supply as exogenous (i.e., in the hands of government rather than private producers or consumers), equilibrium in the money market, given prices, is

$$M/P = L(Y, r), \quad L_1 > 0; \; L_2 < 0.$$

Since the LM curve is monotone (and marginally) increasing in the (Y, r) space, there is a single intersection, yielding the unique equilibrium in income and interest rates. Let us take two more steps. First, we shall use the time parameter t, where t denotes "stock" held at time t or the one period "flow" from $t - 1$ to t. Second, if we assume (as appears common in the simplest models) that taxes collected are a constant proportion u of income and that the consumption and investment equations are simple, linear functions, we get

$$C_t = c(1 - u)Y_t, \quad 0 < c < 1; \; 0 < u < 1 \quad \text{(since } uY = T;$$
$$\text{hence } Y^d = (1 - u)Y),$$

$$I_t = i(Y_t) + \gamma(r_t), \quad i > 0; \; \gamma < 0.$$

Assuming linearity and substituting into the IS equation yield the equilibrium conditions

$$Y_t = c(1 - u)Y_t + iY_t + \gamma r_t + G_t$$
(with $1 - c(1 - u) - i > 0$) to maintain a downward slope),

$$M_t = \alpha Y_t + \beta r_t, \quad \alpha > 0; \quad \beta < 0.$$

The above two equations, then, are the simplest equilibrium "theory" of output and money. In addition to these equilibrium conditions, government policy, which we want to investigate, is subject to a budget constraint. That is, government expenditures must be financed somehow, by taxes or by deficit financing— either printing money or issuing bonds. A simple formulation of the constraint is:

$$G_t = T_t + \Delta M_t + \frac{\Delta B_t}{r_t}.$$

These three equations, then, form the core of the model.

Government fiscal policy can be used to increase real income in three ways. First, the government can purchase more goods or services. This seems to be electorally timed by presidents, especially as they seek renomination. (At least, it is common for them to announce, say, a new highway in Florida, dam in North Carolina, etc., during the primary campaign.) Second, they could provide tax cuts. These, too, may be electorally timed. Third, they can increase transfer payments. Increasing purchases (i.e., $\Delta G > 0$) impacts directly on Y at equilibrium. That is, aggregate demand is stimulated directly. Changes in taxation impact directly on real disposable income, but are not fully realized in consumption, because some proportion of the lowered tax payments go into personal savings. Most models of transfer payments assume they are like negative taxes in this sense. With the simple models here, the multiplier effects of equal changes in G, T, and R are thus

$$\frac{1}{1 - c} \Delta G > \frac{1}{1 - c} (c) \Delta T = \frac{1}{1 - c} (c) \Delta R.$$

We claim that this may be too simplified a view of transfer payments. Since recipients are likely to have relatively low income on average, it seems more reasonable to assume that they will spend much of their increased disposable income (i.e., relatively little will be diverted to savings). Thus, if our argument is correct, an increase in transfer payments should have a larger multiplier effect than a comparable reduction in taxes, although since there may be some diversion to savings, the expansionary effects on consumer demand may be less than a comparable increase in direct purchases by government. To capture this "in betweenness" we define a coefficient d as follows:

$$1 \leqslant d \leqslant \frac{1}{c}.$$

Then, the multiplier effects of comparable changes in the three fiscal measures are

$$\frac{1}{1-c} \Delta G \geqslant \frac{1}{1-c} (c)(d) \Delta R \geqslant \frac{1}{1-c} (c) \Delta T \quad \text{with} \quad \frac{1}{1-c} \Delta G > \frac{1}{1-c} (c) \Delta T.$$

If d equals c, the transfer multiplier will be the same as purchases; if it equals 1, the multiplier will be the same as a tax cut. We assume that the equilibrium conditions are maintained if $\Delta R > 0$. However, the location of the equilibrium will change, stimulating demand and shifting the IS curve up and to the right.

Since virtually all electorally motivated transfer payments are untaxed income, there are no offsetting income tax collections. That is, as national income increases, it is not offset "naturally" by increased income tax. Ordinarily, then, tax collections would be based on uY. However, T must be reduced by the amount of untaxed income $T = u(Y - R)$. Thus, to this point, transfer payments are particularly expansionary compared to tax cuts, since they are diverted to neither savings nor income tax (and, of course, are not subject to withholding).

To this point, then, we have shifted the IS equilibrium curve in an expansionary direction, and left the LM curve unchanged. The problem is, of course, that the government budget constraint is not satisfied. As noted, the constraint can be satisfied by raising taxes (here by the "full amount" since taxable income does not rise with the increase in income at least in the short run), printing money, or issuing bonds. If the transfer payment is a social security benefit increase, the government must raise social security collections. Any other form of increased transfer payments can be expected to be financed by money or bonds. Incumbents are unlikely to increase taxes in an election year. Thus, we have two separate cases.

In simple models such as this one, if the government finances the increased transfer payments out of general revenues and, hence, out of a mix of bond sales and printing money, the short-run effect, so far as we can tell, is to slow the speed of adjustment to the new equilibrium (cf. Turnovsky, 1977, pp. 68-84, for the case of ΔG). The usual case of bond sales is to be expansionary in IS in the long run, leading to a new equilibrium with a higher level of income, consumption, government expenditure, and interest rate (just as with $\Delta R > 0$), but with a lower level of investment. (The extent of these changes depends on the slope of the LM curve from the old to the new equilibrium.) An expansion of the money supply, holding IS constant, leads to a new equilibrium with income, consumption, and investment higher, but interest rates lower. (The LM curve is shifted to the right with a derivative closer to zero in Y.) Thus, we have several long-term changes with slowed adjustment in the short-run.

Social security increases must be financed by increased taxes. Again, we have short-run and long-run questions. In the long run, the "balanced budget multiplier" should hold, since taxes and expenditures are supposed to be in some kind of balance. It is unclear, of course, whether the government strikes a balance, or whether it fails to collect sufficient revenues. (At least, this is what is argued about the already mandated benefits and population changes.) Sentiment may be building to overcollect in the future to offset population dynamics. Ignoring these problems, we assume incrementally balanced social security funds. Ordinarily, the expansionary expenditures are not fully offset by contractionary tax increases due to the constraint of marginal propensity to consume effects on ΔT. If we assume that changes in transfer payments are just like changes in taxation, and if we assume the balanced budget, then the two offset each other exactly. However, we are assuming that changes in transfer payments are somewhere in between government purchases and taxes, so that the effect will be in between the usual case (examining ΔG) and that of full offsetting. The second long-run problem is the peculiarities of social security taxes. With the limitations on collections at higher income levels, it may not be reasonable to assume that these taxes are strictly proportional to income. Instead of being linear, they may be monotonically increasing, marginally decreasing, since if income rises, more people exceed maximal social security payments. For example, we can divide the proportional tax rate u into general tax revenues like income tax u_g and social security taxes u_r with $u = u_g + u_r$. If it happens that social security taxes are proportional to income, then we have $T = u_g(Y) + u_r(Y) = u(Y)$. If not, define b to be between 0 and 1, $0 < b \leqslant 1$. Then social security taxes may be given by $u_r(Y^b)$. If b equals one, we return to the original case. The government can raise taxes by increasing the rate ($\Delta u_r > 0$) or by raising the maximal level of income up to which social security taxes are collected ($\Delta b > 0$ if our assumption is correct). Now, if b is less than one, the effect is an addition to the failure of taxes to fully offset the expansionary effects of increased transfer payments (whether the d term is one or greater than one). Consumption, therefore, takes the following form:

$$C = c(Y^d) = c (Y - T)$$

but Y must be divided into transfer payments where R is an increase in such payments, so that $cY = c(Y - R) + cdR$; hence

$$C = c(Y - R + dR) - cT;$$

but

$$T = uY = u_g(Y - R) + u_r(Y - R)^b ;$$

therefore

$$C = c[(Y - R) + dR - u_g(Y - R) - u_r(Y - R)^b].$$

Of course, if $b = 1$, we can simplify this (since $u = u_g + u_r$) to

$$C = c[(Y - uY) - (R - dR - uR)] = c[(1 - u)Y - (1 - d - u)R].$$

Thus, even if social security taxes are proportional to income and the budget is "balanced," the effect of a transfer payment increase will be expansionary on consumption because $d \geqslant 1, u > 0$.

There is a short-run complication, since Tufte argues that there is ordinarily a delay in social security tax increases until after the election. In the short run, therefore, there is stimulus without the dampening effects of a simultaneous tax increase. The second short-run complication concerns from where the money for R comes over the quarter (or whatever) before taxes are collected. In general, it would seem that expenditures without revenues (especially since recipients are more likely than others to draw cash rather than deposit the check) must have a short-term perturbation of some (possibly small) magnitude, even if no long- or middle-term consequences.

The substantive conclusions may be summarized briefly:

1. We have sketched an argument to the effect that we should expect incumbents as plurality maximizers to increase transfer payments near election day.
2. Available evidence suggests that these increases come, in the usual case, every two years.
3. The long-run effect of each increase is to change the equilibrium, ordinarily in an expansionary direction.
4. Most simple models lead to the conclusion that the short-run effects are to slow the adjustment to the new equilibrium in comparison to changes in equilibrium induced by the other two sectors of the economy.

The point of the example may be summarized as follows. We assume, for purposes of this example, that the economy can be characterized at all times by possessing a unique (global) stable equilibrium. Thus, the system is always either in equilibrium or in the process of converging to it. However, we have reason to believe that there is a predictable, systematic, and regular change in the economic equilibrium induced by the nature of the electoral system. A new equilibrium, moreover, is "created" often, presumably every two years (and it is predictable that the shift in location is expansionary). Given that adjustment is likely to be slower than other induced shifts and that there are likely to be other than usual perturbations disturbing the adjustment process, the most obvious conclusion we can draw is that this global, stable equilibrium is never (or barely) realized. Rather, the system is described better by short-term adjustments and perturbations. While there is a unique, stable equilibrium, simply demonstrating that it exists (and even giving its location) and saying that the system is either at it or on the way there is insufficient. Rather, the actual accounting should—even must—focus on these questions in addition:

1. What exactly are the adjustment processes?
   i. Are they smooth, "unidirectional" convergences, or are there oscillations along the way and/or "overshoots"?
   ii. How rapid is convergence, and how big are oscillations, etc., if any?
2. How big are perturbations, in what directions do they go, etc.?
3. How big are the changes in location of equilibrium and in what directions?
4. How many and what types of people are affected in what ways in the views of the above three questions, and are there any redistributional consequences?

RULES REFORM IN CONGRESS: THE CASE OF STRUCTURE-INDUCED EQUILIBRIUM

Kenneth Shepsle (1979a) has developed the concept of a "structure-induced" equilibrium for a voting situation, which he contrasts with the concept of a global equilibrium we have discussed (which he terms a "preference-induced" equilibrium). Under a structure-induced equilibrium, as Shepsle describes it, the set of alternatives which may be considered may be restricted by institutional rules so that the status quo is preferred to all available alternatives, but other alternatives which would be victorious over the status quo are prevented from consideration.

This concept of structure-induced equilibrium can be broadened to apply to other institutional situations in which the likelihood of a given alternative being victorious is altered from what it would otherwise be due to the existence of a certain set of institutional rules. Consider, for example, a legislative institution—specifically the U.S. House of Representatives. The membership of the House in any given Congress comprises a set of preferences; preferences which are the result of the members own desires about policy questions and of the perceived needs and desires of their constituents. Most conflicts within this body can be (and are) seen as conflicts between "liberal" alternatives (supported primarily by northern Democrats) and "conservative" alternatives (supported primarily by a coalition of southern Democrats and Republicans). The members' preferences are distributed along a set of liberal/conservative issue dimensions offering one side or the other varying chances of winning majority support depending on the issue.

The House, however, is more than just the preferences of its members. It is also a collection of institutional arrangements—rules which define legislative procedures and positions of power within the body and which grant disproportionate influence over outcomes to certain members. During the postwar period through the late 1960s, most of the important positions in the House were held by conservatives (Ornstein and Rohde, 1975). By the late 1960s, moreover, the view was generally held among liberals that the conservatives were—because of their institutional advantages—winning more often than their numerical strength warranted. (Certainly the conservatives won more often than the liberals did in floor votes, except in the aberrant 89th Congress [1965-66] [Manley, 1973].) It was, in effect, the liberals' view that a structure-induced equilibrium occurred which produced outcomes different from those that would have existed had certain biases not been present in the institution's rules.

These institutional biases took many forms, but a few examples will be illustrative. Probably the most widely recognized was the disproportionate power of committee chairmen. Chairmen had a significant impact on the character and fate of legislation that passed through their committees, and because of the operation of the seniority system and the fact that southern Democratic conservatives were more likely to occupy safe seats than their northern counterparts, chairmanships were disproportionately held by southern conservatives. There were many ways a chairman could influence legislation. One was by his right to determine subcommittee jurisdictions and to refer legislation. If a chairman favored a bill, he could refer it to a subcommittee where it would get a favorable hearing; if he opposed a bill, it would go to an unfavorable subcommittee and never be heard from again.

The chairman, moreover, could determine the mix of policy preferences on these subcommittees by his power to appoint subcommittee members and chairmen. And, if no favorable (or unfavorable, as the case may be) subcommittee could be found, the subcommittees could be bypassed entirely by the chairman's whim, and the bill held for consideration by the full committee under the direct control of the chairman.

Another kind of institutional bias was the special position or privilege of certain committees in the House. One example was the Rules Committee, which determined the conditions for debate and the restrictions on amendments for most bills that went to the House floor. In the 1950s and 1960s, the members of the Rules Committee not infrequently stood against the preferences of a majority of the members of the House by refusing to grant any rule to a bill, thus preventing it from being considered at all. Another example was the Ways and

Means Committee, which had a special relation with the Rules Committee. It was argued that the kinds of issues that Ways and Means dealt with (i.e., tax policy) involved such a delicate balancing of interests that the compromises that were reached could not be left open for alteration by the full House. Therefore, bills from Ways and Means were routinely granted *closed rules,* which prohibited any amendments at all, thus presenting House members with a yes or no choice on bills which could not, as a practical matter, be rejected. (This is precisely the kind of device Shepsle considered in his discussion of structure-induced equilibrium.)

A third type of bias existed in the rules for floor consideration of bills. Because the House was so large and its rules of operation were so cumbersome, the parliamentary device of the Committee of the Whole was routinely used for initial consideration of bills. What this meant was that a simpler set of rules was used to consider bills on the House floor and get them near the point of a vote on the final passage, although the "committee" consisted of all House members. At that point the committee would be dissolved and the more formal rules would take over. One of the significant differences between procedures in the Committee of the Whole and normal practice was that in the former case there was no provision for roll call votes on which the position of individual members would be recorded and publicly revealed. This lack of public accountability released members from constituency pressures, but left them open to pressures from committee leaders, thus reducing the likelihood that policies produced by conservative-dominated committees would be changed on the floor.

As we noted, in the view of many liberals these institutional advantages permitted the conservatives to achieve victories they would not have otherwise won. Therefore, they wanted to abolish or reduce these biases in the rules. Yet the problem they faced was how to accomplish this when the very arena in which the decision on any rules changes would be made was the one in which these biases existed. The answer to this problem was to shift the arena of decision. Thus while a few significant changes in House rules were adopted by the full House, most of the "reform" (as it was called) effort centered on the Democratic caucus, where the southern Democratic conservatives did not have the benefit of the votes of their Republican allies. The strategy was to devise rules to be passed by the caucus which thus theoretically restricted only Democrats but which—because of the system of majority party governance that put only Democrats in control of committee leadership positions—worked in effect to bind the institution as a whole.

We can return to our earlier examples of institutional bias to demonstrate what was done. In the case of the power of committee chairmen, the liberals proposed what they termed a "subcommittee bill of rights." This set of rules of the Democratic caucus (adopted in 1973) placed restrictions on the actions of committee chairmen in a number of areas. For example, the power to assign subcommittee jurisdictions was removed from the chairman's hands and was vested in the full committee membership. Further, chairmen could no longer decide which subcommittee to send bills to; the new rules mandated that subcommittees with jurisdiction had to receive a bill within two weeks after it was sent to a committee, or, if the bill were to be held at the full committee level, this could only be done by a majority of the Democrats on the committee. These (and other) reforms effectively broke the dominance of chairmen over policy outcomes within their committees, and shifted much influence over decisions to subcommittees in which the liberal Democrats were significantly better represented.

The liberals also used the Democratic caucus to alter the rules regarding the special position of certain major committees. The Rules Committee was made more responsive to the formal Democratic leadership by vesting the power to appoint both the chairman and the members of that committee in the Democratic Speaker of the House rather than the Democrats' Committee on Committees as had been the practice. The practice of granting closed rules to bills from Ways and Means was restricted when the caucus adopted a rule which permitted a majority of the caucus membership to order the Democratic members of the Rules Committee to permit a floor vote on an amendment to such a bill. Thus a majority of the Democratic caucus could guarantee that any policy alternative would have a chance at a floor vote.

The rules relating to voting in the Committee of the Whole were altered in one of the rare instances of full House action on such rules changes. An amendment was included in the Legislative Reorganization Act of 1970 to permit record votes in the committee. The liberals short-circuited conservative resistance by presenting the issue as one dealing with secrecy versus openness in government rather than relating to the substance of policy outcomes, thereby gaining some conservative support that would not have otherwise been forthcoming (Ornstein and Rohde, 1974).

The aftermath of these and related reforms is less clear than the incentives that led to their passage. By the time all of the rules changes had taken full effect, the Carter administration had come to power, leading the Republicans in the House to become a much more cohesive conservative force than they had been in the past. Moreover, there were significant personnel changes within the Democratic party during this transitional period. There is, however, evidence that these rules changes had some measurable positive impact on the fortunes of liberal Democratic policy proposals (see Ornstein and Rohde, 1977).

More important, however, than the actual impact of these changes are the perceptions and intentions of the actors who proposed and pressed for their enactment. The liberal Democrats in the House believed that the institutional structure was biased against them, producing disproportionate numbers of victories for the conservative opponents—not just occasionally, but systematically over the course of many years. They believed that if the rules were changed, a different equilibrium would result under which they would win more frequently. If they were correct, then under the old rules, knowing where the preference equilibrium was in the system would have provided incomplete and misleading predictions about policy outcomes.

CONCLUSION

The arguments advanced in this paper can be summarized fairly easily. Political scientists have borrowed the notion of equilibrium from economics (and elsewhere). Much of positive political theory can be characterized as attempting to prove the existence of one or more equilibria (or their absence), to demonstrate whether any that exist are stable, and to discover the location of any equilibria that exist. In voting models, in particular, the ordinary conclusions are

1. Equilibria rarely exist at all;
2. If there is one (e.g., under Black's single-peakedness condition and extensions, or Plott conditions and their variations), it is exceedingly unstable to perturbations in its conditions (e.g., symmetry); and/or
3. If there are multiple equilibria (as e.g., Nash equilibria) there are too many and they are vulnerable, too (e.g., to coalitions).

We have argued that the existence of equilibria may be unnecessary to understand politically derived social choices, as are exemplified by the nomination campaign example, and that, even if viewed as possessing equilibria of the stable sort, the knowledge of that fact adds no useful information. We also have argued that the questions asked ordinarily by political scientists in terms of equilibrium analyses are insufficient. We tried to demonstrate this both in the case of the existence of multiple, stable equilibria and in the case of the existence of a globally stable equilibrium.

We hope it is clear that, even though we claim that equilibrium analysis is neither necessary nor sufficient for proper understanding of political choice, we are *not* claiming that these questions are irrelevant. Indeed, we ourselves asked those questions first, and we fully expect and hope that positive theorists address these questions—first. We are making two claims. First, impossibility theorems and their near approximations (as we read, for example, Plott's analysis to be) do not *necessarily* lead to such dismal prospects. Second, positive political theorists should not be satisfied with answering the set of questions we have labeled as belonging to "equilibrium analysis." Answering these questions (affirmatively or negatively) is but the first step toward the development of a satisfactory theory of politics.

Our examples were chosen with a reason. They were all voting models. We choose to examine these precisely because voting theory is the core of positive theory and because voting is precisely where the prospects and problems of equilibrium analysis have played center stage. The examples also shared the characteristic, we believe, that proper understanding of the process being modeled required asking more (and/or different) questions than are ordinarily asked. One crucial point that we have emphasized repeatedly in our examples is the importance of political institutions in structuring choice and outcomes. This theme is one that Riker emphasized (1980a). Further, and we believe this crucial to our argument, all of these examples relied heavily on time dynamics. Calls for greater attention to dynamic processes are common. As we read the general reaction, it is words to the effect that their inclusion makes modeling even harder than it is now. What we hoped we have shown is that, in each case, the nature of the political system, looked at in dynamic terms, adds more structures and constraints to work with, or in other words, adds more political content. These more structured processes, then, provided more material for reaching useful conclusions. In the electoral–economic cycle model, for example, the periodicity and consequent structuring principles of the election calendar are a dynamic property, but one that provides useful information. In short, we are calling for the study of political choice processes, by which we mean the combination of preferences, institutions, and time dynamics.

Our final point is that the sort of analysis we have proposed is not new. The macroeconomics of government fiscal policy, for example, involve ordinarily the study of short-term dynamics. The debate over the Phillips curve, for another example, involves precisely a questioning of what are true short- and long-term effects. The monetarist debate is, precisely, a questioning of the relative impacts of various policies in the short and long term. In effect, what we are saying is that, while equilibrium analysis was borrowed from economics, not enough of its tools and questions were borrowed. Indeed, we believe that what we have learned from twenty years of serious study of public choice is that the key to understanding politics lies in the proper understanding of the political dynamics, not in the study of comparative statics.

7 INSTABILITY AND DEVELOPMENT IN THE POLITICAL ECONOMY

Norman Schofield

Anteater: *Ah, but you fail to recognize one thing, Achilles, the regularity of statistics.*

Achilles: *How is that?*

Anteater: *For example, even though ants as individuals wander about in what seems a random way, there are nevertheless overall trends, involving large numbers of ants, which can emerge from that chaos.*

Achilles: *Oh I know what you mean. In fact, ant trails are a perfect example of such a phenomenon. There, you have really quite unpredictable motion on the part of any single ant — and yet, the trail itself seems to remain well defined and stable. Certainly that must mean that the individual ants are not just running about totally at random.*

— Ant Fugue, in Douglas R. Hofstadter (1979, p. 316)

ESCHER'S STAIRWAY AND THE VOTING THEOREM

This discussion between Achilles and the Anteater very wittily sums up the arguments of classical economic liberalism and populist democratic theory to which Riker (1980a) refers in his recent article.

While every ant might well have a coherent set of goals directing behavior, to an observer the goals are unknowable and the ant's activities appear chaotic. To the anteater, the ant system is nonetheless coherent. In the same way an observer would have insurmountable difficulty in making "rational" the behavior of individual people. In fact it has been argued (Lucas, 1961) that Gödel's incompleteness theorem (1962) implies that it is formally impossible to model human reasoning, by, say, a computer program. Neoclassical economic theory, however, posits that individual behavior *is* internally consistent (irrespective of whether we can verify this consistency) and then goes on to show under certain assumptions that, at the next level of complexity, collective behavior will also be "consistent." More precisely, the fundamental theorem assumes that individuals have well-defined preferences on their own consumption bundles, and shows that the result of free exchange within the market institution is an equilibrium of a certain kind. This theorem has certain structural peculiarities to which I shall return below. Social choice theory is essentially concerned with the limits of validity of this theorem, as it were, by weakening the assumptions. The collective consistency property that is sought is some form of transitivity (either of strict preference and indifference, just strict preference, or, weaker still, acyclicity). The fundamental theorem of social choice shows that as more restrictive forms of consistency are required, then power must be increasingly concentrated (either in dictatorship, oligarchy, or a veto group). While Rae (1980) objects to the reasonableness of transitivity, his examples of nontransitive situations are consequences of the social choice theorem. It is precisely when power is *not* concentrated in a choice mechanism that there is some configuration of individual preferences (possibly just one configuration) which yields a collective preference in violation of the appropriate transitivity property (Arrow, 1951). Even the Pareto principle (for which the oligarchy is the whole society) violates transitivity of strict preference and indifference. One interpretation of the social choice theorem is that there is a profound contradiction between the ability of a collective mechanism to use, in some rich way, the available information on individual preference and its ability to preserve consistency.

Majority rule does, of course, use information "richly" and, by the social choice theorem, can violate even the weak consistency property of acyclicity. It was thought originally by some that the social choice theorem was a phantom; that in fact there would in general be enough homogeneity across individual preferences to guarantee some form of consistency. This was the motivation for the work on restrictions of configurations sufficient for majority rule transitivity. Black's (1948) notion of single-peakedness led to Downs's (1957) argument that in a two-party system on a one-dimensional policy space there will be convergence to a median position (a *core*). Attempts to show the existence of a core in two or more dimensions came up against a result by Plott (1967) that seemed to indicate that no core could exist under majority rule in two or more dimensions. Even so, Tullock (1967) argued that voting cycles, if they exist, will be constrained in two dimensions to a small subset of the Pareto set. Arrow (1969) formalized Tullock's argument and showed, for an infinite electorate with symmetric convex preferences in two dimensions, that a core would exist. Related work by Davis and Hinich (1966) and Davis, Hinich, and Ordeshook (1970), and later Grandmont (1978), examined the symmetry conditions sufficient for core existence.

In two dimensions for a finite electorate of odd size the intuitions of both Plott and Tullock were correct. A majority rule core can almost never exist, while "local" voting cycles must stay in the Pareto set. Moreover, these voting cycles become less significant as the electorate increases in size. In three dimensions, however, Tullock's contention is false. Not only is the core almost always empty, but, for almost any preference configuration, the "local cycle set" is open dense. This means in particular that voting trajectories can be constructed between almost all points.

The behavior of majority rule is completely determined by the dimensionality of the policy space. In one dimensions (the *stable* dimension) no "local" cycles may exist, and when preference is convex a core must exist. In dimension two (the unstable dimension) a core generally does not exist, and Paretian cycles do. In dimension three or more (the chaotic dimensions), anything can happen. In fact any voting game is *classified* in the same way by two integers, its stable and unstable dimensions. This classification theorem makes coherent sense of a large family of results in the spatial theory of voting.[1]

We need the definition of three sets. Suppose D is any decision process, and p is a profile or configuration of individual preferences. Call a point x in W a *local optimum* if there is a neighborhood U of x in W such that there is no y in U that beats x under $D(p)$. Let $DO(p)$ be the set of local optima in W. On the other hand call a point x a *local cycle point* if in *any* neighborhood U of x there is a $D(p)$ cycle (i.e., y_1 beats x, y_2 beats $y_1, \ldots, y_r$ beats y_{r-1}, and x beats y_r). Let $DC(p)$ be the set of local cycle points.

Finally let $PO(p)$ be the set of Pareto optima (i.e., unbeaten by the unanimity rule).

VOTING THEOREM (Schofield, 1978, 1980a, 1981a): Let D be a voting game on Euclidean space W. Then D is *classified* by two integers v, w (with $v \leqslant w$) such that

   i. If $\dim(W) \leqslant v-1$, then $DC(p)$ is empty for any smooth profile p on W.

   ii. If $\dim(W) = v$, then $DC(p)$ (if nonempty) is contained in $PO(p)$.

   iii. If $v + 1 \leqslant \dim(W) \leqslant w$, then both $DO(p)$ and $DC(p)$ may be nonempty.

Moreover, there exists some smooth profile p on W such that DO(p) is empty, and DC(p) is both nonempty and not constrained to the Pareto set PO(p).

iv. If dim(W) $\geq w$, then DO(p) is empty and DC(p) is nonempty, for almost any smooth profile p.

v. If dim(W) $> w$, then DC(p) contains an open dense subset of W for almost every smooth profile p on W.

We shall call $v-1$ the *stable* dimension, w the *unstable* dimension, and $w+1$ the *chaotic* dimension for D.

For any voting game there is an easy algorithm for computing v and w. For example, v is the Nakamura (1978) number, defined as follows: Any family of v distinct winning coalitions in D must intersect, while there is a family of $v+1$ winning coalitions which do not intersect. If the voting game is *collegial* (every family of winning coalitions has a common intersection), then v is defined to be infinity. In this case, when each player has locally acyclic preference, then D(p) is locally acyclic (Brown, 1973, 1975).

If the society has n players, and D is the *q-game* (where every coalition with q players is winning), then

$$\frac{n}{n-q} > v \geq \frac{q}{n-q}.$$

For example, if $(n,q) = (4,3)$, then $v = 3$, since any collection of three coalitions, each with three of the four players, must intersect. On the other hand, if $(n,q) = (6,4)$, then $v = 2$, as can be seen by examining the coalitions $\{1,2,3,4\}$, $\{1,2,5,6\}$, and $\{3,4,5,6\}$. If the voting game is proper (any two winning coalitions must intersect), then $v \geq 2$. For majority rule [other than the case $(n,q) = (4,3)$] the Nakamura number is precisely 2.

It can also be shown, when W is compact Euclidean and convex and DC(p) is empty, that DO(p) is nonempty (Schofield, 1981b). When preference is convex, DO(p) coincides with the usual notion of the core. With standard compactness and convexity assumptions, part (i) of the theorem gives Greenberg's (1979) result that a core exists in a q-game in dimension less than $q/n-q$. For majority rule with $v = 2$, a "local" core exists in one dimension (Kramer and Klevorick, 1974).

Part (ii) of the theorem establishes Tullock's conjecture (1967) that "local" majority-rule cycles are *Paretian* in two dimensions. For the case $(n,q) = (3,2)$, however, the local cycle set is almost always the entire Pareto set (Kramer, 1973; Schofield 1977a) in two dimensions.

There is quite a considerable difference between part (ii) of the theorem and McKelvey's (1976) result on "global" majority cycling in two dimensions. The model underlying the voting theorem is that of small continuous changes in the outcome. McKelvey's chaotic, but discontinuous, cycles have not been observed in experimental two-dimensional voting games (Fiorina and Plott, 1978; Laing and Olmstead, 1978) where the outcomes were located in the Pareto set (just as predicted by part (ii) of the theorem).

For simple majority rule the unstable dimension is two or three, depending on whether the society is of odd or even size (Schofield, 1981c). For example, with the majority game $(n,q) = (6,4)$, one may construct a preference configuration in two dimensions with a "stable" core and one with a stable cycle set (Schofield, 1980b). However, in three dimensions any core can be destroyed by infinitesimal perturbation, while the "top cycle set" includes points far from the Pareto set.

For a q-game the unstable dimension w is no greater than q, while for an arbitrary (weighted) noncollegial voting game, $w \leqslant n - 1$. In the "chaotic" dimensions not only will the core be empty for almost all profiles, but all points can be joined by voting trajectories.

Note that any constant or zero sum "distribution" game is unstable (see Riker and Ordeshook, 1973, p. 135). The voting theorem asserts that only w dimensions are necessary to produce the same kind of instability.

As Rae (1980) observes, a cycle is "like one of Escher's stairways leading always up yet always coming back down to its own foundation." In dimension greater than w a voting game has an extremely chaotic character: around *every* point there exist an infinite number of Escher stairways. No observer looking at the behavior of a formal voting system could say at any time that there was a "coherent" direction of change.

To give a story imagine three men adrift in a boat in the ocean, each of whom thinks land is in a different direction. If they use majority rule they will zig-zag across the ocean. The point is not just that they may go around in circles, but that no coherent sailing policy can be implemented. By the way, the Pareto principle would be worse since they would not move at all. At least under majority rule the random movement of the boat has some chance of hitting land. Perhaps underlying this is the "more intricate altimeter" that Rae believes we need.

MANIPULATION IN THE POLITY AND ECONOMY

Riker (1980a) sees politics as the dismal science since no fundamental equilibria exist, and that, as a consequence, outcomes result not just from "institutions and tastes, but also from the political skill and artistry of those who manipulate agenda, formulate and reformulate questions, generate false issues, etc., in order to exploit the disequilibrium of tastes for their own advantage." It is true that at a locally cyclic point some agenda manipulation may be possible. Indeed it seems that only outside $DC(p)$ may no agenda manipulation be possible (Slutsky, 1979).

With many manipulators, all trying to change the outcome in their favor, chaos enters in again. Complex institutions may go through structural cycles in which "institutional" equilibria are first destroyed, bringing "manipulated" chaos, and then recreated as the institution is reorganized (Dodd, 1977; Schofield, 1980c). In the chaotic dimension, agenda manipulation has to be nearly always nearly everywhere possible.

In a simple plurality system, such as a presidential election, if the policy space is of sufficient dimensionality, then the final outcome is indeterminate. Opinion polls, for example, seem to fluctuate dramatically in response to very small "strategic moves" by the candidates.[2]

While the voting theorem is relevant for general voting games, including committee decision making and coalition government, it must be used with a degree of caution. For example, if both the agenda and the set of outcomes are fixed, then it is quite possible that game theoretic equilibria (the bargaining set, competitive solution, etc.) exist. However, manipulation other than by agenda can occur. One method is to introduce new issues: the choice theory literature (Plott, 1976) shows that strange things can happen, benefiting one or other of the manipulators. A second possibility is for one or more players to lie about their preferences, in a completely consistent fashion, and, by so doing, change the equilibrium in their favor (Farquharson, 1969). Starting with Gibbard (1973) and Satterthwaite (1975), social choice theory has looked at the possibility of *preference manipulation,* and it is now becoming clear that any decision mechanism is susceptible to this kind of "distortion."[3]

Although Rae (1980) seems to think that the way out of voting chaos is to use estimates of intensity of preference (Dahl, 1956), it would appear obvious that any mechanism based on interpersonal comparisons must be completely susceptible to preference manipulation. To validate Rae's argument, one has to design a mechanism which "forces" every individual to reveal preference truthfully.

There are theoretical reasons for believing that this cannot in general be done. While voting mechanisms for preference revelation over public goods do not seem to work, some recent results seem to indicate that one may not even rely on the marketplace to be an effective preference revelation mechanism for private, let alone public, goods.

There is, in fact, a rather subtle problem with the market (and the price) mechanism which puts it at the opposite extreme of voting, but does nothing to diminish our concern about the manner of its operation.

First of all, if every actor is a price taker, then, as in elementary microeconomics, it is rational for each to optimize on the budget or production set to maximize utility or profit, etc. No one gains by behaving other than truthfully. As Riker (1980a) says in a general equilibrium context, "The price of the commodity is jointly and completely determined in a particular describable way by the sum of the sellers' desires to sell."

This is all very well, but the general equilibrium theorem has a very peculiar mathematical form. At a specific price vector, *each* individual engages in optimizing behavior. Since the individual strategy spaces are "linearly independent," no *economic cycles* can occur. In this *Nash* economic game there must be an equilibrium (Schofield, 1981d). The difficulties with the Nash equilibrium concept (Fiorina and Shepsle, this volume) are of course relevant. Second, the most important actor is the "auctioneer" who adjusts the price vector. As far as I know, no decent dynamic model of the auctioneer's behavior exists.[4] Third, there is no general reason to suppose that the Nash economic equilibrium is Pareto optimal, except under very specific assumptions (Brown and Heal, 1979).

The most important difficulty with the Nash competitive equilibrium notion is that no allowance is made for coalition behavior. I do not consider the core existence theorem for production economies (Arrow and Hahn, 1971; Scarf, 1971) at all robust. Indeed I believe that *coalition economies* display the same kind of instability as coalition polities (Schofield, 1977b).

The proof of existence of a competitive equilibrium relies on showing that there is a Nash equilibrium in the game in strategy space (Shafer and Sonnenschein, 1975). For almost any smooth profile, the equilibrium set will consist of zero-dimensional objects (Debreu, 1970, 1976). This means that the market mechanism may be regarded as a map m from the profile $p = (p_1, \ldots, p_n)$ to an outcome, or set of outcomes, $m(p)$ in the space of possible states. A natural question to ask is whether this outcome can be *manipulated*. More precisely, is there a profile p and an individual i who can substitute p_i' for his truthful preference p_i with the result that $m(p_1, \ldots p_i', \ldots p_n)$ is preferred by i to $m(p_1, \ldots p_i, \ldots p_n)$? If we assume that the mapping m is single-valued, then can m be represented as the Nash equilibrium of a game in *preference* space? If not, then even though "truthful" optimization by economic agents will lead to market equilibrium, "second-order rational behavior" by these agents may lead to instability.

For public goods, "It is in the selfish interest of each person to give false signals to pretend to have less interest in a given collective consumption activity than (s)he really has . . ." (Samuelson, 1954). If, in a private goods market (satisfying the private regarding assumptions of the neoclassical model), all actors are infinitesimal, then it is "unprofitable to depart from the rules of perfectly competitive behavior when everyone else continues to abide by the rules" (Hurwicz, 1972). However, Hurwicz was able to produce an exchange economy with two goods and two actors, where actor one by behaving as though preference was p'_1 was able to produce an outcome $m(p'_1,p_2)$ superior to $m(p_1,p_2)$, where p_1,p_2 are the true preferences of the players.

In a later example Orosel (1974) produced an example with three actors and two goods where actor one prefers state y to x, and x is the price equilibrium. If actor one lies and pretends to prefer x to y, then y becomes the equilibrium.

Other types of manipulation abound. Aumann and Peleg (1974) have constructed an example of an exchange economy in which actor one controls the endowment of good 1, and actor two good 2. Actor one has an incentive to destroy some of his good to raise its price, and by doing so correctly can change the price equilibrium in his favor. But both may manipulate, and instability results.

In Gale's (1974) example with three players, actor one donates some of his endowments to actor two. The outcome, after exchange at equilibrium prices, is superior for both players to the exchange outcome that would have resulted had no initial "reallocation" occurred. A more theoretical analysis by Guesnerie and Laffont (1978) has shown that, in any world economy, some nation-state may reallocate its domestic endowments among its members as in the Gale example, so as to produce an outcome after trade with the rest of the world which it prefers to the trade outcome that would have resulted *without* the initial reallocation. For example, income equalization tax policies might put a country onto a higher-growth path than otherwise. It does seem to be the case that it is theoretically possible for a "large" economy to manipulate the world market to its advantage (perhaps through tariffs, export subsidies, tax policies, etc.).

A deeper result by Satterthwaite and Sonnenschein (1979) shows some of the formal structure of the problem. Suppose the market mechanism m maps smooth profiles continuously to a unique price equilibrium. For profile p, let $R(p)$ be the power relation on agents [i.e., $i\,R(p)j$ means that agent i can affect j without cost]. Satterthwaite and Sonnenschein demonstrate that m is nonmanipulable only if $R(p)$ is *acyclic*. In essence this is a smooth analog of Satterthwaite's (1975) theorem that nonmanipulation implies dictatorship. Indeed smooth nondictatorial mechanisms seem almost always to be manipulable by almost everybody (Guesnerie and Laffont, 1981).

To put it crudely, if the market mechanism is nonmanipulable, then, in a sense, the price mechanism (or auctioneer) itself must be essentially a disembodied dictator.

The same argument can be used against the notion of a *structure-induced equilibrium* (SIE) in a political institution (Kramer, 1972; Slutsky, 1977; Shepsle, 1979a). If institutions subdivide the policy problem into one-dimensional jurisdictions, then no local voting cycles may occur, and thus (with the usual assumptions) an equilibrium must exist. Just as in the Nash competitive economy, the equilibrium need not be Paretian and may be susceptible to manipulation. If the institutional structure is "dictatorial," then political decision making will eventually be perceived as unresponsive to electoral preference.

POLITICAL ECONOMY

Riker's dismay about the scientific shortcomings of political theory in contrast to economic theory seems to me to be unfounded. Both the pure theories have been shown to have unsuspected and unattractive features.

In the Nash model of an economy with prices, the equilibrium set will, as we have observed, generally consist of a discrete set of points. The process by which this equilibrium set is tracked is "myopic" (or decentralized) in the sense of being locally defined by first-order conditions: the small trades that can occur at a point are defined at *that* point and are independent of phenomenon far from the point. But this myopia is simply a local form of the independence axiom (Schofield, 1981e). The mathematical model underlying the voting theorem is myopic in the same way. While both a voting system and a market mechanism are "local," they are distinguished by the large cycle sets (and possible agenda manipulation) of the former, and the small equilibrium set (and preference manipulation) of the latter.

As Fiorina and Shepsle (this volume) observe, the results on voting instability (and, of course, the "economic" preference manipulation theorems) are purely theoretical, and need not necessarily inform us about the real world. I believe, however, that these theorems are relevant, not least because they force us to a new perception of both the political and economic world. For one thing it is not obvious that one may justifiably blame political mechanisms for the irrationality of economic events.[5] I concur with Riker that the voting theorem suggests that political institutions be examined afresh to determine how different political structures deal with potential instability (Riker, 1978, 1980b; Schofield, 1981e).

However, I disagree strongly with Fiorina and Shepsle in their assertion that "a model without equilibrium constitutes no more of a scientific improvement in the state of knowledge than wholly complete descriptions of the phenomenon." Indeed I consider the scientific study of the political economy not only compatible with, but necessarily based on, chaos in the micropolitical and microeconomic realm.

Recent work in dynamic systems, particularly in ecological models,[6] evolutionary theory, and celestial mechanics, has suggested that development processes are fundamentally chaotic. Of particular significance is the idea of "bifurcation," that small changes in the initial state can completely transform the process.

As Prigogine (1980) has noted, "The absolute predictability of classical mechanics, or the physics of being, was considered to be an essential element of the scientific picture of the physical world. . . . Over three centuries the scientific picture has shifted towards a new more subtle conception in which deterministic and stochastic features play an essential role." In Prigogine's view, "Irreversibility is the manifestation on a *macroscopic scale* of 'randomness' on a *microscopic scale*."

Prigogine's argument, as I understand it, is that it is *precisely* the chaotic structure of microscopic phenomena that endows macroscopic behavior with a time *direction* and historical meaning.

The ant society is in equilibrium, and therefore comprehensible to the ant-eater, but it is also static. Human societies, I contend, are in *microscopic* turbulence, and it is this that permits *microscopic* development.

As regards general economic equilibrium, since the price equilibrium is continuously dependent on endowments, productive capacities, and preferences, I see no explanation in terms of this theory for rapid changes in commodity prices, exchange rates, interest rates, or, more important, the gross development processes (such as technological innovation) that occur. As Kornai (1971) has observed, the theory offers little explanation for the real motion of the economy. I believe that it is precisely the emphasis on equilibrium at the microscopic level in economic theory that has blocked the development of a general macroeconomic theory.[7]

Keynes's (1936) argument, after all, was that the expectations of economic agents could be inconsistent. The modern literature on preference manipulation supports the same conclusion, that the essential uncertainty held by each agent about other agents' behavior forbids the adoption of an equilibrium strategy of the Nash kind. As Weintraub says, in a comment on Radner's (1968) work, "If agents are uncertain about other agents' behavior, so that *strategic reasoning* intrudes, no equilibrium may exist even with complete futures markets" (Weintraub, 1979, p. 92).

In my view, macroscopic theories of political and economic development must be founded on the likelihood of microscopic indeterminism. In the political realm, institutional structures probably do operate so as to reduce the effects of preference instability, but they may also exhibit structural transformations, or bifurcations. It is precisely this possibility that endows political behavior with a historical dimension.

In the future I expect a rich flow of ideas between economic and political theory at both the micro- and macroscopic levels, as microscopic instability is integrated with macroscopic development. Riker's examination of the significance of micropolitical instability for macropolitical theory is an inspiration on how to proceed with this synthesis.

NOTES

1. See Plott (1967), Sloss (1971, 1973), Kramer (1973), Kramer and Klevorick (1974), McKelvey (1976, 1979), Cohen (1979), Cohen and Matthews (1980), Matthews (1977, 1978, 1980).

2. Consider the French election of May 1981.

3. There is a large literature on this topic. See Dasgupta, Hammond, and Maskin (1979) for a review.

4. See the references to Arrow and Hahn (1971) and Weintraub (1979) in Chapter 5.

5. For examples see the OECD report edited by McCracken (1977), the literature on the political–business cycle or "supply side" arguments such as those presented by Duignan and Rabushka (1980).

6. See Schofield (1980b) for a discussion of some of these developments.

7. See Leijonhufvud (1968, p. 395) for a comment on the bias induced by the "Newtonian conception of what the economic system is like."

8 ON THE PROPERTIES OF STABLE DECISION PROCEDURES

John A. Ferejohn and David M. Grether

Nonunanimous voting processes seldom possess voting equilibria if the number of alternatives is large. The discovery of this fact has led to an intense search for new "solution concepts" for voting games that are capable of predicting outcomes in cases in which equilibria fail to exist. The reader is referred to papers by Kramer (1977), Fiorina and Shepsle (this volume), and Riker (this volume) for examples and further discussion.

That some voting procedures often fail to possess stable outcomes (i.e., alternatives which cannot be defeated by the formation of any powerful coalition) is often taken to be a defect of these procedures. But it is not obvious that alternative procedures exist which can select outcomes that are not vulnerable to coalition formation in just the same way as are the outcomes selected by nonunanimous voting rules.

The purpose of this investigation is to enquire as to the properties of those decision procedures that always select outcomes which are invulnerable to the formation of coalitions. We are able to show that if a decision procedure can select a stable outcome in each environment, then it is either quite indecisive or is essentially oligarchic. This result is established by appealing to several of the classical theorems of social choice theory. Our results suggest that the requirement that a procedure be able to select coalition invulnerable outcomes in every

107

environment is so strong as to exclude many otherwise appealing procedures. In particular, it seems that the fact that majority rule does not generally have stable outcomes is not a very strong criticism of it if all the attractive alternative institutions suffer from the same defect.

In what follows we suggest a general framework for the study of "strategy-proof" or stable decision-making mechanisms and present some new theorems in this direction. The basic concept of a strategy-proof or incentive compatible mechanism has, in previous literature, generally been defined in relation to an equilibrium concept of some sort. For example, Gibbard's notion of a straight-forward mechanism is one for which every agent has a nonempty set of dominant strategies for each preference configuration. In this paper, we say that for any particular concept of equilibrium, a mechanism is *stable* with respect to that concept just in case the set of equilibria is nonempty for each preference configuration. Thus, Gibbard's straightforward mechanisms are stable with respect to dominant strategy equilibrium. Groves and Ledyard's (1977) incentive compatible mechanisms are stable with respect to Nash equilibrium. The principal focus in this paper is on decision-making mechanisms that are stable with respect to strong equilibrium (see Definition 8.2), and we are able to show that such mechanisms are either indecisive or have a concentrated distribution of power.

It will be useful to distinguish our work from the somewhat similar investigations of consistent voting procedures by Peleg (1978) and Dutta and Pattanaik (1978) and implementable social choice functions by Dasgupta, Hammond, and Maskin (1979). A voting procedure is *consistent* with respect to strong equilibrium if one of the outcomes associated with the strong equilibria would have been chosen had the agents voted "truthfully." Thus, for a procedure to be consistent in this sense we must, first, be able to define what truthful behavior is; second, we must require that the set of strong equilibria be always nonempty; and third, we must insist that at least one of the associated outcomes is the same as the outcome associated with truthful revelation. Our condition that a mechanism be stable with respect to strong equilibrium amounts to the second of the above requirements. The following example shows that the requirement that a mechanism satisfy our axiom of strong stability is weaker than the requirement that the mechanism be consistent.

EXAMPLE 8.1: Suppose there are two possible social states $X = \{x,y\}$, and that society consists of two people $N = \{1,2\}$. Let the strategies of the individuals be given by

$$S_i = \left\{ \frac{x}{y}, \frac{y}{x} \right\} \qquad i = 1,2.$$

Thus, the strategy set for each individual contains exactly the strong orderings on X. Let $F: S_1 \times S_2 \to X$ be as follows:

$$F\begin{pmatrix} x & x \\ y & y \end{pmatrix} = y, \qquad F(s^1, s^2) = x$$

for all other $(s^1, s^2) \in S_1 \times S_2$. It is easily checked that F has strong equilibria for each preference configuration but that if the true configuration is

1	2
x	x
y	y

the truthful outcome is y while any strong equilibrium would yield the outcome x. Therefore F is not a consistent voting procedure.

A social choice function (SCF) is a mapping from preference configurations into subsets of the set of alternatives. A SCF is called *implementable* with respect to an equilibrium concept if there is a mechanism (or game form) such that (1) the set of equilibria for that mechanism is nonempty for each preference configuration and (2) the outcomes associated with each equilibrium are contained in the social choice function for every preference configuration. The study of Dasgupta, Hammond, and Maskin (1979) consists of finding classes of social choice functions which are implementable with respect to some equilibrium concept. In so doing they must perforce find stable mechanisms in our sense, but they do not directly examine the effect of simply imposing a stability requirement on decision-making mechanisms. This question seems to us to be the more fundamental one as it does not involve the supposition that a planner has some well-behaved and preexisting notion of the "good" outcomes that he wishes to implement by choice of mechanism. In contrast, we seek only the necessary properties of a stable decision-making mechanism. Obviously, these properties will turn out to delimit the class of implementable SCFs. As an example we may note that any strongly stable mechanism "implements" the SCF that chooses the "weak" Pareto optimals for each preference configuration.

NOTATION AND DEFINITIONS

Let X stand for a collection of alternatives and N for the set of agents. Each agent has a weak ordering R_i (with asymmetric part P_i) that describes the agent's preferences over X. The collection of weak orders on X is written $\mathcal{R}$. A *society* is an n-tuple of weak orders $\pi \in \mathcal{R}^n$.

DEFINITION 8.1: A *social decision procedure* (SDP) is an $(n+1)$-tuple. $\Gamma = \langle S_1, S_2, \ldots, S_n, F \rangle$, where S_i is the strategy set of the ith agent and F is a function that takes strategy n-tuples *onto* the alternatives. Thus, $F: S_1 \times S_2 \times \cdots \times S_n \xrightarrow{\text{onto}} X$. We sometimes will write $s = (s_1, s_2, s_3, \ldots, s_n) = (s^c, s^{N-c})$, where $s^c \in \Pi_{i \in c} S_i \equiv S^c$ and $s^{N-c} \in \Pi_{i \in N-c} S_i \equiv S^{N-c}$, and $c \subseteq N$.

Several definitions will be useful in the following developments.

DEFINITION 8.2: $\bar{s} \in S^N$ is a *strong equilibrium* for $\langle \Gamma, \pi \rangle$ if

$$\forall c \subseteq N, \ \forall s^c \in S^c, \quad \exists \, i \in c \quad \text{with} \quad F(\bar{s}) R_i F(s^c, \bar{s}^{N-c}).$$

We let $H(\pi)$ denote the set of strong equilibria for F given the preference configuration π. The notion of strategy proofness we employ here is parallel to that given by Gibbard:

DEFINITION 8.3: F is *strongly stable* if for each $\pi \in \mathcal{R}^n$, there is a strong equilibrium.

The following example shows that there exist social decision procedures which are strongly stable but which are not straightforward in the sense that for some $\pi \in \mathcal{R}^n$, some agent fails to possess a dominant strategy.

EXAMPLE 8.2: Let $X = \{x, y\}$, $N = \{1, 2, 3\}$, $S_i = \{s_1^i, s_2^i\}$, and F be described by the following normal form:

	s_1^1				s_2^1	
	s_1^3	s_2^3			s_1^3	s_2^3
s_1^2	x	y		s_1^2	y	y
s_2^2	x	y		s_2^2	x	x

Note that agent one controls the choice of matrix, agent two the rows, and agent three, the columns. It is easily checked that if agent one has, say, yP_1x, he has no dominant strategy. On the other hand, strong equilibria exist for each π.

If F is strongly stable, we can find a correspondence H that takes each preference n-tuple into its (nonempty) set of strong equilibria. And, we can define functions that select from H. Thus, we let $h(\pi) \in H(\pi) \quad \forall \pi \subset \mathcal{R}^n$ be a function that selects a particular, strong equilibrium for each $\pi \in \mathcal{R}^n$.

For each π we can define a family of associated configurations, $\pi(Z) = (R_1(Z), R_2(Z), \ldots, R_n(Z))$ as follows:

$$\forall x, y \in Z, \quad \forall i \in N, \quad x R_i(Z) y \Leftrightarrow x R_i y,$$

$$\forall x \in Z, \ y \notin Z, \quad x P_i(Z) y,$$

$$\forall x, y \notin Z, \quad x R_i(Z) y \Leftrightarrow x R_i y.$$

Thus $\pi(Z)$ is an n-tuple of weak orders which agrees with π on Z and $X - Z$ but in which everyone ranks the elements of Z above those in $X - Z$. It will now be possible to show that a choice function may naturally be defined from $\langle \Gamma, \pi \rangle$. Let $\mathcal{P}(X)$ denote the power set of X.

DEFINITION 8.4: C is a *social choice function* (SCF) if

$C: [\mathcal{P}(X) - \phi] \times \mathcal{R}^n \to \mathcal{P}(X) - \phi$ and

$\forall \pi \in \mathcal{R}^n, \ \forall A \in \mathcal{P}(X) - \phi, \ \phi \neq C(A, \pi) \subseteq A.$

Let $C_F(A, \pi) = F(H(\pi(A))) \ \forall A \in \mathcal{P}(X).$

PROPOSITION 8.1: C_F is a social choice function if F is strongly stable.

Proof: That $C_F(A, \pi)$ is nonempty follows from the fact that F is strongly stable, and so $H(\pi(A)) \neq \phi$.

If $x \in C_F(A, \pi)$ and $x \notin A$, there is a $z \in A$ such that $\forall i \in N, \ zP_i(A)x$. But then the coalition N can find a strategy to obtain z since F maps onto X. Q.E.D.

PROPERTIES OF THE INDUCED CHOICE FUNCTION

In this section we shall show that C_F satisfies various "classical" properties from the theory of social choice. In particular, it will be shown to satisfy the Pareto and independence of irrelevant alternative axioms, as well as a weak regularity condition proposed some years ago by Sen (1970).

DEFINITION 8.5: C satisfies *independence of irrelevant alternatives* (IIA) if, whenever π and π' agree on A,

$C(A, \pi) = C(A, \pi').$

DEFINITION 8.6: C satisfies *Pareto* if $xP_iy \ \ \forall \ i \in N$, and if $x, y \in A$, then $y \notin C(A, \pi)$.

PROPOSITION 8.2: If F is strongly stable, then C_F satisfies Pareto and IIA.

Proof: Pareto is obvious. For IIA note that if π and π' agree on A, then $H(\pi(A)) = H(\pi'(A))$. Q.E.D.

DEFINITION 8.7: A choice function satisfies *Sen's α* if and only if for $A \subseteq B$,

$A \cap C(B, \pi) \subseteq C(A, \pi).$

PROPOSITION 8.3: C_F satisfies Sen's α.

Proof: Assume that $A \subseteq B$ and that $x \in A \cap C_F(B, \pi)$. Because $x \in C_F(B, \pi)$, there is an $\bar{s}^N \in S^N$ with $F(\bar{s}^N) = x$ such that there does not exist a triple (c,y,s^c) for which $c \subseteq N$, $y \in X$, and $s^c \in S^c$ such that

$$y = F(s^c, \bar{s}^{N-c}) P_i(B) F(\bar{s}^N) \ \forall \ i \in c.$$

Since $A \subseteq B$, no such c,y, and s^c exist with y restricted to lie in A. Thus $\bar{s}^N$ is a strong equilibrium for $\pi(A) \Rightarrow x \in C_F(A, \pi)$. Q.E.D.

PROPOSITION 8.4: If choice function satisfies Sen's α, then the binary relation induced from its two-element sets is acyclic.

Proof: Let $B = \{x_1, x_2, \ldots, x_k\}$ be chosen such that $\{x_i\} = C(\{x_i, x_{i+1}\}, \pi)$ mod k. Now notice that $\{x_i, x_{i+1}\} \cap C(B, \pi) \subseteq C(\{x_i, x_{i+1}\}, \pi)$ implies that $x_{i+1} \notin C(B, \pi)$ and that this holds for each i (mod k). Q.E.D.

DEFINITION 8.8: Given a social decision procedure F, the binary relation $R_F(\pi)$ is defined as follows:

$$x R_F(\pi) y \Leftrightarrow x \in C_F(\{x,y\}, \pi) \ \forall x, y \in X.$$

REMARK 8.1: Note that if F is not stable, it may happen that $C_F(\{x,y\}, \pi)$ is empty or contains only elements other than x and y. In this case the relation $R_F(\pi)$ would not be complete.

REMARK 8.2: As a matter of convention, if C_F satisfies P and/or IIA and R_F is defined as above, then we shall say that R_F satisfies P and/or IIA.

We may now state the main theorem of this section.

THEOREM 8.1: If F is strongly stable, there exists a mapping which satisfies Pareto and IIA, $R_F: \mathcal{R}^n \to \mathcal{A}$, where $\mathcal{A}$ is the family of complete, reflexive, acyclic binary relations on X.

Proof: Follows immediately from Propositions 8.1, 8.3, and 8.4. Q.E.D.

We can obtain a related result of some interest by using the following stability concept:

DEFINITION 8.9: F is *uniquely strongly stable* (USS) if for each $\pi \in \mathcal{R}^n$ $F(H(\pi))$ is a singleton.

THEOREM 8.2: If F is uniquely strongly stable, then there is a mapping $R_F: \mathcal{R}^n \to \mathcal{R}$ which satisfies Pareto and IIA.

Proof: Note that if H is single-valued, $x R_F(\pi) y$ and $y R_F(\pi) x \Rightarrow x = y$. Thus, in this case, $R_F(\pi)$ is acyclic if and only if it is a linear order. Q.E.D.

REMARK 8.3: Note that on $\mathcal{P}^n$, the set of n-tuples of linear orders, F in Example 8.1 is USS but not straightforward.

PROPERTIES OF THE COLLECTION OF DECISIVE SETS

In this section we shall prove that if F satisfies strong stability (or unique strong stability), then the associated collection of decisive sets constitutes a prefilter (or an ultrafilter). First we need some definitions.

DEFINITION 8.10: A collection of subsets $W \subseteq \mathcal{P}(N)$ is a *prefilter* if it satisfies

   i. $N \in W, \phi \notin W$,
   ii. $c \in W, c \subseteq d \Rightarrow d \in W$,
   iii. $\cap_{c \in W} c \neq \phi$.

DEFINITION 8.11: A collection of subsets $W \subseteq \mathcal{P}(N)$ is an *ultrafilter* if it satisfies (i) and (ii) above and also

   iii'. $c, d \in W \Rightarrow c \cap d \in W$,
   iv. $\forall c \in N$, either c or $N - c \in W$.

DEFINITION 8.12: $c \subseteq N$ is *decisive for* (x, y) if

$$x P_i y \ \forall i \in c \Rightarrow \{x\} = C_F(\{x, y\}, \pi).$$

DEFINITION 8.13: If $\forall x \in X, [x P_i y \ \forall i \in c, \ \forall y \in X - \{x\}] \Rightarrow \{x\} = C_F(X, \pi)$, then c is a *decisive* set. Let W stand for the collection of decisive sets.

We may easily relate the decisive sets for (x, y) to the decisive sets as follows:

PROPOSITION 8.5: If F is strongly stable, then $c \subseteq N$ is a decisive set for each $(x, y) \Leftrightarrow c$ is a decisive set.

Proof: Let $P_F(\pi)$ stand for the asymmetric component of the binary relation $R_F(\pi)$. Let $c \subseteq N$ be decisive for each (x, y) but not decisive. Then there would be a $\pi \in \mathcal{R}^n$ such that

$$\forall i \in c, \ x P_i y \ \forall y \in X - \{x\} \quad \text{and} \quad \{x\} \neq C_F(X, \pi).$$

Take $y \in C_F(X, \pi), y \neq x$, and note that

$$y \in \{x, y\} \cap C_F(X, \pi) \subseteq C_F(\{x, y\}, \pi) = \{x\}.$$

Conversely, if c is not decisive for all (x, y), there is a π and a pair (x, y) with $x P_i y \ \forall i \in c$ and $\{x\} \neq C_F(\{x, y\}, \pi) = F(H(\pi(\{x, y\})))$. But note that in $\pi(\{x, y\})$,

$xP_i z \quad \forall i \in c, \quad \forall z \in X - \{x\}$ and $\{x\} \neq C_F(X, \pi(\{x,y\}))$

$= C_F(\{x,y\}, \pi(\{x,y\}))$.

Thus c is not decisive. Q.E.D.

REMARK 8.4: While we have defined the decisive sets by starting with the induced choice function C_F, we could as well have given a definition directly based on F, namely: A set $c \subseteq N$ is called *winning* if for each $x \in X$ there is an $\bar{s}^c \in S^c$ such that $F(\bar{s}^c, s^{N-c}) = x \ \forall s^{N-c} \in S^{N-c}$. It is easy to check that a set is winning just in case it is decisive.

PROPOSITION 8.6: c is winning if and only if it is decisive.

Proof: If c is winning for F, then it is obvious that c is decisive.

Conversely, if c is decisive, then, for an arbitrary $x \in X$ let $\pi \in \mathcal{R}^n$ be such that

$xP_i y \quad \forall i \in c, \quad \forall y \neq x,$

and

$yP_i x \quad \forall i \in N\text{-}c, \quad \forall y \neq x.$

Clearly, $\{x\} = F \circ H(\pi)$, which implies $\exists s \in H(\pi)$ such that $x = F(s) = F(s^c, s^{N-c})$. Now assume that there is a $t^{N-c} \in S^{N-c}$ such that $F(s^c, t^{N-c}) = z \neq x$. Then s cannot be a strong equilibrium for π. Therefore $F(s^c, t^{N-c}) = x$ for all $t^{N-c} \in S^{N-c}$, and so since x is arbitrary, c is winning for F. Q.E.D.

THEOREM 8.3: (Brown): If $|X| \geq n$ and F is strongly stable, then the collection of winning sets constitutes a prefilter.

Proof: Note that the mapping R_F is acyclic-valued and satisfies IIA and Pareto. P implies that N is a winning set and that ϕ is not winning. The collection of winning sets is trivially monotone. Thus either the winning sets form a prefilter, or there is a collection of k winning sets $\{c_i\}$ with $\cap_{i=1}^k c_i = \phi$. In the second case for each $i = 1, \ldots, k$ let the members of c_i have preferences $x_i P x_{i+1}$ (mod k). And

$\forall z \in X - \{x_1, \ldots, x_k\}, \quad x_i P_j z \quad \forall i \in 1, \ldots, k$ and $\forall j \in N.$

Note that no individual is in more than $k - 1$ such sets so that the individuals may have weak order preferences. Then $\{x_i\} = C_F(\{x_i, x_{i+1}\}, \pi)$ (mod k), which implies that $R_F(\pi)$ is not acyclic. Q.E.D.

Some easy corollaries of Theorem 8.3 may be given. For example, we may say an individual $i \in N$ has a *veto* on (x,y) if $xP_i y \Rightarrow x \in C_F(\{x,y\}, \pi)$. If there is no individual who has a veto on any pair of alternatives, then we say that F satisfies NV. Note that F satisfies NV only if each subset of n-1 individuals is decisive on each pair of alternatives.

COROLLARY 8.1 (Peleg): If $|X| \geqslant n$, there is no F satisfying NV and strong stability.

Proof: The collection of winning sets contains all subsets of $n - 1$ members and thus is not a prefilter. Q.E.D.

The following definition is given in Peleg (1978).

DEFINITION 8.14: F satisfies D_k if each $c \subseteq N$ such that $|c| > k$ is winning.

COROLLARY 8.2: If $|X|$ is finite, there is no F satisfying D_k and strong stability if k is such that $n/(n - k - 1) \leqslant |X|$.

Proof: This is proved by Peleg but it also follows from an application of Propositions 8.3 and 8.4 above and Theorem I of Ferejohn and Grether (1978). This is accomplished by noting that $R_F(\pi)$ is acyclic, so that if the decisive sets associated with R_F contain all sets of at least $k + 1$ members, there can be no more than $n/(n - k - 1)$ elements in X. Q.E.D.

We can obtain another theorem using similar reasoning.

THEOREM 8.4 (Arrow): If $|X| \geqslant 3$ and F satisfies USS, then the collection of winning sets forms an ultrafilter.

An easy corollary of this theorem is analogous to the Gibbard–Satterthwaite theorem. First we need a definition.

DEFINITION 8.15: $i \in N$ is a *dictator* if for each $x \in X$ there is an $\bar{s}_i \in S^i$ such that $F(\bar{s}_i, s^{N-i}) = x \quad \forall s^{N-i} \in S^{N-i}$.

COROLLARY 8.3: If $|X| \geqslant 3$, there is no F satisfying USS and nondictatorship. Since dictatorships have dominant strategy equilibria for each configuration, we can see that if F satisfies USS, then it is strategy-proof in the sense of Gibbard.

Finally, Theorem 8.3 allows us to show that the strongly and fully implementable social choice functions are oligarchical in exactly the same sense as are the SDPs.

DEFINITION 8.16: A *social choice rule* is a mapping G from $\mathfrak{R}^n$ into X.

REMARK 8.5: A social choice rule is simply a social choice function with domain restricted to $\{X\} \otimes \mathfrak{R}^n$.

DEFINITION 8.17: A social choice rule G is *strongly and fully implementable* if there is an SDP $\langle S_1, \ldots, S_n, F \rangle$, such that $G(\pi) = F \circ H(\pi) \quad \forall \pi \in \mathfrak{R}^n$. In this case we say that $\langle S_1, \ldots, S_n, F \rangle$ strongly and fully implements G.

DEFINITION 8.18:   A coalition $c \subseteq N$ is *prevalent for a social choice rule* G if $\forall \pi \in \mathcal{R}^n$ such that $xP_i y$ $\forall i \in c$ $\forall y \in X - \{x\} \Rightarrow \{x\} = G(\pi)$.

The following proposition may be established by the same argument as was given in the proof of Proposition 8.6.

PROPOSITION 8.7:   If F strongly and fully implements a social choice rule G, then c is prevalent for G if and only if c is winning for the SDP $\langle S_1, \ldots, S_n, F \rangle$.

COROLLARY 8.4:   If $|X| \geqslant n$ and a social choice rule G is strongly and fully implementable, then the collection of prevalent coalitions for G is a prefilter.

Thus we see that the strongly and fully implementable social choice rules have the property that there are coalitions which, when they unanimously prefer an alternative to every other alternative, it is the unique chosen alternative. Further, there is a privileged collection of individuals who belong to every such (prevalent) coalition.

Note that if the SDP $\langle S_1, \ldots, S_n, F \rangle$ is merely required to strongly implement G in the sense that $F \circ H(\pi) \subseteq G(\pi)$ $\forall \pi \in \mathcal{R}^n$, then we can conclude from Corollary 8.4 that the prevalent coalitions can actually ensure the choice of any unanimously preferred alternative.

CONVERSELY

Our results suggest that if a social decision procedure always has strong equilibria, then it must either be indecisive or power must be distributed quite unequally. If, in addition, the equilibrium set is always single-valued, then there is a dictator. These results are obviously connected to those of Gibbard (1973) and Satterthwaite (1975) in that the existence of a certain type of equilibrium forces the normal form F to have certain strong and undesirable properties.

We should note that, in general, converses of our theorems are not available since the following example demonstrates that there are social decision procedures whose decisive sets form a prefilter but which fail to satisfy strong stability.

EXAMPLE 8.3: $X = \{x, y, z\}$, $N = \{1, 2\}$, $S_i = \{s_1^i, s_2^i\}$, and F is described by the following matrix game in which the strategies of player one and two correspond to the rows and columns, respectively.

	s_1^2	s_2^2
s_1^1	x	y
s_2^1	y	z

Let π be such that

R_1	R_2
x	y
z	z
y	x

Then note that the only decisive set is $\{1,2\}$ and that this is obviously a pre-filter; but F has no strong equilibrium at π.

While the property that the winning or decisive sets form a prefilter is not generally sufficient for the existence of strong equilibria at each configuration, we can impose an additional regularity condition on F that will allow us to establish this sufficiency. A coalition, c, is called *winning for x against y* if there is a strategy n-tuple $\bar{s}$ with $F(\bar{s}) = y$ and $s^c \in S^c$ such that $x = F(s^c, \bar{s}^{N-c})$. The collection of coalitions which are winning for x against y is denoted $W_F(x,y)$. Clearly the winning sets W are contained in $W_F(x,y)$ for each (x,y). In conclusion we give the following result.

THEOREM 8.5: *If* $\infty > |X|$, $W = W_F(x,y)$ *for all* $(x,y) \in X \otimes X$, *and* W *is a prefilter, then there exists a strong equilibrium for each* $\pi \in \mathcal{R}^n$.

Proof: Suppose there is no strong equilibrium at $\pi \in \mathcal{R}^n$ and that $F(s_1) = x_1$. Then there exists $c_1 \subseteq N$ and $s^{c_1} \in S^{c_1}$ such that

$$x_2 = F(s^{c_1}, s_1^{N-c_1}) P_i F(s_1) = x_1 \quad \forall i \in c_1.$$

Thus $c_1 \in W$. Now let $s_2 = (s^{c_1}, s_1^{N-c_1})$; since s_2 is not a strong equilibrium, we can find $c_2 \subseteq N$ such that

$$x_3 = F(s^{c_2}, s_2^{N-c_2}) P_i F(s_2) \; \forall i \in c_2.$$

Proceeding in this fashion we can construct sequences $\{x_i\}$ and $\{c_i\}$ such that $c_i \in W$, for all i and $x_{i+1} P_j x_i \quad \forall j \in c_i$. Since $|X| < \infty$, there is a smallest k such that $x_{k+1} = x_m$ for some $m \in \{1, 2, \ldots, k\}$. But then since W is a prefilter, there is an individual $j \in \cap_{i=m}^{k} c_i$ with cyclic preferences. Q.E.D.

REMARK 8.6: It is clear that the preceding argument uses only (iii) of Definition 8.10. Thus there are a variety of weaker conditions which are sufficient for the existence of strong equilibria. We present Theorem 8.5 because it provides a partial converse to Theorem 8.3, though we recognize it does not give the weakest possible sufficient condition.

9 AN EXPERIMENTAL TEST OF SOLUTION THEORIES FOR COOPERATIVE GAMES IN NORMAL FORM

Richard D. McKelvey and Peter C. Ordeshook

There is a growing belief among scholars, as expressed by Riker (1980a), that political processes necessarily exhibit some indeterminancy unless the game-theoretic representation of those processes possesses a (Nash) equilibrium or a core. Here, however, we offer some evidence to support the proposition that the existence of such equilibria need not render a game's outcome determinate, given existing theory. This paper reports on a series of experiments on cooperative games in normal form, designed to test the adequacy of solution theory for such games. Although there is much literature on cooperative games in normal form, there does not seem to be any entirely satisfactory solution concept for such games. We investigate here two such solution concepts—the strong equilibrium and the core—and find them both to be poor in terms of their ability to account for our experimental results.

The most common approach to analyzing cooperative normal form games is to translate them into characteristic function form games and then analyze this form via various solution concepts such as the core, V-set, and so on (cf. Luce and Raiffa, 1957, Chapter 8; Aumann, 1961). Although it is generally recognized that information is lost in reducing a game to characteristic function form, there nevertheless is widespread use of this method, if only for lack of a better alternative.

A second, more recent approach is to deal directly with the normal form, and to look for points in the normal form that are stable against group defections. Such points are called strong equilibria and are but an especially stable subset of Nash equilibria. While such points are not guaranteed to exist, this solution concept, which appears initially in Aumann (1967), is used extensively in theoretical work attempting to construct incentive compatible social choice processes immune to group manipulation (cf. Drèze and de la Vallée Poussin, 1971; Kalai, Postlewaite, and Roberts, 1979; Maskin, 1978).

This paper investigates the usefulness of these approaches (as well as a variety of noncooperative solutions) in the context of two three-person normal form games. The second section gives formal definitions of these solutions. The third section discusses the experimental outcomes. The final section presents some conclusions and interpretations on why the solution theories do not adequately account for our data.

SOLUTIONS FOR NORMAL FORM GAMES

A *normal form game* consists of a set $N = \{1,2,\ldots,n\}$ of *players*, for each $i \in N$ a finite set S_i, called the set of *pure strategies* for player i, and a function $\psi: S \to \mathbb{R}^n$, where $S = \Pi_{i \in N} S_i$. The function ψ is called the *payoff function*, or *payoff matrix*, for the game, and for any $i \in N$, and $s \in S$, $\psi_i(s)$ represents the *payoff to player* i under the strategy n-tuple s.

Any subset $C \subseteq N$ is called a *coalition*, and we use the notation $S^C = \Pi_{i \in C} S_i$ to denote the pure strategies available to the coalition C.

Next, we let Λ^C denote the set of probability distributions on S^C, and write $\Lambda = \Lambda^N$, $\Lambda^i = \Lambda^{\{i\}}$, and $\underline{\Lambda} = \Pi_{i \in N} \Lambda^i$. Thus, Λ^i represents the set of correlated mixed strategies available to the coalition C. If $\lambda^C \in \Lambda^C$, and $\lambda^{\overline{C}} \in \Lambda^{\overline{C}}$, we write $\lambda = (\lambda^C, \lambda^{\overline{C}})$ to denote the mixed strategy $\lambda \in \Lambda$ obtained by taking the product of the two measures λ^C and $\lambda^{\overline{C}}$. Similarly, if $\lambda_i \in \Lambda^i$, for $i = 1,\ldots,n$, we write $\lambda = (\lambda_1,\ldots,\lambda_n)$ to denote the probability measure $\lambda \in \underline{\Lambda} \subseteq \Lambda$ obtained by taking the product of the λ_i. In either case, the payoff function is extended to Λ in the usual manner consistent with $\psi_i(s)$ representing a von Neumann-Morgenstern utility. Namely, for any $\lambda \in \Lambda$, take

$$\phi_i(\lambda) = \sum_{s \in S} \psi_i(s)\lambda(s).$$

If the game ψ is played noncooperatively, then there are a number of solution concepts that are available to predict the outcome of ψ. Our interest is in cooperative games here, but we give a brief summary of these solutions for completeness. For noncooperative games we must stick to the strategy space $\underline{\Lambda} \subseteq \Lambda$, since there is no possibility of correlation of strategies. The most widely used solution concept is that of a Nash equilibrium: A *Nash equilibrium* is any $\lambda^* = (\lambda_1^*,$ $\ldots, \lambda_n^*) \in \underline{\Lambda}$ satisfying, for all $i \in N$ and $\lambda_i \in \Lambda^i$,

$$\psi_i(\lambda^*) \geqslant \psi_i(\lambda_i | \lambda^*).$$

Here the notation (λ_i / λ^*) represents the vector obtained by replacing the ith component of λ^* by λ_i. The measure λ_i is degenerate if it assigns some pure strategy a probability of one. A Nash equilibrium λ^* is a pure strategy Nash equilibrium if each λ_i is degenerate.

The problem with Nash equilibria is that there are frequently too many of them. Therefore, other solution concepts have been developed to weed out the "unreasonable" equilibria. We do not formally define these procedures here, but refer the reader to other sources. One procedure for doing this is the "trembling hand," or *perfect* equilibrium developed by Selten (1975). Intuitively, an equilibrium is perfect if each player's component remains a best response even when the other players have some small probability of making mistakes. A second method of isolating reasonable equilibria is by successive elimination of dominated strategies. Thus, in the original game ψ, with pure strategies S, all players eliminate any dominated strategy. This results in a smaller game, and again players can eliminate dominated strategies in this game. The strategies that remain after no further reduction in the game can take place are referred to as *ultimately admissible strategies*, denoted $S^u \subseteq S$. Any equilibria to this reduced game are called *sophisticated equilibria*. The ultimality admissible strategies are also of interest in their own right. (This procedure is discussed in Luce and Raiffa, 1957, under the terminology wide domination, and is developed more fully by Farquharson, 1969, for specific classes of voting games.)

If the game ψ is played in a cooperative context, then there are two solution concepts of interest. The first of these is a simple extension of the Nash equilibrium, called a strong equilibrium. A strategy n-tuple $\lambda^* = (\lambda_1, \ldots, \lambda_n) \in \underline{\Lambda}$ is a *strong equilibrium* if for all $\lambda \in \underline{\Lambda}$, and $C \subseteq N$,

$$\psi_i(\lambda^*) \geqslant \psi_i(\lambda|_C \lambda^*)$$

for some $i \in C$. Here the notation $(\lambda|_C \lambda^*)$ is used to denote the vector in which we replace all components λ_i^* of λ^* by λ_i if $i \in C$. Note that the strong equilibrium requires λ^* to be stable against coalition defections, but does not take advantage of correlation of strategies.

The second cooperative solution concept is based on moving to the characteristic function representation for the normal form game. The characteristic function of a game is a function which, for each coalition, determines the set of outcomes that coalition can in some sense guarantee. To be precise, we say that, for any $C \subseteq N$, C is α *effective* for a vector $x \in \mathbb{R}^n$ if there is a $\lambda^C \in \Lambda^C$ such that for all $\lambda^{\overline{C}} \in \Lambda^{\overline{C}}$, and all $i \in C$,

$$\psi_i(\lambda^C, \lambda^{\overline{C}}) \geqslant x_i.$$

C is said to be β *effective* for x if, for each $\lambda^{\overline{C}} \in \Lambda^{\overline{C}}$, there is a $\lambda^C \in \Lambda^C$ such that, for all $i \in C$,

$$\psi_i(\lambda^C, \Lambda^{\overline{C}}) \geqslant x_i.$$

For any $C \subseteq N$, we set $v_\alpha(C)$ to be the set of payoff vectors in $\mathbb{R}^n$ for which C is α effective, and set $v_\beta(C)$ to be the set of payoff vectors in $\mathbb{R}^n$ for which C is β effective. The functions $v_\alpha: \mathcal{P}(N) \to \mathbb{R}^n$ and $v_\beta: \mathcal{P}(N) \to \mathbb{R}^n$ are referred to as the α and β characteristic functions, respectively (see Aumann, 1967, for more details). Now various cooperative solutions can be defined in the usual manner. In particular, for any $x, y \in \mathbb{R}^n$, we say x dominates y, written x D y, if for some $C \subseteq N$, $x_i > y_i$ for all $i \in C$ and $x \in v_\alpha(C)$. Set $H = \psi(\Lambda)$ to be the image of the payoff function in $\mathbb{R}^n$; then the α *core* of H is the set of undominated payoff vectors:

$$C_\alpha = \{x \in H | \nexists \; y \in \mathbb{R}^n \;\; \text{such that } y \text{ D } x\}.$$

The β core can be defined similarly using the β characteristic function.

EXPERIMENTAL STRUCTURE

The experiments consist of two series of three-person, normal form games, in which each player has two alternative strategies. The payoff matrices for these two series are given in Tables 9.1 and 9.2. The experiments were conducted so as to allow for cooperation and correlation of strategies. We discuss here some important features of the experimental design. The complete instructions read to the subjects appear in the appendix to this chapter.

At the beginning of the experiment, each subject is presented with a "worksheet" that contains a payoff matrix as in Tables 9.1 or 9.2. In addition, each subject is given a different "stake." This is a dollar amount representing the amount of money the subject will earn if he is successful in the experiment. The entries in the payoff matrix then represent the probability that each subject will win his or her stake if that is the cell chosen in the experiment. (In each cell, the first number refers to player 1, the second to player 2, and the third to player 3.) At the termination of the experiment, a fair lottery is conducted for each subject, so that each subject wins his stake with the probability corresponding to the probability of the cell selected. If the subject loses in the lottery, he is paid $1.00. With this procedure, then, the entries in each cell are equivalent

Table 9.1. Payoff Matrix for Experimental Design 1

c_1	b_1	b_2	c_2	b_1	b_2
a_1	0.75 0.75 0.30	0.10 0.10 0.15	a_1	0.20 0.20 0	0.90 0.10 0.90
a_2	0.10 0.10 0.15	0.80 0.80 0.35	a_2	0.10 0.90 0.90	0.30 0.30 0.80

Table 9.2. Payoff Matrix for Experimental Design 2

c_1	b_1	b_2	c_2	b_1	b_2
a_1	0.65 0.50 0.20	0 0.60 0.35	a_1	0.55 0.20 0	0.30 0.30 0.40
a_2	0.70 0.55 0.30	0.10 0.90 0.60	a_2	0.50 0.00 0.80	0.20 0.10 0.70

to a von Neumann–Morgenstern utility. Note that each subject knows his own utilities as well as those of the other subjects, but subjects are not aware of, nor are they allowed to talk about, the stakes of the other subjects. The prohibition prevents side payments and collusive agreements prior to the experiment.

Each experiment begins with a fifteen-minute discussion period during which the subjects can discuss what strategies they might adopt and what agreements they might want to enter into. During this period, however, they cannot make any formally binding agreements. This discussion period is intended to ensure that the subjects have an opportunity to internalize the important features of their payoffs and to appreciate some of the strategic possibilities of the experiment before reaching a final decision.

After the initial discussion period, subjects are allowed to choose their individual strategy at any time by filling out and signing a card. They are allowed to reveal this choice of strategy to none, one, or both of the other subjects. When all three subjects have filled out their cards, and placed them on the table, the experimenter asks whether anyone wishes to change his strategy. If no one does, the experiment terminates. If any one subject wishes to change his strategy, all cards are returned, and the above process is repeated. This termination procedure, then, is intended to satisfy two conflicting requirements. First, the choice of strategies should be simultaneous. Second, there should be the possibility of correlating strategies, of commitment, etc. In this design, the final choice of strategy can be thought of as occurring when the experimenter asks whether anyone wishes to change his strategy; hence the final choice is simultaneous, as required. Also, each subject is permitted to reveal selectively his choice of strategy to other subjects prior to finalizing his choice formally. This allows for the required commitment and correlation of strategies.

EXPERIMENTAL OUTCOMES

The particular game matrices portrayed in Tables 9.1 and 9.2 have several interesting properties, and are designed to yield situations in which the characteristic function might not model well the "value" of a coalition. Table 9.3 gives various solutions—both noncooperative and cooperative—for the two experimental designs. The first design has a relatively large core, one element of which is also a Nash equilibrium. The second design, on the other hand, contains one cell—$a_1b_2c_2$—which has all sorts of nice properties, both from a cooperative and noncooperative point of view. It is a unique Nash equilibrium (even if mixed strategies are allowed), it is a unique perfect equilibrium, and it is a unique ultimately admissible strategy (i.e., the strategy which remains when all players successively eliminate dominated strategies). In addition, this cell is a unique strong equilibrium, and is the only pure strategy which is in either the α or the β version of the core.

The rationale for the choice of these two designs is that in neither does the characteristic function appear to give a good representation of the value of various coalitions. The characteristic functions for the two-person coalitions in both designs are drawn in Figure 9.1. In the first experimental design note that the coalition {1,2} with the α version of the characteristic function can only ensure itself of (0.30, 0.30). The β version assigns this coalition a somewhat larger set, but still the coalition cannot ensure itself of any more than a sum of 1.0 divided among its components. In fact, looking at the normal form of the game, we see that if the coalition takes advantage of the rationality of the complementary coalition (player 3), then there are strategies available to {1,2} which give it more than (0.30, 0.30), namely: if {1,2} commits itself to the strategy a_1b_1, then player 3 is left with a choice of 0 or 0.30. If he is rational and picks strategy c_1, then players 1 and 2 each get 0.75. From here, if they desire, they can bargain via the coalition of the whole to the Pareto-superior point $a_2b_2c_1$, which gives players 1 and 2 each 0.80. (Of course player 3 has obvious incentives to defect from $a_2b_2c_1$, but can be kept from defecting by the threat by players 1 and 2 to return to a_1b_1). In short, the characteristic function seems to be an underrepresentation of the true power of the coalition of 1 and 2.

In the actual outcomes of the first series, which are reported in Table 9.4, we see that the above observation seems confirmed. Of the 14 trials of this experiment, 13 were in the α core. Of these 13 core outcomes, all but two were in the cells $a_1b_1c_1$ and $a_2b_2c_1$, where the coalition {1,2} obtains at least (0.75, 0.75).

The above experiment raises some questions about the adequacy of the characteristic function, yet the solution based on this characteristic function (namely the core) does quite well, explaining thirteen of fourteen outcomes. The only

Table 9.3. Solutions for Experimental Designs 1 and 2

	Design 1		Design 2	
	Strategy	Payoff	Strategy	Payoff
Nash equilibrium	$a_1 b_1 c_1$	(0.75, 0.75, 0.30)	$a_1 b_2 c_2$	(0.30, 0.30, 0.40)
Perfect equilibrium	$a_1 b_1 c_1$	(0.75, 0.75, 0.30)	$a_1 b_2 c_2$	(0.30, 0.30, 0.40)
Ultimately admissible strategies	all	—	$a_1 b_2 c_2$	(0.30, 0.30, 0.40)
Strong equilibrium	ϕ	—	$a_1 b_2 c_2$	(0.30, 0.30, 0.40)
Core (α version)	$a_1 b_1 c_1$ $a_2 b_2 c_1$ $a_2 b_1 c_2$ $a_1 b_2 c_2$ $a_2 b_2 c_2$	(0.75, 0.75, 0.30) (0.80, 0.80, 0.35) (0.10, 0.90, 0.90) (0.90, 0.10, 0.90) (0.30, 0.30, 0.80)	$a_1 b_2 c_2$	(0.30, 0.30, 0.40)
Core (β version)	$a_1 b_1 c_1$ $a_2 b_2 c_1$ $a_2 b_1 c_2$ $a_1 b_2 c_2$	(0.75, 0.75, 0.30) (0.80, 0.80, 0.35) (0.10, 0.90, 0.90) (0.90, 0.10, 0.90)	$a_1 b_2 c_2$	(0.30, 0.30, 0.40)

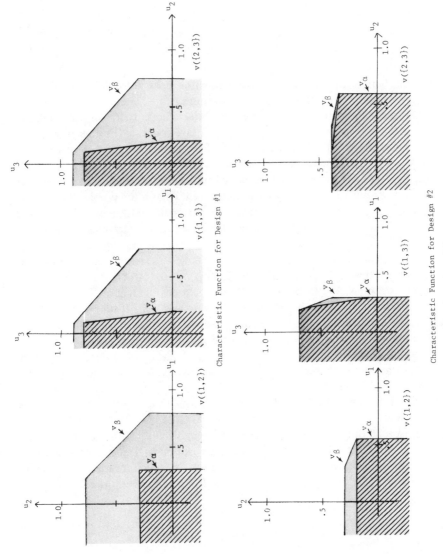

Characteristic Function for Design #1

Characteristic Function for Design #2

Figure 9.1. Characteristic Functions for Designs 1 and 2

Table 9.4.   Experiment 1: Outcomes

c_1	b_1	b_2		c_2	b_1	b_2
a_1	3	0		a_1	1	0
a_2	0	8		a_2	1	1

problem here is that the characteristic function does not account for the frequency distribution of outcomes within the core.

Our second experiment is perhaps more interesting in that it provides a direct test of the usefulness of the cooperative solution concepts. Further, this design contains a strong equilibrium as well. In fact, in this design, there is one cell, $a_1 b_2 c_2$, which uniquely has just about all the desirable properties we could imagine. Yet a glance at the experimental outcomes (see Table 9.5) reveals that only 3 of 17 outcomes actually result in this cell. What is the problem?

Again, the problem seems to be that none of the existing solution notions take adequate account of strategies in which one coalition can commit itself and take advantage of the rational response of the complementary coalition. If we look at either the α or β versions of the characteristic function of this game, we see that the cell $a_1 b_2 c_2$, with payoffs (0.30, 0.30, 0.40), is stable for all two-person coalitions. Yet in this design, both coalitions {1,2} and {2,3} have strategies by which they can get more than they do at $a_1 b_2 c_2$ if they commit themselves to the strategies and count on a rational response. The coalition {1,2}, by adopting the strategy $a_1 b_1$, can force player 3 into choosing c_1, thereby giving this coalition (0.65, 0.50), a payoff which each coalition member prefers to the core. This outcome, of course, depends on a rational response by player 3. Similarly, {2,3} can adopt the strategy $b_2 c_1$, forcing a rational response of a_2 by player 1. This gives 2 and 3 (0.90, 0.60), which they prefer to these payoffs at the core.

In fact, 10 of the 13 deviations from the core involve just such outcomes. The two outcomes in the cell $a_1 b_1 c_1$ involve a coalition of 1 and 2. The four outcomes in the cell $a_2 b_1 c_1$ also involve a coalition of 1 and 2, followed by a Pareto move to $a_2 b_1 c_1$. Finally, the outcomes in $a_2 b_1 c_1$ are a coalition of 2 and 3.

Table 9.5.   Experiment 2: Outcomes

c_1	b_1	b_2		c_2	b_1	b_2
a_1	2	1		a_1	0	3
a_2	4	4		a_2	1	1

CONCLUSIONS

The experiments reported here show that in these particular normal form games, neither of the cooperative solution concepts is entirely adequate to explain the observed outcomes. In the first experiment, although most of the outcomes are in the core, the core does not give any explanation as to why the outcomes cluster in a particular subset of the core. In the second experiment, both the core and the strong equilibrium predict one cell, whereas the observed outcomes scatter widely outside of this cell. We have concluded that the failures in these experiments are due to the inability of either of the cooperative solution concepts to take adequate account of the threat and commitment strategies available to the subjects.

Before concluding, we anticipate one objection to the above experiments. This objection is that, experimentally, we have not really induced the game whose normal form is that of Tables 9.1 and 9.2. Rather, because of our experimental procedures, the strategy sets available to each player are really much larger than the two strategies indicated in the tables. Thus, the argument would go, in our experimental design, players have strategies involving the timing of communication, commitment, and the like. Hence, the extensive form to the game being played is quite complex, involving many chance moves, and the corresponding normal form would be much more complex than that used here.

Our defense against the above objection is that anyone taking this position must also take the position that cooperative game theory is itself conceptually flawed. One cannot talk about cooperation, correlation of strategies, etc., in a given normal form game without conceding that the underlying extensive form has failed to include these possibilities as explicit moves. Nash (1951) originally suggested that a more appropriate way to model cooperative games was precisely to include all such possibilities for communication and cooperation as moves in the extensive form, and then to analyze this extensive form as a noncooperative game, looking for Nash equilibria to this game. Harsanyi and Selten (see, e.g., Harsanyi, 1978) have also advocated this point of view and have developed more sophisticated methods for isolating unique and reasonable equilibria for such games. Unfortunately, the obvious problem with this approach is specification of the extensive form when any reasonably rich possibilities for communication are available.

It has been the hope of cooperative game theorists to circumvent these problems by not including cooperative moves in the extensive form, but rather summarizing the possibilities for cooperation in the characteristic function. In these particular experiments we must conclude, nevertheless, that this particular form of simplification is inadequate. Certainly, more thought must be given to the definition of a cooperative game, and perhaps we shall find that Nash's earlier suggestion is the most promising route to an adequate solution theory.

APPENDIX: INSTRUCTIONS FOR NORMAL
FORM EXPERIMENTS

This experiment is designed to study individual choice in a group setting. In this experiment, each of you has been given two choices. Player 1 must choose between A_1 and A_2, player 2 must choose between B_1 and B_2, and player 3 must choose between C_1 and C_2. The entire purpose of the experiment is for each of you to decide which of your two choices to make, and your payment from the experiment is determined by the choices that you make.

To assist you in understanding the experiment, each of you has been given a sample worksheet. At the beginning of the experiment, you will each be given a similar worksheet, although the entries there may differ from those on this sample.

Since each of you has two alternatives, there are eight possible outcomes of this experiment. They are indicated on the sample worksheet in the two tables. In these tables, player 1's choice corresponds to a choice of the row in the tables. Thus, if player 1 chooses A_1, the outcome of the experiment will be in the first row of the tables. If he chooses A_2, the outcome will be in the second row. Player 2's choice, on the other hand, corresponds to a choice of the column of the tables. If player 2 chooses B_1, the outcome will be in the first column of one of the tables, whereas if he chooses B_2, the outcome will be in the second column of one of the tables. Finally, player 3's choice corresponds to a choice of which table the outcome will be in. Thus, if player 3 chooses C_1, the outcome will be in the left-hand table, whereas if he chooses C_2, the outcome will be in the right-hand table.

A choice by all three players determines a cell in the tables. For example, one possible outcome would be the following: Player 1 chooses A_2, player 2 chooses B_2, and player 3 chooses C_3. This would correspond to the cell in row 2, column 2, and Table 9.2 —i.e., the lower right-hand cell in Table 9.2.

Now each cell in the table has associated with it an outcome, which determines the payoffs of each of the three players. Specifically, each cell contains three numbers, which correspond to the probability that each of the three players will win his stake. (The "stake" is the money amount entered in the lower part of the worksheet.) For example, in the cell corresponding to $A_2B_2C_2$, we find the numbers (0.7, 0.6, 0.5). These numbers are probabilities for players 1, 2, and 3, respectively. Thus player 1's probability is 0.7, player 2's is 0.6, and player 3's is 0.5. At the termination of the experiment, for each of you, a lottery will be conducted, and you will win your stake with probability corresponding to your entry in the cell which is chosen. If you do not win, you will be paid the minimum of $1.00 for participation. Thus, in this example, if $A_2B_2C_2$ is the choice, player 1's probability is 0.7. So he would draw a random number between 0 and 0.9. If the number selected is *less than* 0.7, he would win his stake, and be paid $6.00 for his participation in the experiment. If the number selected is greater than or equal to 0.7, he would lose, and be paid only the minimum of $1.00 for participation in the experiment. Other players are paid in a similar fashion. Hence player 2 has a 0.6 chance of winning his stake, and player 3 has a 0.5 chance of winning his stake. On the other hand, if $A_1B_2C_1$ is chosen, player 1's probability is 0, so he has no chance of winning his stake. In the worksheets which you receive, *your* probabilities will be underlined. Thus, in this sample, which is a sample for a fictitious player 1, the first number in each cell is underlined, and represents his probability of winning his stake if that cell is chosen. If you are player 2, the second entry in each cell will be underlined, and represents your probability of winning your stake. The probabilities for the other players are provided for your information.

In the actual worksheet that you receive at the beginning of the experiment, the probabilities assigned to alternatives and the stakes for which you will be playing will, of course, differ from those in this table. Further, as you can see in the sample worksheet, the probabilities that you associate with a given outcome may differ from those of another player. Thus, one outcome may be much more attractive to one player than it is for another. Finally, the stake each of you will be playing for may differ from player to player, so that even if two of you associate the same probability with the committee's decision and even if both of you win your stake, you need not ultimately receive the same payoff from participating in this experiment. One essential rule of this experiment, moreover, is that *at no time are you to mention the value of your stake or to make any mention of money.* Further, at no time are you permitted to discuss schemes for dividing your winnings at the termination of play. At the termination of the experiment, in fact, each of you will be paid in the absence of other players, so there is no need to *ever* reveal your total winnings, should you decide not to do so.

Let me now discuss the way in which the experiment will proceed. The experiment is divided into two phases, a *discussion* and a *decision* phase. At the beginning of the experiment, I will hand out your actual worksheets and you will begin with a 15-minute discussion period. During this period, you may discuss what your final choices might be and what agreements you might want to enter into, but you may not implement any binding agreements. At the end of the discussion phase, you will begin the decision phase. During this phase, which lasts for 5 minutes, you are permitted to continue your discussion but, at the beginning of this phase I will hand out to each of you a choice card on which you are to indicate your choice between your two alternatives. You may show your choice to none, any, or all players, and at the end of this phase each of you will be required to place your choice card on the table face down. Once all cards are on the table, I will record these and ask whether anyone wishes to change his choice. At this point, you will have 15 seconds to consider whether you wish to change. If no one so indicates, the experiment will terminate and you will each be paid as described earlier. If one person wishes to change, you will each retrieve your individual choice cards and begin the decision phase anew. In order to ensure some finite end to this process, if the choices recorded by the experimenter coincide with a previously recorded set of choices, the experiment will terminate at that point.

III EQUILIBRIUM ANALYSIS IN PRACTICE

10 POLITICAL INEQUALITY:
An Economic Approach
Peter H. Aranson

*After close to two centuries of intermittent agitation, democratic ide-
ologists have firmly established the democratic principle of universal,
equal suffrage as an article of the American faith. And further, democratic politicians have actually embodied much of that ideal in institutional practice. It is no mean praise of the achievement of seven
generations that this chapter on suffrage in American democracy could
concentrate so much on the* lapses *from the ideal. That very emphasis
itself suggests that Americans need not be convinced of the value of
voting and that the basic steps toward realization of the ideal have been
taken. We are well over half-way on our road to the operational goal of
democratic theory.*

*Important as some of the derelictions from the ideal of "one-man,
one-vote" still are, we can take hope from the fact that the democratic
conscience is now quite aroused.*

William H. Riker (1965a, p. 82)

*I dissent in each of these cases, believing that in none of them have the
plaintiffs stated a cause of action.*

Mr. Justice John M. Harlan, *Reynolds* v. *Sims,*
377 U.S. 533 at 625 (1964)

133

POLITICAL INEQUALITY AND POLITICAL EQUILIBRIA

Since the publication of Duncan Black's *Theory of Committees and Elections* (1958) and earlier Anthony Downs's *An Economic Theory of Democracy* (1957), the theoretical search for conditions underlying political equilibria or their absence has largely been carried on under assumptions of political equality among voters in single, well-defined constituencies electing representatives to unicameral legislatures. This is as it should be in normal science, for the study of conditions guaranteeing the presence or absence of equilibria has been sufficiently difficult without introducing the asymmetries associated with political voting inequality, peculiarities of particular representational districting schemes, or bicameralism.

We have been aware that matters such as districting could add rich detail to our understanding of political allocations, however. For example, Hinich and Ordeshook (1974) describe a series of electorates with preferences distributed over R^2. In some of these hypothetical electorates there exists no pure strategy equilibrium for candidates to adopt. But when one of these electorates is appropriately divided into separate election districts, a pure strategy equilibrium emerges in each district. Furthermore, if the legislators elected to represent these districts act as reasonable approximations of Burkean "delegates" with a "district-wide focus" (Eulau et al., 1959), then the resulting legislature (committee) also might have a pure strategy equilibrium, although none existed in the underlying electorate. (Of course, such a pure strategy committee equilibrium may be absent.) In other hypothetical electorates, a pure strategy equilibrium exists until a districting scheme is imposed. Then, each individual district may or may not have a pure strategy electoral equilibrium, and the same indeterminateness may characterize the legislature drawn from these districts.

Naturally, if the two chambers of a bicameral legislature, as well as an electoral college, are drawn from the same (or different) constituencies, differently drawn, then the problem of political equilibria grows that much more complicated. And, we have little beyond Buchanan and Tullock's (1962) discussion of rational constitutional construction of bicameralism to illuminate the matter.

But we have not yet considered the effects of political inequality on the existence and location of political equilibria. Despite Professor Riker's optimism, which reflected the larger felicity of a mid-1960s liberalism, collective decision making in the United States remains crenelated with real and imagined political

The author thanks J. Morgan Kousser and Samuel Krislov for useful discussions about many of the ideas in this paper. Neither agrees with the paper's major arguments, and therefore neither should be held responsible for its conclusions.

inequalities. A formal, constitutional inequality of votes underlies the apportionment of the United States Senate and the electoral collegè. Both the General
Assembly and the Security Council of the United Nations institutionalize malapportionment (based on population), and therefore inequality, on an international scale. Domestic political inequality continues to be accepted *sub silentio.*
Examples include the possibility of political inequality because of economic and
educational inequality as well as such ongoing practices as the gerrymander
[*Gomillion* v. *Lightfoot*, 379 U.S. 249 (1960), *Gordon* v. *Lance*, 403 U.S. 1
(1971), *Whitcomb* v. *Chavis*, 403 U.S. 124 (1971), *Gaffney* v. *Cummings*, 412
U.S. 735 (1973), *White* v. *Regester*, 412 U.S. 753 (1973), *United Jewish Organizations of Williamsburg* v. *Carey*, 403 U.S. 144 (1977)]. Indeed, we may have to
accept such inequalities or trade off the achievement of other goals as desirable
as the one-man, one-vote standard (Niemi and Deegan, 1978).

Positive analyses of political inequality are extremely limited, both in number
and in subject matter. The principal theoretical tool for measuring political inequality has been the Shapley *value,* which when adapted to political situations
is called the Shapley–Shubik *power index* (Shapley, 1953; Shapley and Shubik,
1954; Riker and Ordeshook, 1973, Chapter 6). However, the Shapley value is
only useful for explaining the opportunity cost of being (or not being) in a certain situation, and not the public policies (equilibrium strategies) chosen once
there. (Though opportunity costs and public policies are clearly related, usually
no connection is drawn in this literature.) Other measures of political inequality
are designed to reflect particular forms of unequal treatment, such as malapportionment (David and Eisenberg, 1961; Dauer and Kelsay, 1955; Schubert and
Press, 1964a,b). However, as noted later in this paper, variations in the level of
measures of inequality correlate poorly with variations in public policy.

Reasons of parsimony explain the neglect of political inequality by scholars
of public choice and positive political theory. As a consequence of this neglect,
it is not yet clear what additional phenomena the presence or absence of political inequality might explain or how political inequality itself might be explained.
Nevertheless, the motives behind, and the effects of, practices such as gerry-
mandering and malapportionment, though complex in execution, seem straightforward enough to understand. Furthermore, specific examples of political
inequality seem too *ad hoc* for us to utter general sentences about them.[1]

While political inequality has not received much theoretical attention, such
inequality is nevertheless a salient characteristic of collective decision making.
Indeed, perhaps because political inequality has been ignored, several explanatory problems remain. For example, we do not know why the malapportionment of the United States Senate or of the electoral college fails to correlate
with any noticeable differences in federal public policies toward the states. Nor

can we explain the failure of the presence or extent of malapportionment to correlate with any public policy differences *among* the states or the failure of reapportionment to bring about systematic and measurable intrastate changes in public policies. Furthermore, we cannot explain why poor people, who share a putative lack of political influence, have nevertheless become net beneficiaries of collective action since the beginning of the Johnson administration (Leffler, 1978).

The complexities of spatial models are now apparent, and we do not expect such models to explain very general aspects of political inequality. Accordingly, this essay examines political inequality using certain very elementary notions from economic analysis. The second section reviews the basic economic framework. In particular, it describes the pricing of assets and adjustments in those prices over time as a function of alternative investment opportunities. The third section suggests that political scientists have overstated the importance of economic inequality as a cause of political inequality, because the presence of economic inequality fails to provide an a priori reason for believing that those less well off economically should also occupy a position of political inferiority. The fourth section interprets the effects of the reapportionment revolution and by inference the effects of other forms of political public policy. The argument in the fourth section rests on two sets of assumptions. If the first set holds true, then the gains or losses from malapportionment or reapportionment would be entirely transitional. If the second set holds true, then there are no such gains: in the absence of transactions costs and in the presence of fully fungible political resources and a perfect capital market, the only gains or losses from reapportionment or malapportionment are experienced by politicians themselves, not the citizenry. The fifth section analyzes recent judicial attempts to equalize the benefits flowing from public policy. The essay concludes by reflecting on the public policy effects of reforming political procedures.

THE PRICING OF ASSETS

We take as our underlying model of political inequality the pricing of assets, such as securities, in efficient markets. To avoid unnecessary complications, we define a security as a property right to a future stream of income or consumption goods. Hence, stocks and bonds are securities, as are other assets such as homes and rental units (Fama and Miller, 1972, Chapters 3, 7). Asset pricing is very much like the pricing of other economic goods. As the expected return of a security (its net present value) increases relative to the expected return of other securities, then, *ceteris paribus,* so too does its unit price. The price of a security is also inversely related to the perceived riskiness of its future income stream.

Very generally, securities markets quickly equilibrate the prices of securities, so that at any given time the unit prices of securities in the same risk class are approximately equal, reflecting a normal rate of return (zero economic profit). Any remaining price fluctuations are random (Samuelson, 1965, 1973; Stone, 1975). The forces leading to this equilibrium are not merely supply and demand, as in ordinary market exchange, but also variations in supply and demand brought about by the continuing presence of alternative investment opportunities in assets bearing a normal rate of return. Two examples help to explain the manner in which asset markets reach these equilibria.

The Bond Market

The simplest example is that of the bond market. A bond is "a certificate or evidence of a debt on which the issuing company or governmental body promises to pay the bondholders a specified amount of interest for a specified length of time, and to repay the loan on the expiration date. In every case a bond represents a debt — its holder is a creditor of the corporation and not a part owner as is a shareholder" (*Black's Law Dictionary,* 1979). Usually, a bond belonging to a particular risk class (as assigned by a bond-rating service such as *Moody's* or *Standard and Poor's*) is issued at an interest rate determined by market forces to be the normal rate of return. Bondholders are then free to buy and sell such a bond or futures contracts to it, and this activity will continue until the bond matures.

The trading price of bonds shows the effects of a general market in securities on the market for a particular security. Bonds are commonly issued in denominations of $1,000. Suppose a bond is issued at 10% interest, reflecting the prevailing annual interest rate for its risk class on the date of issuance. If the prevailing interest rate of subsequently issued securities of that risk class should fall, perhaps correlated to a fall in the prime interest rate (or other indices of the price paid for money), then the trading price of the bond will increase to reflect the extent to which its nominal interest is above the normal rate of return. Indeed, the trading price of the bond will increase (usually instantaneously) until those who buy it will be earning only a normal rate of return on their investment. Similarly, if the prevailing interest rate paid by newly issued securities should increase, then the trading price of the bond will decline until it again reflects an investment at a normal rate of return for those who purchase it. In this way, the prices of all investments continuously approach an equilibrium price, although that equilibrium itself may change from day to day. Notice that the gains and losses associated with changes in the prices of preexisting bonds accrue only to those who own them before the changes occur. *Ceteris paribus,* there is no advantage to be gained from purchasing a bond whose price has recently increased, because that increase reflects the impact of all anticipated and actualized market occurrences.

Transitional Regulatory Gains

The second example, one closer to politics, has been known to economists for some time but has recently been examined by Tullock (1975). He investigates the problem of greater-than-normal rates of return created by regulatory cartelization. For example, in regulating taxicab services, city governments commonly set fares at above market-clearing prices and then issue medallions (licenses) to a limited number of suppliers to prevent additional entries into this now more lucrative market. In the absence of close substitutes for taxicab services, the result is a greater-than-normal rate of return on the investment of those who owned taxicabs before regulation and were issued medallions by the regulatory authorities.

An investment in a taxicab company is very much like an investment in any other asset, however. Just as declines in interest rates affect bond prices, so too after the imposition of regulation, the price of taxicab companies (medallions) would be bid up until subsequent owners of taxicabs would only enjoy a normal rate of return on their investments. Accordingly, the gain induced by regulation would be merely transitional. Even if the original owner of the taxicab company did not recognize the opportunity for a transitional gain, it would soon be exploited by other entrepreneurs more familiar with the effects of government regulation. As James Madison pointed out in *Federalist Paper* No. 62, "Every new regulation concerning commerce or revenue, or in any manner affecting the value of the different species of property, presents a new harvest to those who watch the change, and trace its consequences; a harvest, reaped not by themselves, but by the toils and cares of the great body of their fellow-citizens." In sum, the value of the asset would quickly adjust to reflect the cartel profits induced by regulation, and subsequent owners of taxicab companies would experience only a normal rate of return.

ECONOMIC INEQUALITY AND POLITICAL INEQUALITY

We stop briefly before analyzing institutionalized political inequality to discuss one alleged effect of that inequality as well as an alleged cause of it, namely, economic inequality. In its starkest form, the argument that economic inequality results in political inequality is part of the power elite thesis. Indeed, economic power and political power have been interpreted as being equivalent phenomena. For those who believe in this thesis, there is a "power elite in America . . . composed of men whose positions enable them to transcend the ordinary environments of ordinary men and women: they are in positions to make decisions having major consequences." These men "command . . . the major hierarchies in organizations of modern society . . . rule the big corporations . . . run the machinery of state and claim its prerogatives . . . direct the military establishment . . . [and] occupy the strategic command posts of the social structure in which are now centered the effective means of the power and the wealth and the celebrity which they enjoy" (Mills, 1951).

While the power elite view equates political and economic power, another view sees in capitalism itself a source of political inequality:

> Capitalism is a power relation including dominant and subordinate elements in which some interests are the vassals of others. Pressure politics expresses economic authority as well as interest. In the business world opinions are communicated from the higher levels to the lower, but rarely in the other direction. Influence is a possession of those who have established their supremacy in the invisible empires outside of what is ordinarily known as government. From this point of view the function of pressure politics is to reconcile formal political democracy and economic autocracy. If the overlords of business are not masters of the state, they seem at least to negotiate with it as equals. (Schattschneider, 1963)

Not surprisingly, those who believe that wealth promotes political advantage have not considered the possibility that the poor might also use politics to their benefit. For an underlying and unexamined corollary of this thesis equating economic inequality and political inequality is that those without wealth cannot buy public policy, either directly or indirectly. One obvious corrective, which has already been taken in the United States and in other western democracies, is to broaden the suffrage so that there are no formal bars to political participation by those of a lower economic station. However, many believe that even that broadening cannot fully equalize political influence in the presence of economic inequality, because the poor may have the ability to understand neither the political issues before them nor their real interests in public policy.

What are we to make of these claims? From an economic perspective, economic inequality is neither a necessary nor a sufficient condition for generating political inequality. In the exchange between a politician and a citizen (or group of citizens), the benefits of a public policy flow from the politician to the citizen, and payment in one form or another flows from the citizen to the politician. In this sense, the politician is selling an asset, a security, to the citizen. The claim that poor citizens are less able to pay for such securities than are wealthy citizens does not ring true in the presence of perfect capital markets. Payment for political action, for favorable public policies, even by those of little wealth, can be provided out of the proceeds or returns expected to be generated by the public policy. Such a practice is not uncommon. (Indeed, the Hatch Acts grew out of the fears of many southern legislators, and particularly southern senators, that CCC and other New Deal beneficiaries would help Franklin D. Roosevelt "purge" the Congress of opponents. The acts' sponsors predicted exactly the kind of future payment—to Roosevelt and his allies—from the expanding New Deal bureaucracy that we postulate here.)

It may be argued that the poor do not have the necessary knowledge and skill to create such a market in present public policies in exchange for the future payments those policies will make possible. But recipients need not have this knowledge and skill. Creating the market and the exchanges therein is the task of the political entrepreneur, and those entrepreneurs who are most successful at making such markets are also those who will find ways to circumvent the putative political inertia bred of ignorance or growing out of free-rider problems (Frohlich, Oppenheimer, and Young, 1971; Olson, 1971; Salisbury, 1969; Wagner, 1969).

It may also be argued that wealthy citizens have a larger wealth base with which to buy public policy than do poor citizens. But again, this argument cannot stand economic scrutiny. Suppose a public policy is worth $100 to a wealthy citizen and the same amount to a poor one. Even though the wealthy citizen controls millions of dollars, and even when bidding against a poor person, he will not spend more than $100 to secure the passage of such a public policy. In this regard rich and poor are equal. To believe otherwise would be to impute a kind of irrationality to the wealthy that contradicts at least one premise under which political inequality was said to result from economic inequality, a difference in education and skill.

Still, it might be argued that rich and poor differ in their ability to withstand expropriation. That may be so, but first, a wealthy citizen will not pay more to prevent expropriation by the state than that expropriation is worth. Second, if such expropriation did exist, it would be in the direction of equality, which trend would eventually eliminate inequality. And third, the public policy bias predicted by this claim is itself clearly directed against the wealthy and not against the poor.

Finally, it might be argued that the poor must borrow against a future income stream to arrange for desired public policies. Even if capital markets are perfect as supposed, the use of others' money or resources has a cost, which the wealthy need not pay. But this objection overlooks the opportunity costs (in forgone interest) of spending the money or resources the wealthy might use to buy public policy directly. In a perfect capital market, this cost will equal the interest rate that poor citizens must pay.

In sum, there is no a priori case for expecting the wealthy to have more political influence than the poor. The only remaining justification for such a belief would be the claim that a public policy dollar spent on a wealthy person creates more income than the same dollar spent on a poor person would create. If this claim holds true, then the wealthy person would be able to pay the political entrepreneur a larger amount for the public policy than would the poor person. The empirical conditions underlying the validity of such a claim are less than clear, as are the public policy implications of it. (For example, one condition would be marginally *increasing* returns to investment in human capital.) In the absence of such differences in productivity, which themselves could not be changed by public policy, economic inequality should not be correlated with political inequality.

THE EFFECTS OF MALAPPORTIONMENT
AND REAPPORTIONMENT

The reapportionment cases came to the Supreme Court following a long history of rejected jurisdiction by the Court, because the issue involved a "political question" [*Colegrove* v. *Green,* 328 U.S. 549 (1946)]. In the eyes of many Americans, malapportionment in the United States was as scandalous as the rotten boroughs were to many in Great Britain before modest reapportionment in that country. Before reapportionment, the population of the Connecticut state legislature's largest district was 242 times as large as the population of its smallest district, and the Nevada senate ratio was 223 to 1. Other states were not far behind, and in many places there had not been a thorough reapportionment based on population since the turn of the century or earlier. Plaintiffs in these cases pressed a consistent claim, one that the Court heeded. In particular, "These plaintiffs and others similarly situated are denied the equal protection of the laws accorded them by the Fourteenth Amendment to the Constitution of the United States by virtue of the debasement of their votes" [*Baker* v. *Carr,* 369 U.S. 186 at 194 (1962)]. The Court stated the matter thus in the first case accepted, concerning malapportionment of the Tennessee state legislature:

> These appellants seek relief in order to protect or vindicate an interest of their own, and of those similarly situated. Their constitutional claim is, in substance, that the 1901 Statute constitutes arbitrary and capricious state action, offensive to the Fourteenth Amendment in its irrational disregard of the standard of apportionment prescribed by the State's constitution or of any standard, effecting a gross disproportion of representation to voting population. The injury which appellants assert is that this qualification disfavors the voters in the counties in which they reside, placing them in a

position of constitutionally unjustifiable inequality *vis-à-vis* voters in irrationally favored counties. A citizen's right to a vote free of arbitrary impairment by state action has been judicially recognized as a right secured by the Constitution. . . . (*Baker* v. *Carr,* 369 U.S. 186 at 207–208 [1962])

The Court concluded:

It would not be necessary to decide whether appellants' allegations of impairment of their votes by the 1901 apportionment will, ultimately, entitle them to any relief, in order to hold that they have standing to seek it. If such impairment does produce a legally cognizable injury, they are among those who have sustained it. They are asserting "a plain, direct and adequate interest in maintaining the effectiveness of their votes . . ." not merely a claim of "the right, possessed by every citizen, to require that the government be administered according to the law. . . ." They are entitled to a hearing and to the District Court's decision on their claims. "The very essence of civil liberties certainly consists of the right of every individual to claim the protection of the laws, whenever he receives an injury." (*Baker v. Carr,* 369 U.S. 186 at 208 [1962])

Malapportionment, Reapportionment, and Transitional Gains

But what is the "legally cognizable injury"? The reapportionment cases include scant references to real injuries beside the deprivation of a constitutional right attributable to "dilution" of one's vote. Indeed, in *Baker* v. *Carr,* the first and central case in the reapportionment series, only in the dissenting opinion of Mr. Justice Frankfurter do we find reference to a claim of injury outside of the constitutional matrix. ("Appellants also alleged discrimination in the Legislature's allocation of certain tax burdens and benefits. Whether or not such discrimination would violate the Equal Protection Clause if the tax statutes were challenged in a proper proceeding . . . these recitative allegations do not affect the nature of the controversy which appellants' claims present" [369 U.S. 186 at 298, n. 21].) In *Reynolds* v. *Sims* [377 U.S. 533 (1964)], and in *Wesberry* v. *Sanders* [376 U.S. 1 (1964)], the story is much the same: there is no accounting of plaintiffs' claims of real injury other than that the value of their vote had been diluted.

Despite the absence of claims of damages other than those of the constitutional variety, let us suppose that plaintiffs could actually show that malapportionment affects public policy to their detriment. Compared with the benefits of public policy flowing to citizens of districts more favorably represented, their deprivations may be of three sorts. First, because of their enlarged numbers relative to the populations in other districts, malapportionment's victims may suffer from a lack of ombudsman services supplied by their legislators. These services have grown in importance in recent years as the public sector itself grows larger (Fiorina, 1977). Second, elsewhere Ordeshook and I have pointed out in theory, and others have pointed out in practice, that legislators are really about the business of providing private goods to their constituencies only and to identifiable groups within their constituencies, where such constituencies and groups are taken as households (Aranson and Ordeshook, 1977, 1978; Fiorina, 1977; Mayhew, 1974; Weingast, Shepsle, and Johnson, 1981). Citizens electorally disadvantaged by malapportionment might therefore claim that their districts received a reduced stream of benefits from the public sector as a consequence. Indeed, the flow might be negatively valued, as occurs with the unfavorable siting of dumps, public housing projects, nuclear power plants, and airports. Third, we should also include reference to the psychological injury created by living in a district in which certain voters share "less" of a legislator than do those in other districts.

These effects of malapportionment may again be divided into two sorts. The first sort includes effects that can be *expected,* anticipated, either because they have occurred before or because one can reliably predict that they will occur in the future, based upon some robust model of the political process. The second sort includes effects that are entirely unpredictable, unanticipated, partaking of complete Knightian uncertainty. The second sort need not concern us here, because people do not make decisions based upon entirely unanticipated events.

The first sort of effects are of great interest, however. In particular, notice that the citizen in the district *advantaged* by malapportionment is in a position exactly analogous to that of a person buying a taxicab company *after* the imposition of a favorable regulatory regime. That is, the three causes of damage brought about by malapportionment, translated for him into added benefits, must already have impacted upon the price of any property owned in the advantaged district. A person who then buys the property pays more for it, and the person who buys property in a district disadvantaged by malapportionment will have paid less for it. (He is in a position analogous to that of a person buying a taxicab company that has already been deregulated or buying a bond after prevailing interest rates exceed its interest rate at issue.) Both citizens will nevertheless expect to earn a normal rate of return either in terms of consumption or in terms of an income stream. Therefore, malapportionment has only transitional effects, creating gains or losses only at the time of the last change, and then only if the change created unanticipated effects.

In the case of the malapportionment of the United States Senate, the expected effects were evident in 1789, and therefore all transitional gains were fully capitalized long ago. In *Baker* v. *Carr,* the Tennessee malapportionment complained of developed after an apportionment last made in 1901, and the shift from a rural to an urban population was more or less smooth over the intervening six decades. Therefore, whatever effects malapportionment might have had in Tennessee, they were fully capitalized in the early 1960s.

It might be argued that *legislative* reapportionment as a political tool, occurring as it now does every ten years in most states, provides no basis for predictability. For example, we cannot know in advance from one decade to the next which district will receive a new road system, or a new school, or a new state park, because reapportionment might change the political balance. However, such changes fall in our second category of effects. To the extent that they are unanticipated (cannot be insured against), there is no reason to believe that they will be capitalized into the value of the affected property. That is, if apportionment is random or cannot be predicted, *ex ante* it works no inequality as between those who benefit and those who lose from periodic reapportionments.

It might also be argued that as formulated here, malapportionment or reapportionment affects only property owners. However, the value of property would also influence the costs faced by renters. And, to the extent that we emphasize psychic costs or acknowledge real differences in public services consequent to malapportionment, such as in education or amenities, wage rates must also equilibrate to reflect the differences involved.

In sum, malapportionment will have only a transitional impact on the welfare of those respectively advantaged or disadvantaged. Furthermore, notice that the judicial imposition of reapportionment will create a windfall profit for those living in districts previously disadvantaged, since their property will suddenly yield a greater-than-normal rate of return because of public policy decisions subsequent to reapportionment. Similarly, those previously advantaged by malapportionment will experience a windfall loss for parallel reasons.

Reapportionment as an Inconsequential Change

In the preceding discussion, we state *ex hypothesis* that the stream of benefits flowing to a particular district from the public sector would increase or decrease as a function of legislative apportionment. However, as noted earlier, the Court's opinions on reapportionment contain little evidence of such variations. Furthermore, empirical research has found no significant differences between malapportioned and well-apportioned states in the public policies their legislatures adopt or in the distributive aspects of those policies as between rural and urban districts.[2] This lack of difference in the public policies of both malapportioned and well-apportioned states (both before and after reapportionment) must figure as counterintuitive. The expected impact has been taken as a self-evident truth by those who wrote about malapportionment before evidence to the contrary was gathered. As noted, "In the past, proponents of reapportionment have been very enthusiastic about its expected consequences. Having attributed a lack of party competition, unfair distributions of state funds, conservative tax schemes, unprogressive education policies, and penny-pinching welfare programs to rural overrepresentation, they naturally expect to see these conditions changed by reapportionment" (Dye, 1965). But the evidence indicates that such expectations are unfounded.

Accordingly, political scientists have sought alternative explanations for a finding of no difference in public policies between malapportioned and well-apportioned states. For example, some cite the apparent lack of cleavages between urban and rural areas, while others suggest that reapportionment might have affected public policy if the competitive political structure in the state were different (Derge, 1958; Lockard, 1963).

An alternative explanation for finding no significant differences between malapportioned and well-apportioned states (before and after reapportionment), and one consistent with economic theory, can be offered, but first we must reject the assumption *ex hypothesis* that there are (transitional) gains and losses associated with malapportionment or reapportionment. The argument for rejecting this assumption relies on our reasoning for rejecting economic inequality as a source of political inequality. A similar argument applies here *on a per capita basis.*

Suppose transactions costs are minimal, political resources are completely fungible, and capital markets are perfect. Now, what differences should we expect in public policy toward malapportioned districts, be they in-state legislative districts or the states themselves *vis-à-vis* the Senate or the electoral college? Clearly, the answer is *none.* The political entrepreneur will search for an investment according to the productivity of the dollar spent in a particular district. That productivity will be the same whether it is spent in a district that is advantaged or disadvantaged by malapportionment. The benefits involved are fully fungible. That is, the politician could well build a project in district A and collect the proceeds from his entrepreneurial actions. Residents in A would have had to pay him for the project, even if the contract to build it went to a firm in district B, the materials having been bought in district C, and another project having been developed in district D. Each project or contract will be evaluated on its political productivity alone (*vide* Abscam).

Here, we ignore the value of a vote. However, the friction caused by different voting strengths has not merely been assumed away by specifying that the political process is without transaction costs and that resources are fully fungible. Rather, we argue that even if voting presents a problem for allocating resources in districts that have less than their fair share of representatives (legislative votes),

the political marketplace will facilitate the necessary exchange, and inventiveness in the fungibility of resources will be the mark of the successful (surviving)
political entrepreneur.

To summarize, from the point of view of the political entrepreneur, if a
superior use is found for a million-dollar project in district A compared to all
other projects in all other districts, then district A will get the project *even if it
has no representatives at all*. Provided the payment to the political entrepreneur
is fungible, the representatives of all other districts can be paid off from the
proceeds, if that is necessary. But A will still get its project, and payoffs to the
representatives of all other districts or to the districts themselves will be judged
according to *their* political productivity. Alternatively, perhaps no payment to
the other districts will be forthcoming in the absence of a truly competitive
political process. The political entrepreneur will simply capture the rents, and
he will do so no matter what the apportionment system might be.

Notes on Political Entrepreneurs

A consistent application of the preceding analysis clears up a few mysteries
and casts serious doubt on certain lines of research. First, Riker and Ordeshook
(1973, p. 169) report that the weighted voting scheme used in the legislature of
Nassau County, New York, in 1964 had six members with 31, 31, 28, 21, 2, and
2 votes, respectively. They note that the members with votes of 21 and 2 are
Shapley-value dummies because they have no opportunity to pivot. Riker and
Ordeshook conclude that "it is hard to believe that citizens of any political
unit would consciously consent to a system in which their representatives can
never win in the sense that their representatives' votes are *never* pivotal. Probably
the bizarre defects of this legislature result entirely from a careless oversight"
(1973, p. 169). Similarly, Riker and Ordeshook point out that in the wake of
Baker v. *Carr,* many state legislators from rural districts proposed weighted voting
schemes to maintain their positions in the legislature while complying with the
one-man, one-vote standard. Since the rural districts would nevertheless lose
legislative opportunities to pivot from such an arrangement, Riker and Ordeshook
labeled this a ruse. "Both advocates and opponents thus behaved irrationally in
terms of the interests of their constituents. Urban legislators, who opposed,
should have favored weighted voting; and rural legislators, who proposed it,
should have kept silent" (1973, p. 170).

In light of our analysis of the noneffects of reapportionment, it seems apparent that Riker and Ordeshook failed to understand the problems involved in
both of these instances. In the Nassau County legislature case, the Shapley
value has no consequence for the people living in districts whose legislators are

Shapley-value dummies. Rather than being an oversight, the fact of not having an opportunity to pivot in legislative votes may be irrelevant as long as the district has *any* representative who can act as an entrepreneur in proposing county projects and in arguing for their superior productivity (from the point of view of himself and other political entrepreneurs). Nor were the state legislators being foolish after *Baker* v. *Carr.* Rural legislators were at least maintaining their jobs, while not really compromising on public policy, while urban legislators were probably maneuvering to dominate positions of legislative leadership by the expedient of increasing their own numbers.

Our discussion of reapportionment itself implies that the entire argument was really carried on from the point of view of political entrepreneurs and not of citizens whom they represent. We do not fully understand the contours of this argument because it is completely cast in the language of constitutional rights. However, I strongly suspect the argument is really over *leadership* in the Congress and in the respective state legislatures. Therefore, we may find in the reapportionment revolution more a phenomenon of political ambition and less a battle over the politics of distributive public policies than we had supposed.

Finally, we note in passing that attempts to identify the effects of the electoral college on public policy have assumed that political activity, such as visits to particular states by presidential candidates, may provide a useful surrogate for measuring public policy promises made to the residents of those states (Brams and Davis, 1974, 1975; Colantoni, Levesque, and Ordeshook, 1975a,b). If the argument of our preceding discussion holds true, then visits to states by presidential candidates may prove to be exactly that—attempts to win public office with no public policy consequences. For, our entire discussion of apportionment suggests that the operation of the electoral college today has no public policy consequences whatever.

THE JUDICIAL IMPOSITION OF PUBLIC POLICY EQUALITY

We may think of the Court's reapportionment revolution and present attempts to abolish the electoral college as steps in a struggle to achieve political equality of opportunity. More recently, the California Supreme Court and several federal district courts (in one instance the Supreme Court itself) have faced the problem of adjudicating claims to the political equality of result.

In *Serrano* v. *Priest* [5 Cal. 3d 584 (1971)], the California Supreme Court declared that unequal per capita expenditures for education in various districts violated the equal protection clause of the California constitution. In *Hobson* v. *Hansen* [269 F. Supp. 401 (D.D.C. 1969), aff'd. sub. nom. *Smuck* v. *Hobson,* 408 F. 2d 175 (D.C. Cir. 1969)], *Hadnot* v. *City of Pratville* [309 F. Supp. 967

(D. Ala. 1970)], and *Hawkins* v. *Town of Shaw* [437 F. 2d 1286 (1971), *aff'd en banc,* 461 F. 2d 1175 (5th Cir. 1972)], various federal district and circuit courts faced the problem of equalizing municipal services provided to racially segregated neighborhoods. As a general rule, the federal courts have ordered a rearrangement of spending patterns where the expenditures are paid out of general tax revenues, but not where taxing districts specific to a particular neighborhood are involved. Furthermore, in *San Antonio Independent School District* v. *Rodriguez,* the Supreme Court held that a Texas system of unequal expenditures for schools does not violate the Equal Protection Clause of the Fourteenth Amendment. "Though concededly imperfect, the system bears a rational relationship to a legitimate state purpose. While assuring a basic education for every child in the State, it permits and encourages participation in and significant control of each district's schools at the local level" [411 U.S. 1 (1973)]. However, in *Smuck* v. *Hobson,* the Circuit Court of Appeals (District of Columbia circuit) held that the Equal Protection Clause could be applied to correct inequalities in District of Columbia schools [408 F. 2d 175 (1969)]. Clearly, attempts to equalize expenditures are and will be a continuing source of litigation.

The preceding discussion sheds some light on this problem. In particular, if we hold as we did *ex hypothesis* earlier that there are real differences among districts as a result of some form of inequality (there it was simple malapportionment, now it is expanded to include racial discrimination), then we must also conclude that such differences have fully impacted on the prices of property and labor in the affected districts. Similarly, property and labor prices in advantaged districts will be commensurately higher to reflect the value of the alleged advantage. The judicial overturning of these patterns, it follows, will result in respective windfall profits and losses. We do not conclude that such equalization is unwarranted. We only conclude that the economic marketplace has already created a redistribution to adjust for the inequalities flowing from the political system.[3]

Second, suppose we reject the assumption *ex hypothesis* of inequality, as we did in the second part of the discussion of malapportionment. If so, we must conclude that differences in expenditures as between districts or neighborhoods actually stem from the calculations of political entrepreneurs that such expenditures as an equalization would imply would be nonproductive. We then face the interesting problem, one purposely ignored throughout this essay, of deciding whether the calculations of the political entrepreneurs make sense, perhaps by applying a standard of technological efficiency. Our answer to this question need not be dispositive of the public policy problems involved. However, that answer will certainly condition public policy recommendations made under the most cautiously worded normative positions.

CONCLUSION

This essay provides an elementary economic analysis of various forms of political inequality. We find in most instances that such inequality has no public policy consequences. On the other hand, even if we assume that such consequences exist, in the absence of information about the efficiency effects of the implicit subsidies or taxes imposed by inequality, we can only conclude that the gains or losses are windfall and transitional.

The assumptions leading us to these results include a perfect capital market, the fungibility of political resources, and zero transactions costs. We have not examined the sensitivity of our analysis to these assumptions. Nevertheless our own inclination is that the results would hold up even in the presence of non-trivial transactions costs, partial bars to fungibility, and various imperfections in capital markets.

Several recent developments in statutory and case law have acted to reduce the fungibility of political resources and to increase transactions costs, however. We number among these recently passed statutes concerning campaign contributions and freedom of information and "sunshine" acts both at the national and state and local levels. Paradoxically, the intent of these acts is to increase certain transactions costs and to reduce fungibility. However, as we have seen in this essay, the logical implication of both substantial increases in transactions costs between political entrepreneurs and citizens and marked reductions in the fungibility of political resources might be to exacerbate the public policy effects of existing political inequalities.[4]

NOTES

1. The problems of political inequality and districting might interact with the problems of electoral and legislative equilibria in as yet unanticipated ways. Plainly, the members of a legislature trying to devise a new districting scheme may face endless cycles, as proposed district boundaries are hypothetically moved about. Hence, the existence and location of *public policy* equilibria in electorates and legislatures may affect and be affected by the existence and location of legislative equilibria concerning election rules in general and districting arrangements in particular. While districting decisions have commonly been viewed as serving venal purposes, the legislative decision problems associated with districting and other electoral rules have been paid scant attention. For a discussion of decision making concerning one such rule, the extension of the franchise to new voters, see Aranson (1981, Chapter 8).

2. The initial findings of no significant differences are reported in Jacob (1964), Dye (1965), and Hofferbert (1966); see also Fry and Winters (1970). These studies are cross sectional. Three later time series or before-and-after analyses did show some differences. See Pulsipher and Weatherby (1968), Frederickson and Cho (1974), and Hanson and Crew

(1973). However, these time series studies are found to have serious problems of multi-collinearity, and on respecification of the models, no differences are found. See Newcomer and Hardy (1980).

3. The Court seems to have recognized the Tiebout (1956) effects of interpolity competition in *San Antonio*. Furthermore, serious objections of a different nature have been raised against the decision in *Serrano*. Posner argues, "the correlation between the real estate tax base and the income of the families who patronize the public schools may often be negative. In New York City, for example, there are many wealthy people and much valuable real estate. But since the wealthy people do not send their children to public schools and much of the property tax is levied on commercial rather than residential property, the effect of this method of school financing is to redistribute income to the poor. If expenditures per pupil were equalized on a statewide basis, New York City would be classified as a wealthy district and its expenditures per pupil reduced, although many of those pupils are poor. The primary beneficiaries of equalization would be rural inhabitants.

"In addition, equalization would weaken the public school system by reducing the incentive of wealthy communities to tax themselves heavily to pay for high quality public education. No community is entirely homogeneous. Invariably some of its residents will be drawn from lower income strata, and they will enjoy a high quality education subsidized by their wealthy neighbors" (Posner, 1977, p. 505). For an economic analysis, though one based on a superficial application of public choice theory, see Student Note (1972).

4. A similar, though less general prediction is offered in Kazman (1976). A similar argument concerning job discrimination is provided in Demsetz (1965).

11 SOPHISTICATED VOTING UNDER THE PLURALITY PROCEDURE

Richard G. Niemi and Arthur Q. Frank

Plurality voting—the system of voting in which each individual casts a ballot for one alternative and the alternative with the most votes wins—is perhaps the most obviously manipulable of all voting procedures. Political observers have long noted that when most of the votes will be split between two candidates, supporters of minor candidates are torn between "wasting" their vote on an obvious loser while expressing their first preference and voting for their second choice but perhaps making a difference in the outcome. The collection of preference order data for representative samples now makes strategic voting possible even in large electorates, such as in state and national elections.

Despite the obviousness of strategic voting in plurality elections, the topic does not readily lend itself to systematic study. Only Farquharson (1969) and Joyce (1976) have investigated the problem. Farquharson's analysis, it turns out, is severely limited. Joyce's ideas perhaps represent an improvement, but his definition of sophisticated voting has no theoretical rationale and its properties and consequences are not specified.

We would like to thank John Langeland for writing the computer program used to calculate Farquharson strategies and outcomes. We gratefully acknowledge support from the National Science Foundation under grant SES 80-07138.

In this paper we present a new, alternative definition of sophisticated voting. Insofar as possible, we show how it is related to Farquharson's definition, and we show how our definition treats sincere and Condorcet winners. However, we begin by showing the inadequacies of Farquharson's approach. Since Farquharson's definition of sophisticated voting is so well known, and since the idea of eliminating dominated strategies seems so unassailable—and yet is so flawed in the context of plurality voting—it seems appropriate to use his approach as a foil for presenting an alternative definition.

Our work here is limited to the case of three alternatives. Contrary to Farquharson's euphoric statement (1969, p. xii) that his results can "readily be extended to any number of alternatives," we shall see that the case of three alternatives is sufficiently complicated to satisfy many a masochist. We begin by defining the model we shall use, justifying especially the need for the key assumption of bloc voting. Then we take up Farquharson's approach and our own definition in turn.

THE MODEL

We assume the following: voters have strong preference orderings (no indifference); voters have complete knowledge of others' preference orderings; the plurality procedure includes a provision for random selection (among the two or three with the most votes) in the case of ties; voters with the same preference ordering vote as a bloc; blocs act independently of one another (noncooperative game).

The strong preference, complete knowledge, and noncooperative assumptions are relatively standard in formal voting models. In the context of plurality voting with three alternatives, the assumption of no indifference is a harmless simplifying device. One could easily assume that voters with preferences such as $a(bc)$ — meaning that these voters prefer a to both b and c and are indifferent between the latter two—vote with certainty for their first choice and that voters with preferences such as $(ab)c$ vote for each of the tied alternatives with a probability of 0.5. However, little would be gained by such an assumption. Requiring complete knowledge of preference orderings avoids, as usual, the plethora of situations involving partial knowledge. In a real-world voting situation, one would have to deal with incomplete information by making (perhaps ad hoc) assumptions about the missing information. Having made such assumptions, one would then analyze the situation just as if there were complete knowledge. Hence, this assumption seems relatively innocuous. The assumption of a noncooperative game is useful as a starting point. As with other voting rules, work might eventually be extended to cover activities such as vote trading.

Since the presence of ties considerably complicates an already complex situation, we shall minimize the number of ties that we need to deal with by using strict inequalities in our later analysis and by showing examples, whenever possible, without tied votes. Still, some provision must be made for tie votes since ties can occur even if we assume an odd number of voters. Farquharson assumed that one voter, the chairman, has both a regular vote and a tie-breaking vote. However, at least in the American context we are unaware of any institutions with this arrangement. Rather, ties are typically broken by a random device such as choosing names out of a hat. (In binary choices, a tie may be defined as not winning—as in court cases—or a chairman may have a tie-breaking vote only—as the vice-president has in the Senate.) Therefore, we assume that in a two-way tie for first place, each of the top vote getters wins with a probability of $1/2$; in case of a three-way tie, each candidate wins with a probability of $1/3$.

The assumption of bloc voting is unusual, but it seems eminently appropriate. Bloc voting could occur as a result of explicit coordination (i.e., specifically altering the assumption of noncooperation), as where groups of voters act as disciplined parties. Or it could be a result of tacit coordination. The latter assumption is not unreasonable. Each voter is likely to see his interests as identical to those of all the voters who hold the same opinion as himself, and likewise for those holding other opinions, and as a consequence presumably analyzes the strategic situation in terms of blocs (of known size) of like-minded individuals.

In any event, the assumption of bloc voting is a virtual necessity. Since we can show that no voter will ever vote for his third preference (see below), the three-alternative case can be considered a game in which each voter has two strategies, voting for his first preference or for his second preference. But without blocs, this means that each voter has to consider 2^{n-1} contingencies—combinations of all possible votes for all other players—in deciding how to vote. Even though the appropriate strategy would be obvious in many of these contingencies, their sheer number when there are more than, say, eight or nine voters precludes effective analysis. Moreover, consider the following simple situation. There are six voters with the preference ordering abc and four voters with the preference ordering cba. It seems patently obvious that the first set should vote for a, even in the absence of any explicit coordination. Yet without assuming bloc voting, this is not necessarily the best strategy. Each of the voters with the preference ordering abc must consider the contingency in which all four with the preference ordering cba vote for c and the other five with the preference ordering abc split three for b and two for a. In this contingency, voting for b dominates a because it would give the voter in question a 0.5 chance of getting his second choice, while voting for a would guarantee selection of his last choice.

As this example suggests, without the assumption of bloc voting, almost all cases would be indeterminate both in the sense that voters could not eliminate either first or second place voting and in the sense that one could not determine what the outcome of strategic voting would be. With the bloc voting assumption, plurality voting with three alternatives can be conceived of as a noncooperative game with six or fewer players, since there are six different preference orderings, and a bloc of voters with the same preference ordering behaves as a single player. The limitation to six players makes analysis possible and sharply increases the number of voting situations that have determinate strategies and outcomes.

FARQUHARSON'S DEFINITION OF SOPHISTICATED VOTING AND ITS WEAKNESSES

Farquharson (1969, Chapter 8) defines sophisticated voting in terms of the elimination of dominated strategies. For a given player (bloc), we say that one of his strategies dominates another if the former strategy yields at least as favorable an outcome as the latter for every possible voting pattern of the other n-1 voters (blocs) and a more favorable outcome for at least one such voting pattern. An undominated, or admissible, strategy is one which is not dominated by any other strategy.

For a plurality voting system, voting for one's third preference is always dominated by the strategy of voting for one's first preference since (a) there will be at least one situation for which voting for one's first preference will result in that alternative winning but voting for one's third preference will result in one of the other two alternatives winning; and (b) one can never obtain a better result by voting for one's third preference rather than one's first preference.[1] Hence we assume that no voter will ever vote for his third preference; consequently we can analyze the three-alternative case as a game in which each voter has two strategies, voting for either his first or second preference.

Following Farquharson we assume that voters only use *primarily* admissible strategies, i.e., strategies that are undominated when all other blocs are permitted to vote for either their first or second choice. In some situations at least one voter has a unique primarily admissible strategy. The existence of at least one such voter means that we can eliminate from consideration all voting patterns in which that player (or players) employs a dominated strategy. But when we limit our consideration to those voting patterns, some bloc(s) that have two primarily admissible strategies may find that one of these strategies dominates the other. If so, we assume that such blocs will not use the dominated strategy, and we can eliminate from consideration all voting patterns in which these voters use what is now a dominated strategy. We continue in this fashion until, for the remaining voting patterns, no voter employs a dominated strategy. The remaining strategy or strategies for each player are called "ultimately admissible" or "sophisticated."

Farquharson's definition appears to be relatively unassailable on logical grounds. By the very definition of domination, one could hardly advocate using primarily *in*admissible strategies. And if these strategies are not used, it seems just as logical to consider only what might happen with the reduced set of strategies, and this leads to further reductions. It turns out, however, that there are two serious problems with Farquharson's definition. First, it is exceedingly difficult to work with the Farquharson procedure, either analytically or practically. While computer programs can be written to perform the reductions, ordinary voters could not be expected to use this complex a procedure. And even approached analytically, Farquharson's definition defies easy analysis. For this reason alone, a new definition is much needed.

The other problem with Farquharson's definition is that in the context of plurality voting it very often leads to indeterminate outcomes. Though we have so far been unable to characterize the situations in which indeterminacy occurs, it appears to be a very large class. In part this is owing to the nature of the plurality procedure. Yet we can show situations in which Farquharson's method produces indeterminacy although there is an obvious determinate outcome. Consider, for example, the case shown in Table 11.1. Since a majority of the voters (18 out of 29) have a as their first choice, it seems reasonable to suppose that any definition of sophisticated voting should have blocs abc and acb voting sincerely—i.e., for a. Yet Farquharson's procedure shows this to be a case of complete indeterminacy: No voter can eliminate any strategy and the outcome might be any of the three alternatives. Surely a definition with this property is not acceptable.

A NEW DEFINITION OF SOPHISTICATED VOTING

In light of the weaknesses of Farquharson's definition, we have developed a new definition of sophisticated voting. An obvious advantage is that it is considerably easier to work with than is Farquharson's. Using a classification system based on a series of inequalities, it is possible to determine quickly the sophisticated strategies and sophisticated outcome for any distribution of preferences over three alternatives.

More significantly, our definition yields determinate outcomes in a number of situations in which Farquharson's definition leads to indeterminacy. This includes situations such as that described above in which there is a majority alternative. And even where there is indeterminacy, the precise nature of the indeterminacy is clear and might be resolved by additional information or by minimal amounts of cooperation between blocs.

Finally, from the perspective of how people act in real situations, it is a virtue of our definition that it is based on the sincere vote and on voters' reactions to

Table 11.1. A Situation in Which One Alternative Is Ranked First by a Majority and the Farquharson Procedure Is Indeterminate

Bloc Number	Number of Voters	Preference Ordering	Voting Patterns															
			1	2	3	4	5	6	7	8	9	10	11	12	13	14	15	16
1	6	abc	a	a	a	a	a	a	a	a	b	b	b	b	b	b	b	b
2	12	acb	a	a	a	a	c	c	c	c	a	a	a	a	c	c	c	c
3	8	bac	b	b	a	a	b	b	a	a	b	b	a	a	b	b	a	a
4	—	bca																
5	3	cab	c	a	c	a	c	a	c	a	c	a	c	a	c	a	c	a
6	—	cba																
		Outcomes	a	a	a	a	c	c	c	a	b	a	a	a	c	b	c	c

Analysis: Neither first- nor second-place voting is dominated for any player, as shown for each bloc below:

Bloc 1: Comparing, e.g., patterns 1 and 9, voting for *a* is preferred; patterns 6 and 14, voting for *b* is preferred.

Bloc 2: Comparing, e.g., patterns 1 and 5, voting for *a* is preferred; patterns 9 and 13, voting for *c* is preferred.

Bloc 3: Comparing, e.g., patterns 9 and 11, voting for *b* is preferred; patterns 6 and 8, voting for *a* is preferred.

Bloc 5: Comparing, e.g., patterns 13 and 14, voting for *c* is preferred; patterns 9 and 10, voting for *a* is preferred.

the outcome implied. Though Farquharson's definition may be logically unassailable, it hardly mirrors the thought processes that individual voters are likely to undertake in determining how they should vote. Our definition much more clearly reflects the way individuals are likely to think about a voting situation.

As noted, our definition does not always yield a determinate result. While we shall continue to look for ways out of such situations, we suspect that any reasonable definition of sophisticated voting under the plurality rule will contain some indeterminacy. This is owing to the nature of the plurality system itself—specifically to the fact that the choice is not binary—and is not traceable to deficiencies in our definition per se.

With this background in mind, let us define our new approach to sophisticated voting under the plurality rule. We begin by labeling the voting blocs according to the preference ordering of all voters therein:

Bloc 1:   *abc*;
Bloc 2:   *acb*;
Bloc 3:   *bac*;
Bloc 4:   *bca*;
Bloc 5:   *cab*;
Bloc 6:   *cba*.

Define n_i = the number of voters in bloc i, $i = 1, 2, \ldots, 6$. Then to specify a particular game we need only specify n_i, $i = 1, \ldots, 6$. Since we will deal extensively with inequalities among sets of blocs, we define $N(i, j, \ldots)$ to be the number of voters in blocs $i, j, \ldots$ combined. Assuming no ties, we can assume, without loss of generality, that

$$N(1,2) > N(3,4) > N(5,6). \tag{11.1}$$

In other words, *a* will always be the sincere winner and *c* will receive the fewest first place votes.

We now define sophisticated voting in terms of three steps:

1. Voters consider the current situation, a situation being a description of how all blocs vote and the outcome implied by that voting. At the beginning the current situation is sincere voting by all blocs.
2. Each bloc determines whether it can improve the outcome by altering its own vote while assuming that all other votes remain the same. Improving the outcome means changing the result from (a) one's last choice to: one's second choice; one's first choice; a tie between one's last choice and second choice; a tie between one's last choice and first choice; a tie between one's second choice and first choice; a tie between one's last,

second, and first choice; or (b) one's second choice to: one's first choice;
a tie between one's second and first choice.

It turns out that no more than two blocs can improve the outcome in
this way.

3a. If no bloc can improve the outcome, the current situation is a Nash equi-
     librium, and the current situation contains the sophisticated strategies
     and the sophisticated outcome.

3b. If exactly one bloc can improve the outcome, it changes its vote accord-
     ingly, and the process reverts to step 1.

3c. If two blocs can improve the situation, we examine the two-person game
     described below. The result of the game is that only one bloc will change
     its vote or the situation is what Luce and Raiffa (1957, pp. 90–91) call
     a "battle-of-the-sexes." In the former case, the one bloc changes its vote
     and the process reverts to step 1. In the latter case, the sophisticated
     outcome is indeterminate.

     The two-person game is one in which each bloc has two strategies —
     voting its first or second choice — and is based on the assumption that all
     other players will not change their votes. Each bloc checks for domi-
     nated strategies in the manner described earlier, and only strategies that
     are ultimately admissible in this game are used. Since it is a 2 × 2 game,
     there are no more than two simple reductions involved.

Whether a bloc can improve the outcome depends on one or more inequalities. Therefore, in practice this definition of sophisticated voting amounts to
testing inequalities among sets of blocs. At a minimum there is one stage; two
inequalities determine that the sincere winner is also the sophisticated winner.
At a maximum there are five stages with ten inequalities to check.

Application of the definition leads to the results shown in Figure 11.1. We
begin with the sincere situation shown at the top. Each bloc considers voting for
its first choice. Alternative a would win under this situation.

Now take step 1 described above. Blocs 1 and 2 obviously cannot improve
the situation since they are already getting their first choice. Blocs 3 and 5 are
not getting their first choice, but if they voted strategically it would only add to
the margin by which their second choice won. Thus the votes of at least four
of the six blocs will remain unchanged. Next consider bloc 4. If bloc 4 votes
strategically for c, c will win (assuming all other votes remain the same) if
$N(4,5,6) > N(1,2)$. Therefore, this is one of the crucial inequalities at this stage.
Likewise, consider bloc 6. If it votes for b, b will win if $N(3,4,6) > N(1,2)$.
Hence this is a second crucial inequality.

Depending on the direction of these two inequalities, we move to step 3a, 3b,

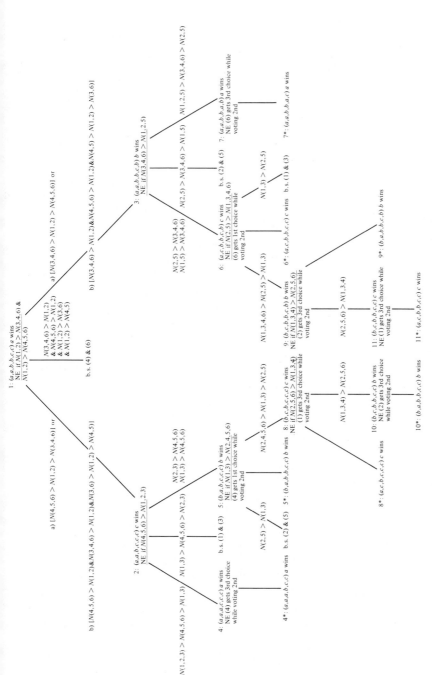

Figure 11.1. Niemi–Frank Sophisticated Voting and the Associated Inequalities. *Notes:* (1) Niemi–Frank sophisticated voting underlined. (2) "b.s." means "battle-of-the-sexes." "NE" means "Nash equilibrium." (3) Strategies indicated for bloc *i* are irrelevant if $n_j = 0$. (4) For the battle-of-the-sexes situation, the outcome is indeterminate (and strategies are indeterminate for the "battling" blocs only). (5) Situations 4*–9* are NE. In 10* and 11*, blocs 1 and 2, respectively, can improve the outcome by shifting their votes to *a*. But this is the starting point—the sincere situation.

or 3c. In terms of Figure 11.1, we determine whether we stop at situation 1 or move down one of the paths leading from that situation:

1. If $N(1,2) > N(3,4,6)$ and $N(1,2) > N(4,5,6)$, neither bloc 4 nor bloc 6 can upset the sincere situation. The sophisticated strategies and outcomes are as shown in situation 1.
2. If either $N(3,4,6) > N(1,2)$ or $N(4,5,6) > N(1,2)$, but not both, then either bloc 4 or bloc 6 will switch its vote, thereby moving the process to situation 2 or 3 in Figure 11.1.
3. If both $N(3,4,6) > N(1,2)$ and $N(4,5,6) > N(1,2)$, we have to consider the two-person game between blocs 4 and 6. Since each bloc is considering only two strategies, the game can be represented as a 2 × 2 game. The outcome, however, depends on certain other inequalities. The relevant inequalities and the resulting outcomes of the game are shown in Figure 11.2. Below each matrix is shown the result of the elimination of dominated strategies. In two cases, blocs 4 and 6 arrive at a common strategy which involved one of the blocs switching its vote from that in situation 1. In these cases, the relevant bloc switches its vote and the situation in Figure 11.1 moves down to situation 2 or 3. (As noted by the inequalities, there are thus two different ways in which one might arrive at situations 2 and 3.) In the third matrix shown in Figure 11.2, neither bloc can eliminate either strategy. If both vote the same way, the alternative they vote for will win. If they split their votes—by each voting sincerely or each voting for its second choice—alternative a will win. Since the game is noncooperative, there appears to be no way to resolve this dilemma. It is a classic "battle-of-the-sexes."

As a result of the steps taken so far, the game has ended at situation 1, has resulted in a battle-of-the-sexes, or has moved to situation 2 or 3. In the latter two situations, we begin again with step 1. In either situation, four of the six blocs cannot improve the outcome. Depending on several inequalities, we again are confronted with an equilibrium (situation 2 or 3), a battle-of-the-sexes, or we move to one of two new situations (4 or 5 from situation 2, 6, or 7 from situation 3). The process continues in the same fashion, although there may be only one or two branches leading from a given situation rather than three. In each case, however, all that is necessary is to determine a few inequalities until we arrive at a Nash equilibrium or determine that the situation is a battle-of-the-sexes. With fixed bloc sizes, of course, only one path can be traversed. Therefore, it is a simple matter to determine the sophisticated strategies and the sophisticated outcome—or to establish that the situation is indeterminate—for any given set of blocs. This will be obvious from examples that follow.

Preferences Bloc 4: *bca*
Bloc 6: *cba*

$N(4,5) > N(1,2) > N(3,6)$ $N(3,6) > N(1,2) > N(4,5)$

Bloc 6   Bloc 6

		c	*b*			*c*	*b*
Bloc 4	*b*	*a*	*b*	Bloc 4	*b*	*a*	*b*
	c	*c*	*c*		*c*	*c*	*b*

Reduction 1 $\begin{cases} \text{Bloc 4: } b,c \\ \text{Bloc 6: } b \end{cases}$ Reduction 1 $\begin{cases} \text{Bloc 4: } c \\ \text{Bloc 6: } c,b \end{cases}$

Reduction 2 $\begin{cases} \text{Bloc 4: } b \\ \text{Bloc 6: } b \end{cases}$ Reduction 2 $\begin{cases} \text{Bloc 4: } c \\ \text{Bloc 6: } c \end{cases}$

$N(1,2) > N(3,6)$
$N(1,2) > N(4,5)$

Bloc 6

		c	*b*
Bloc 4	*b*	*a*	*b*
	c	*c*	*a*

Reduction 1 $\begin{cases} \text{Bloc 4: } b,c \\ \text{Bloc 6: } c,b \end{cases}$

Figure 11.2. Two-Person Game between Contending Blocs

Before examining some of the properties of our definition, we need to point out an interesting anomaly. In some cases the sophisticated strategies are such that a bloc is voting its second choice but the outcome is its first or third choice (situations 5-6 and 4, 7-11, respectively). One might wish to assume that a bloc in this situation would change its vote to its first choice. After all, voters probably benefit psychologically, if in no other way, from voting for their first choice. Since their vote is apparently not serving any purpose in these situations, they might just as well vote sincerely.

In six of the situations when this occurs (4-9), the vote switch does not change the outcome and the situation after the switch (as well as before) is a Nash equilibrium. This is shown in Figure 11.1 as situations 4^*-9^*. In the remaining two situations (10, 11), the vote switch has a destabilizing effect as explained in note 5 to Figure 11.1. Viewed from this perspective, sophisticated strategies and outcomes cannot be determined for situations 10 and 11 even though they represent Nash equilibria. Significantly, strategies and outcomes for these cases are also indeterminate using Farquharson's definition (see below).

THE NIEMI-FRANK AND FARQUHARSON DEFINITIONS AND THE RELATION BETWEEN SINCERE, CONDORCET, AND SOPHISTICATED WINNERS

As an initial exploration of the properties of sophisticated voting, we set out to determine the relation between Farquharson's definition and our own and to determine how both definitions treat sincere and Condorcet winners. While a more complete analysis is underway, a series of examples is sufficient to show a number of important results. Therefore, in Table 11.2 we present examples that fit each of the 11 situations delineated in Figure 11.1. This form of presentation also has the virtue of showing that the inequalities defining each situation are not inconsistent (except in one case). Apart from 12a, distributions of bloc sizes exist that satisfy all of the inequalities defining each case.[2]

The examples have been chosen with care, but they are not necessarily exhaustive of the kinds of distributions satisfying the requirements for any given situation. In each case (except number 1, in which the distinction does not apply, and number 8) we show one distribution satisfying the "a" and one satisfying the "b" inequalities set down in Figure 11.1 (between situations 1 and 2 and 1 and 3). We also picked examples for each situation in such a way that the Cordorcet winner varies. Thus, for example, in situation 2 we show a case in which c is the Condorcet winner and another in which there is a cycle; in situation 4 we show one case in which a and one case in which b is the Condorcet winner; and so on. Finally, we have looked for examples that vary on whether

Table 11.2. Distributions of Bloc Sizes and Sincere, Condorcet, and Sophisticated Winners

Situation Number (from Figure 11.1)	Total Voters	Bloc Size	Sincere Winner	Condorcet Winner	Farquharson Sophisticated Voting — Strategies	Farquharson Winner	Niemi–Frank Sophisticated Voting — Strategies	Niemi–Frank Winner
1	29	(6, 12, 8, –, 3, –)	a	a	$((a,b),(a,c),(b,a), \ - \ ,(c,a), \ - \ )$	Indet.	(a,a,b,c,c)	a
2(a)	50	(10, 11, –, 15, 10, 4)	a	none	$((a,b),(a,c), \ - \ ,(b,c), \ c \ , \ c \ )$	Indet.	$(a,a,-,c,c,c)$	c
(b)	30	(11, –, 3, 7, –, 9)	a	b	$(a \ , \ - \ , \ b \ , \ c \ , \ - \ , \ c \ )$	c	$(a,-,b,c,-,c)$	c
3(a)	31	(5, 10, 8, 6, –, 2)	a	b	$(a \ , \ a \ , \ b \ , \ b \ , \ - \ , \ b \ )$	b	$(a,a,b,b,-,b)$	b
(b)	42	(15, –, –, 14, 3, 10)	a	b	$((a,b), \ - \ , \ - \ ,(b,c), \ c \ ,(c,b))$	Indet.	$(a,-,-,b,c,b)$	b
4(a)	36	(10, 6, 3, 8, 9, –)	a	a	$(a \ , \ a \ , \ a \ , \ c \ , \ c \ , \ - \ )$	a	$(a,a,c,c,-)$	a
(b)	66	(12, 11, 13, 9, 7, 14)	a	b	$((a,b),(a,c),(b,a),(b,c),(c,a),(c,b))$	Indet.	(a,a,c,c,c)	a
5(a)	452	(103, 60,125, 20,144, –)	a	a	$(b \ , \ a \ , \ b \ , \ c \ , \ c \ , \ - \ )$	b	$(b,a,b,c,c,-)$	b
(b)	84	(20, 9, 25, 3, 8, 19)	a	b	$((a,b), \ a \ ,(b,a),(b,c),(c,a),(c,b))$	Indet.	(b,a,b,c,c,c)	b
6(a)	461	(60,106,150, –,125, 20)	a	a	$(a \ , \ c \ , \ b \ , \ - \ , \ c \ , \ b \ )$	c	$(a,c,b,-,c,b)$	c
(b)	104	(12, 25, 13, 21, 28, 5)	a	c	$(a \ ,(a,c),(b,a),(b,c),(c,a),(c,b))$	Indet.	(a,c,b,c,b,b)	c
7(a)	144	(50, 11, 30, 30, 19, 4)	a	a	$(a \ , \ a \ , \ b \ , \ a \ , \ b \ , \ b \ )$	a	(a,a,b,a,b)	a
(b)	21	(8, –, 2, 5, 4, 2)	a	none	$((a,b), \ - \ ,(b,a),(b,c),(c,a),(c,b))$	Indet.	$(a,-,b,a,b)$	a
8(a)		never occurs						
(b)	102	(15, 20, 27, 7, 20, 13)	a	a	$((a,b),(a,c),(b,a),(b,c),(c,a),(c,b))$	Indet.	(b,c,b,c,c,c)	c
9(a)	463	(68,100,150, 17,120, 8)	a	a	$(b \ , \ c \ , \ b \ , \ b \ , \ c \ , \ b \ )$	b	(b,c,b,c,b,b)	b
(b)	174	(35, 30, 17, 46, 40, 6)	a	none	$((a,b),(a,c),(b,a),(b,c),(c,a), \ b \ )$	Indet.	(b,c,b,c,b,b)	b
10(a)	47	(10, 7, 12, 4, 14, –)	a	a	$((a,b),(a,c),(b,a),(b,c), \ c \ , \ - \ )$	Indet.	$(b,c,b,c,-)$	b
(b)	93	(17, 16, 23, 9, 8, 20)	a	b	$((a,b),(a,c),(b,a),(b,c),(c,a),(c,b))$	Indet.	(b,c,b,c,c)	b
11(a)	45	(6, 10, 15, –, 12, 2)	a	a	$((a,b),(a,c), \ b \ , \ - \ ,(a,c),(c,b))$	Indet.	$(b,c,-,c,c)$	c
(b)	267	(39, 61, 17, 67, 66, 17)	a	none	$((a,b),(a,c), \ b \ ,(b,c),(c,a),(c,b))$	Indet.	(b,c,b,c,c)	c

Notes: (1) Distributions (a) and (b) refer to the inequalities between situations 1 and 2 or 1 and 3 in Figure 11.1.
(2) Situation 8a never occurs. Proof:

i. $N(4,5,6) > N(3,4,6) \Rightarrow N(5) > N(3)$.
ii. Given (i), $N(1,3) > N(2,5) \Rightarrow N(1) > N(2)$.
iii. $N(1) > N(2) \ \& \ N(3,4) > N(5,6) > N(1,3,4) > N(2,5,6)$, which contradicts the condition for situation 8.

163

Farquharson's definition yields a determinate solution. In situation 7, for example, Farquharson's definition yields a single sophisticated strategy for each player with one distribution but is completely indeterminate with the other distribution. Still, these examples do not exhaust all of the possibilities.

Consider now the relation between Farquharson's prescriptions and our own. As noted at the outset, an important drawback of Farquharson's definition is that it is so often indeterminate. From Table 11.2 we can see that it fails to identify sophisticated strategies in at least some distributions satisfying all of the 11 situations. In contrast, our definition determines a unique set of strategies and a unique outcome for every distribution in every one of these cases.[3] Equally important, there are no instances (in Table 11.2 or in the battle-of-the-sexes situations we have examined) in which the situation is indeterminate under our definition and determinate under Farquharson's. Thus we conjecture that our definition is an extension of Farquharson's definition in the sense that (a) whenever Farquharson's definition yields a determinate outcome, our definition yields the same determinate result; and (b) when Farquharson's definition is indeterminate, our definition is also indeterminate or yields a unique set of strategies and a unique outcome that are "sophisticated" in Farquharson's sense (i.e., the strategies are all ultimately admissible).[4]

If our conjecture is correct,[5] it provides further support for favoring our definition over Farquharson's. The conjecture says that in no instance does an outcome occur under our definition that would be ruled out if blocs were following Farquharson's prescriptions. If Farquharson's definition yields just one outcome, ours picks the same one. In addition, when our procedure leads to a determinate result when Farquharson's does not, no strategies are used by the blocs that would be ruled out by Farquharson (though other strategies may be ultimately admissible as well). And, as situation 1 in Table 11.2 shows, Farquharson's definition can lead to indeterminacy in circumstances in which the outcome is obvious, while our definition prescribes the obvious strategies and outcome.

Having argued that our definition of sophisticated voting is better than Farquharson's, let us consider how it treats sincere and Condorcet winners. The examples in Table 11.2 make it clear that neither sincere nor Condorcet winners are guaranteed victory under our definition (or Farquharson's definition) of sophisticated voting. Indeed, even a Condorcet winner that is also the sincere winner may lose (situations 5a, 6a, 9a, 10a, and 11a). This suggests that sophisticated voting under the plurality rule has a different character than sophisticated voting under binary procedures. McKelvey and Niemi (1978) and Miller (1977) show that under binary procedures sophisticated voting produces an outcome that is the same as that produced by sincere voting or is preferred to the latter when there is a Condorcet winner and that it produces an outcome in the "top cycle" if there is no such winner.[6] It appears that one cannot argue so strongly for the superiority of sophisticated voting under plurality rule.

At the same time, there are situations (3a, 3b, 5b, 6b, and 10) in which a Condorcet winner loses under sincere voting but wins under sophisticated voting. Thus one cannot malign sophisticated voting as always yielding worse results either. Moreover, sophisticated voting has one major advantage over sincere voting. If voting is sincere, a "Condorcet loser"—an alternative that loses to both other alternatives—may win. Under sophisticated voting (where there is a determinate outcome), this cannot occur.[7] An example is shown in Table 11.2 (3b). Alternative a loses to both b and c if paired against them. Yet it would win if voting were sincere. In contrast, sophisticated voting under our definition would result in b winning. Thus in this weaker but still important sense, sophisticated voting is apparently preferable to sincere voting under the plurality procedure as well.

CONCLUSION

Considerable work remains to be done in determining fully the properties of sophisticated voting under the plurality system. In addition to proving the conjecture relating our definition to Farquharson's, there is the obvious question of whether our definition can usefully be extended to cover more alternatives and two-stage procedures (run-offs). A probability model might also prove useful in giving us some notion of the frequency with which Condorcet winners can be expected to win or lose under sophisticated voting.

At least for the case of three alternatives, however, we are confident that we have developed a definition of sophisticated voting that is realistic in the sense of how voters might be expected to think, if they have perfect information, and justifiable from a theoretical point of view. If this is so, then—since the plurality system is so ubiquitous and three candidates a fairly common occurrence—we have developed an idea with considerable applicability to the real world of politics. This, above all, should please the person we are honoring with this conference today.

APPENDIX

Here we show that Farquharson's definition of sophisticated voting always leads to indeterminacy when the inequalities defining situation 11 in Figure 11.1 are satisfied. This also shows (for situation 11) that the indeterminacy of the starred

extension of the Niemi–Frank definition of sophisticated voting implies the indeterminacy of the Farquharson definition.

First let us consider situation 11(a), which is defined by the following inequalities:

    i. $N(1,2) > N(3,4) > N(5,6)$;
    ii. $N(3,4,6) > N(1,2) > N(4,5,6)$;
    iii. $N(2,5) > N(3,4,6)$;
    iv. $N(1,5) > N(3,4,6)$;
    v. $N(1,3,4,6) > N(2,5) > N(1,3)$;
    vi. $N(2,5,6) > N(1,3,4)$.

Using these inequalities, we can obtain the possible outcomes for each of the
64 voting patterns of the six blocs, as given in Diagram 11.A1. For 60 of the 64
patterns, the above six inequalities determine a single outcome. Many of these
outcomes are immediate consequences of one of these inequalities (that pattern
2 yields outcome b follows immediately from inequality ii, for example),
while to demonstrate others requires some algebraic manipulations. For example, to show that pattern 23 necessarily yields outcome a, we need to show that
$N(1,5) > N(2,4,6)$. Now (ii) and (iv) imply that $N(1,5) > N(3,4,6) > N(1,2) >
N(4,5,6)$, so that $N(3) > N(5) > N(2)$. Hence $N(1,5) > N(3,4,6) > N(2,4,6)$,
and so a is the outcome.

For patterns 6, 35, 40, and 54, there are two outcomes which are consistent
with the six inequalities. To show this, consider the following two combinations
satisfying the conditions of situation 11(a): (1)–(6,10,15,0,12,2); (2)–(57,105,
140,14,120,20). Combination (1) yields outcome b for pattern 6, while (2)
yields outcome a. For pattern 35, (1) yields b and (2) yields a. For pattern 40,
(1) yields b and (2) yields a. And for pattern 54, (1) yields b and (2) yields c.
It is obvious for all four patterns that the third alternative cannot win.

Now from Diagram 11.A1 we can easily demonstrate that Farquharson's
definition yields indeterminacy. By comparing pattern 1 with 33 and pattern
18 with 50, we see that both of bloc 1's strategies are primarily admissible. By
comparing patterns 1 with 17 and 2 with 18 we see also that both of bloc 2's
strategies are primarily admissible. For bloc 3, only voting for b is primarily
admissible. Bloc 4 is either a dummy or has voting for b as its only admissible
strategy. By comparing pattern 2 with 4 and 17 with 19, we see that both of
bloc 5's strategies are primarily admissible. By comparing pattern 1 with 2 and
49 with 50, we see also that both of bloc 6's strategies are primarily admissible.
Thus the first reduction yields $((a,b),(a,c),b,b,(c,a),(c,b))$.

Hence we can eliminate from consideration those patterns where either bloc
3 or 4 uses an inadmissible strategy, namely patterns 5–16, 21–32, 37–48, and

Diagram 11.A1

	1	5	9	1 3	1 7
n_1	aaaa	aaaa	aaaa	aaaa	aaaa
n_2	aaaa	aaaa	aaaa	aaaa	cccc
n_3	bbbb	bbbb	aaaa	aaaa	bbbb
n_4	bbbb	cccc	bbbb	cccc	bbbb
n_5	ccaa	ccaa	ccaa	ccaa	ccaa
n_6	cbcb	cbcb	cbcb	cbcb	cbcb
Outcomes	abaa	abaa a	aaaa	aaaa	ccaa

	2 1	2 5	2 9	3 3	3 7
n_1	aaaa	aaaa	aaaa	bbbb	bbbb
n_2	cccc	cccc	cccc	aaaa	aaaa
n_3	bbbb	aaaa	aaaa	bbbb	bbbb
n_4	cccc	bbbb	cccc	bbbb	cccc
n_5	ccaa	ccaa	ccaa	ccaa	ccaa
n_6	cbcb	cbcb	cbcb	cbcb	cbcb
Outcomes	ccaa	ccaa	ccaa	bbbb a	bbab a

	4 1	4 5	4 9	5 3	5 7	6 1
n_1	bbbb	bbbb	bbbb	bbbb	bbbb	bbbb
n_2	aaaa	aaaa	cccc	cccc	cccc	cccc
n_3	aaaa	aaaa	bbbb	bbbb	aaaa	aaaa
n_4	bbbb	cccc	bbbb	cccc	bbbb	cccc
n_5	ccaa	ccaa	ccaa	ccaa	ccaa	ccaa
n_6	cbcb	cbcb	cbcb	cbcb	cbcb	cbcb
Outcomes	aaaa	aaaa	cbbb	cbbb c	ccaa	ccaa

53-64. However, the comparisons in the previous paragraph used none of these patterns, and so the same comparisons show that blocs 1, 2, 5, and 6 all have two secondarily admissible strategies. Thus no further reduction is possible, and the Farquharson sophisticated strategies are $((a,b),(a,c),b,b,(c,a),(c,b))$, so that the outcome is indeterminate.

Now let us consider situation 11(b), which is defined by the same inequalities

RICHARD G. NIEMI AND ARTHUR Q. FRANK

as 11(a) except that (ii) is replaced by (ii') $N(3,4,6) > N(1,2)$ & $N(4,5,6) >$ $N(1,2)$ & $N(4,5) > N(1,2) > N(3,6)$. The possible outcomes for each of the 64 voting patterns are given in Diagram 11.A2. For 40 of the 64 patterns the inequalities that define situation 11(b) determine the outcome. To show that two outcomes are compatible with these inequalities for the other 24 patterns, we consider the following three combinations which satisfy (i), (ii'), and (iii)–(vi):

Diagram 11.A2

	1	5	9	13	17
n_1	aaaa	aaaa	aaaa	aaaa	aaaa
n_2	aaaa	aaaa	aaaa	aaaa	cccc
n_3	bbbb	bbbb	aaaa	aaaa	bbbb
n_4	bbbb	cccc	bbbb	cccc	bbbb
n_5	ccaa	ccaa	ccaa	ccaa	ccaa
n_6	cbcb	cbcb	cbcb	cbcb	cbcb
Outcomes	abaa	ccaa	aaaa b	aaaa cc	ccaa

	21	25	29	33	37
n_1	aaaa	aaaa	aaaa	bbbb	bbbb
n_2	cccc	cccc	cccc	aaaa	aaaa
n_3	bbbb	aaaa	aaaa	bbbb	bbbb
n_4	cccc	bbbb	cccc	bbbb	cccc
n_5	ccaa	ccaa	ccaa	ccaa	ccaa
n_6	cbcb	cbcb	cbcb	cbcb	cbcb
Outcomes	ccaa cc	ccaa	ccaa cc	bbab b	bbaa cc b

	41	45	49	53	57	61
n_1	bbbb	bbbb	bbbb	bbbb	bbbb	bbbb
n_2	aaaa	aaaa	cccc	cccc	cccc	cccc
n_3	aaaa	aaaa	bbbb	bbbb	aaaa	aaaa
n_4	bbbb	cccc	bbbb	cccc	bbbb	cccc
n_5	ccaa	ccaa	ccaa	ccaa	ccaa	ccaa
n_6	cbcb	cbcb	cbcb	cbcb	cbcb	cbcb
Outcomes	aaaa bbbb	aaaa cc	cbbb	ccbb cc	cbaa cbb	ccaa cc

(1)-(50,60,0,95,70,18); (2)-(35,37,55,15,58,11); (3)-(39,61,17,67,66,17). For 23 of the 24 nonunique patterns, (1) and (2) yield different outcomes. For pattern 35, (1) and (2) both yield outcome b, but (3) yields a. It is easy to see for each of these 24 patterns that the third alternative cannot win.

From Diagram 11.A2 we can readily show that Farquharson's definition yields indeterminacy. By comparing pattern 1 with 33 and 18 with 50, we see that both of bloc 1's strategies are primarily admissible. Likewise, comparing pattern 1 with 17 and 2 with 18 shows that both of bloc 2's strategies are primarily admissible. Bloc 3's situation is complicated, and will be dealt with below. By comparing pattern 1 with 5 and 2 with 6, we see that both of bloc 4's strategies are primarily admissible. Similarly, comparing pattern 2 with 4 and 5 with 7 shows that both of bloc 5's strategies are primarily admissible, and comparing pattern 1 with 2 and 49 with 50 shows that both of bloc 6's strategies are primarily admissible.

If bloc 3 is a dummy or if both of bloc 3's strategies are primarily admissible, we are finished—in that case Farquharson's definition yields complete indeterminacy. If bloc 3's only primarily admissible strategy is voting for b, then we eliminate from consideration patterns 9-16, 25-32, 41-48, and 57-64. However, the comparisons in the previous paragraph used none of these patterns, and so in this situation the same comparisons show that blocs 1, 2, 4, 5, and 6 all have two secondarily admissible strategies. Thus no further reduction is possible, and the Farquharson sophisticated strategies are $((a,b),(a,c),b,(b,c),(c,a),(c,b))$.

Thus, if bloc 3 is a dummy or if both its strategies are primarily admissible or if only voting for b is admissible, the Farquharson definition yields an indeterminate outcome. Hence, to complete this proof, we need only show that bloc 3 never has voting for a as its only primarily admissible strategy, i.e., that voting for a cannot dominate voting for b. We now proceed to show this.

Suppose bloc 3 has voting for a as its only admissible strategy. Then for all 32 of the voting patterns of the other five blocs, voting for a must yield as good as or better an outcome than voting for b, and in at least one of the 32 patterns it must yield a better outcome. For a to be always at least as good a strategy as b, all the following inequalities must hold (see Diagram 11.A2):

1. From patterns 2 and 10, we get $N(4,6) > N(1,2,3)$;
2. From patterns 33 and 41, we get $N(1,4) > N(2,3)$;
3. From patterns 34 and 42, we get $N(1,4,6) > N(2,3)$;
4. From patterns 35 and 43, we get if $N(1,3,4) > N(2,5)$, then $N(1,4) > N(2,3,5)$;
5. From patterns 36 and 44, we get $N(1,4,6) > N(2,3,5)$;
6. From patterns 37 and 45, we get $N(4,5,6) > N(1,3)$;
7. From patterns 38 and 46, we get $N(4,5) > N(1,3,6)$;

8.   From patterns 40 and 48, we get $N(2,5) > N(1,3,6)$;
9.   From patterns 50 and 58, we get $N(1,4,6) > N(2,5)$;
10. From patterns 51 and 59, we get $N(1,4) > N(3,5)$;
11. From patterns 52 and 60, we get $N(1,4,6) > N(3,5)$;
12. From patterns 55 and 63, we get $N(2,4,6) > N(1,3)$;
13. From patterns 56 and 64, we get $N(2,4) > N(1,3,6)$.

These thirteen inequalities are not independent of each other: in fact (2) implies (3), (7) implies (6), (5) implies (9), and (13) implies (12). Hence we can eliminate inequalities (3), (6), (9), and (12) from the list. By using the inequalities that define situation 11(b), we can eliminate others as well. Inequalities (ii') and (iv) imply that $N(1,5) > N(3,4,6) > N(1,2)$, so that $N(5) > N(2)$. Inequalities (i) and (vi), which say that $N(2,5,6) > N(1,3,4)$ and $N(3,4) > N(5,6)$, imply that $N(2) > N(1)$. Inequality (i), which says that $N(1,2) > N(5,6)$, together with $N(5) > N(2)$, implies that $N(1) > N(6)$. Hence any combination of bloc sizes satisfying the inequalities that define situation 11(b) also satisfies

vii. $N(5) > N(2) > N(1) > N(6)$.

Now $N(5) > N(6)$, together with inequality (5), implies (2). Similarly, $N(2) > N(6)$, together with (5), implies (10), and $N(2) > N(1)$, together with (5), implies (11). Hence we can also eliminate inequalities (2), (10), and (11) from the list. To summarize, any combination of bloc sizes which satisfies the conditions of situation 11(b) and for which bloc 3 has voting for a as its only admissible strategy must satisfy inequalities (i), (ii'), (iii)–(vii), (1), (4), (5), (7), (8), and (13).

In addition, voting for a must yield for bloc 3, for at least one of the 32 voting patterns of the other five blocs, a better outcome than voting for b. Hence, in addition to satisfying all of the inequalities listed above, the combination of bloc sizes must satisfy at least one of the following (see Diagram 11.A2):

14. From patterns 5 and 13, $N(1,2,3) > N(4,5,6)$;
15. From patterns 6 and 14, $N(1,2,3) > N(4,5)$;
16. From patterns 23 and 31, $N(1,3,5) > N(2,4,6) > N(1,5)$;
17. From patterns 24 and 32, $N(1,3,5) > N(2,4) > N(1,5)$;
18. From patterns 37 and 45, $N(2,3) > N(4,5,6) > N(1,3)$;
19. From patterns 38 and 46, $N(2,3) > N(4,5) > N(1,3,6)$;
20. From patterns 55 and 63, $N(3,5) > N(2,4,6) > N(1,3)$;
21. From patterns 56 and 64, $N(3,5) > N(2,4) > N(1,3,6)$.

Now to complete the proof, we need to show that there cannot be a combination of bloc sizes satisfying any one of (14)–(21), and also satisfying all of (i), (ii'), (iii)–(vii), (1), (4), (5), (7), (8), and (13). Since a combination that fails to satisfy (15) will also fail to satisfy (14), we can drop (14) from the list. We consider (15)–(21) one at a time below.

(15), together with (1), yields $N(4,6) > N(1,2,3) > N(4,5)$, which implies that $N(6) > N(5)$, contradicting (vii).

(16) is contradicted by (vii) and (5), for if $N(2) > N(1)$, and $N(1,4,6) > N(2,3,5)$, then $N(4,6) > N(3,5)$, so that $N(2,4,6) > N(1,3,5)$.

(17) requires a consideration of two cases to prove its incompatibility with (i)–(13). First, suppose $N(4) \geqslant N(5)$; then $N(1,3,4) \geqslant N(1,3,5) > N(2,4) \geqslant N(2,5)$, so that $N(1,3,4) > N(2,5)$. Then (4) implies that $N(1,4) > N(2,3,5)$. Since, from (vii), $N(2) > N(1)$, we have $N(2,4) > N(1,4) > N(2,3,5) > N(1,3,5)$, which contradicts (17). Next, suppose $N(5) > N(4)$. Then (5) yields $N(1,4,6) > N(2,3,5)$, so that $N(1,6) > N(2,3)$. From (vii), $N(2) > N(1)$, so we have $N(6) > N(3)$. But $N(5) > N(4)$ and $N(6) > N(3)$ imply that $N(5,6) > N(3,4)$, contradicting (i).

(18) and (19) are contradicted by (vii) and (1), for $N(4,6) > N(1,2,3)$ and $N(1) > N(6)$ imply that $N(4) > N(2,3)$; hence $N(4,5,6) > N(2,3)$ and $N(4,5) > N(2,3)$.

Finally, (20) and (21) are contradicted by (vii) and (5), since $N(2) > N(6)$ and $N(1,4,6) > N(2,3,5)$ imply that $N(1,4) > N(3,5)$. But $N(2) > N(1)$, so that $N(2,4) > N(3,5)$; hence also $N(2,4,6) > N(3,5)$.

Therefore bloc 3 cannot have voting for a as its only admissible strategy. Q.E.D.

NOTES

1. An exception is when one's bloc is a dummy, i.e., when it can never affect the outcome. For example, if there are four blocs with 8, 6, 4, and 1 voters, respectively, then the one-voter bloc is a dummy, and all three of his strategies are admissible. In such a case, it is harmless to assume that the members of the dummy bloc get some personal satisfaction out of voting for their first preference, and hence in this situation also we exclude the possibility of voting for one's third preference.

2. Distributions also exist for each of the battle-of-the-sexes shown in Figure 11.1.

3. Farquharson's definition, like ours, appears to be indeterminate whenever there is a battle-of-the-sexes. Also, as noted, the extension of our definition as diagrammed in the starred nodes of Figure 11.1 is indeterminate for situations 10* and 11*.

4. Part b of the conjecture is not true with the starred extension of our definition. For example, consider situation 5(a) in Table 11.2. Farquharson's definition yields the unique strategies $(b,a,b,c,c,-)$, while our starred extension yields $(b,a,b,c,-)$. Hence the starred extension of our definition does not always yield a sophisticated equilibrium.

5. For case 11 we show that the conjecture is true, as follows. We show in the Appendix that Farquharson's definition is always outcome indeterminate. This shows that part

a of our conjecture is correct since Farquharson's definition never yields a determinate outcome. That part b is correct can be seen by observing the following: As shown in the Appendix, only blocs 3 and 4 have Farquharson-determinate strategies, and they are the same strategies that are prescribed for these blocs by our definition; for the other blocs, both first- and second-place voting is Farquharson sophisticated, so the unique strategies prescribed by our definition are necessarily sophisticated in that sense. Similar proofs are planned for other situations.

6. In addition, Bjurulf and Niemi (forthcoming) argue on probabilistic grounds for the superiority of sophisticated voting when there is no Condorcet winner.

7. That a Condorcet loser cannot win under our definition of sophisticated voting can be easily seen:

Blocs 1, 2, and 5 prefer a to b, while 3, 4, and 6 prefer b to a.
Blocs 1, 2, and 3 prefer a to c, while 4, 5, and 6 prefer c to a.
Blocs 1, 3, and 4 prefer b to c, while 2, 5, and 6 prefer c to b.

From Figure 11.1, we get

a wins in situation 1, in which it is the Condorcet winner.
c wins in situation 2, in which a majority prefer c to a.
b wins in situation 3, in which a majority prefer b to a.
a wins in situation 4, in which a majority prefer a to c.
b wins in situation 5, in which a majority prefer b to c.
c wins in situation 6, in which a majority prefer c to b.
a wins in situation 7, in which a majority prefer a to b.
c wins in situation 8, in which a majority prefer c to b.
b wins in situation 9, in which a majority prefer b to c.
b wins in situation 10, in which a majority prefer b to c.
c wins in situation 11, in which a majority prefer c to b.

Thus the Niemi–Frank sophisticated outcome is always preferred by a majority to at least one of the other two alternatives.

12 THE ROLE OF IMPERFECTIONS OF HEALTH INSURANCE IN VOTER SUPPORT FOR SAFETY REGULATION

Melvin J. Hinich

The federal government in recent years has steadily increased its activities aimed at protecting consumers from potentially harmful goods and services.[1] A general policy to regulate the market to improve product safety has resulted from democratic decision making in Congress.

There are two basic approaches that a consumer protection agency can use to improve product safety. In the first approach, the agency acts as a police force whose goal is the identification of producers of potentially unsafe products or plants where the production process could conceivably cause harm. Once identified, the agency then attempts to penalize these firms and their management in order to force them to comply with standards adopted by the agency and the judiciary, or go out of business. In the second approach, the agency provides consumers with information on product safety in the form of compulsory labeling, advertising, or an agency seal of approval. Armed with presumably reliable information, consumers could freely exercise their preferences in the marketplace. Regulatory agencies in this field tend to prefer the first approach.

The banning of such products by a governmental agency is preferred to the information dissemination approach by voters if they believe there are

Part of this research effort was supported by a grant from the National Science Foundation.

173

large costs imposed on them by the consumption of hazardous products by a large subgroup in the population whose choice behavior will not be changed if information is freely provided. Even if product safety information were freely available, *some* people would consume hazardous products. A self-interest-based majority-rule choice to restrict consumer choice is formalized in this paper using a simple cardinal utility model for consumers. A parametric utility model is used to obtain the derived demand function and the market equilibrium price and contamination level. The market equilibrium results are then used to derive voter preferences for or against banning.

The purpose of the exercise is to formalize the analysis of the political demand for restrictions on consumer choice in the market, under the assumption that the distribution of voter preferences influences government policy on this issue. It will be shown that once a social cost is introduced in the consumer's utility function, consumers who overestimate the risk subsidize those who underestimate the risk and will prefer a total ban on hazardous products to free choice. The extreme version of this argument states that there exist many ignorant individuals whose consumption patterns pose a threat to a cautious consumer which is costly to avoid by individual action. The model illuminates the social choice pressures for restricting market choice without assuming the extreme position or assuming that regulation is solely due to producer action.

Support for the restriction of market choices also comes from consumers who prefer to have the government force their choices and thus cut the costs of decision making. This is a self-paternalism argument for regulation. It is unclear under what circumstances a self-paternalist will favor the banning approach over requiring mandatory warnings. In the last section of this paper, a comparison is made between the self-paternalistic approach and the social cost argument when technological change reduces the unit cost of production. This paper focuses on the process of generating political support for regulation, rather than taking a normative or economic efficiency approach.

INDIRECT UTILITY FUNCTIONS AND SUBJECTIVE SOCIAL COST

Consider a world where there are only two types of goods, contaminated ambrosia and perfect gruel. Let k_{ji} denote the jth consumer's subjective assessment of the amount of contamination in a unit of the ith brand of ambrosia. Assume that k_{ji} is *proportional* to the true contamination rate k_i, i.e., $k_{ji} = \kappa_j k_i$. Assume that consumers can estimate k_i by reading consumerist literature, and by trusting certain brands. It is rational for a consumer to put some faith in a brand name since the goodwill invested in it can be quickly lost if the public becomes aware of serious problems with products bearing the brand.

Let $q_j = (q_{j1}, \ldots, q_{jn})$ denote the number of units of the various brands of ambrosia consumed per period by the jth consumer, and let s_j be the amount of gruel consumed per period. Assume that the consumer's utility function is of the form

$$U_j(q_j, s_j) = \alpha_j \sum_{i=1}^{n} q_{ji} - H_j\left(\sum_{i=1}^{n} k_{ji} q_{ji}\right) + s_j, \tag{12.1}$$

where α_j is the marginal utility of *perfect* ambrosia and the marginal utility of gruel is set equal to one with no loss of generality. The term $H_j(\Sigma_{i=1}^{n} k_{ji} q_{ji})$ represents the subjective disutility suffered by the jth consumer as a result of consuming $\Sigma_{i=1}^{n} k_{ji} q_{ji}$ units of contaminated ambrosia in the period. Assume that it is a convex monotonically increasing function of its argument. The next step is to show that the equilibrium price and contamination rate for each brand are simple functions of α_j and the marginal cost of production.

Let p_i and 1 be the unit prices of the two foods, and T_j be the budget constraint of the consumer, i.e., $\Sigma_{i=1}^{n} p_i q_{ji} + s_j \leqslant T_j$. The consumer will spend all of his food budget T_j on some mix of gruel and ambrosia, or all of one type. Thus from (12.1),

$$U_j(q_j, s_j) = \sum_{i=1}^{n} (\alpha_j - p_i) q_{ji} - H_j\left(\kappa_j \sum_{i=1}^{n} k_i q_{ji}\right) + T_j, \tag{12.2}$$

where $\kappa_j = k_{ji}/k_i$. Clearly $q_{ji} = 0$ if $p_i \geqslant \alpha_j$. Setting $\partial U_j/\partial q_{ji} = 0$ for each $i = 1, \ldots, n$, we have

$$\frac{\alpha_j - p_i}{k_i} = \kappa_j H_j'\left(\sum_{i=1}^{n} k_{ji} q_{ji}\right),$$

where H_j' is the slope of H_j.

By the Kuhn–Tucker conditions, the brands which are purchased have a price and contamination rate lying along the indifference contour in the (p,k) plane, $(\alpha_j - p_i)/k_i = M_j$, where $M_j = \max_i [(\alpha_j - p_i)/k_i]$ assuming that at least one price is less than α_j. It will be convenient to reparameterize the contamination rate by setting $g = 1/k$ as a measure of "goodness."

For a given value of α, assume there are a large number of consumers with that marginal utility of perfect ambrosia. The competitive market solution will set price equal to marginal cost of the industry. Suppose that for any fixed level of output, the marginal cost of ambrosia with contamination $g = 1/k$ is independent of demand and is a convex monotonically increasing continuous function of g, e.g., marginal cost $= c_i g$, $c_i > 0$ for the ith firm. If price equals marginal cost, $[\alpha - p(g)]g$ is a unimodal function of g in the interval $0 \leqslant g \leqslant p_i^{-1}(\alpha)$. Thus the ith firm in a competitive market will select a g_i satisfying the equation $\alpha = p_i(g_i) + p_i'(g_i)g_i$.

Consider the subset of consumers who have the same α and thus the same indifference curve. For this group there is a unique quality and price for ambrosia in the competitive equilibrium if the marginal cost curves for all firms are the same. For example, if $p(g) = cg$, then $g = \alpha/2c$ is the market solution.[2] The fact that the variation of subjective contamination does not affect the quality equilibrium is due to the proportionality assumption.

Since the consumer's budget constraint puts an upper limit of T_j/p on the amount of ambrosia consumed, assume that T_j is sufficiently large relative to α_j and H' such that at the equilibrium all consumers purchase some gruel, i.e., $s_j > 0$. The corner solutions could have been avoided by making the utility concave in q and s, but we would lose the advantage of having a closed form for the equilibrium price and quality.

In order to derive the demand for ambrosia, which is needed for the social cost argument, it is necessary to use a specific functional form for H. For simplicity let H be a quadratic function of its argument, namely,

$$H_j = \beta_j \left(\sum_{i=1}^{n} k_{ji} q_{ji} \right)^2, \tag{12.3}$$

where β_j is the consumer's sensitivity to the contaminant. If the marginal cost for all firms is cg, the jth consumer purchases

$$q_j = \frac{\alpha_j - cg}{2\sigma_j} g^2, \qquad g = \frac{\alpha_j}{2c} \tag{12.4}$$

units of ambrosia, where $\sigma_j = \beta_j \kappa_j^2$. Thus the total amount of contamination consumed is $\alpha_j^2/8c\sigma_j$.

Suppose, however, that all consumers pay the same premium to a social insurance fund which compensates them for the financial losses from illness caused by their consumption of contaminated ambrosia. This is an abstraction of the interlocking and overlapping coverage by group health and accident plans, private insurance, and government subsidized health services. Since the individual consumption of ambrosia is inversely proportional to σ_j, individuals who are less sensitive to contaminants, or who underestimate the risk (low σ individuals) consume more ambrosia than sensitive or pessimistic individuals (high σ individuals). Thus light users subsidize heavy users. If the premium could be adjusted upward for the heavy users, the income transfers would be reduced, but assume that the correct variation of premiums is too costly to enforce.[3]

In order to bring social cost into the individual utility functions, suppose that the expected compensation from the health insurance fund is proportional to the expected disutility of consuming contaminated ambrosia in the period. For simplicity, assume that everyone has the same α.

Because of the proportional reduction in disutility, it is easy to check that the indirect utility function of our consumer is the same as (12.2) with T_j replaced by $T_j - \pi$ and σ_j replaced by $\delta\sigma_j$, where π is the insurance premium and δ is the fraction of the disutility *not* compensated, where for simplicity δ is assumed to be the same for all. Thus the ambrosia demand is shifted to the right but the market equilibrium price and quality are the same as before, i.e., $g = \alpha/2c$ and $p = \alpha/2$.

As an alternative to free competition, suppose that the government forces producers to set g above a level g_0 which is greater than the market quality. Setting $g_0 \geqslant \alpha/c$ is equivalent to banning ambrosia for those consumers whose $\alpha_j \leqslant \alpha$.

Given δ, assume that the budgets are sufficiently great so that $q_j < T_j/p$ for all consumers. It then follows from (12.4) that $kq_j = (\alpha - cg_0)g_0(2\delta\sigma_j)^{-1}$. By averaging over the population the insurance premium (ignoring administration costs) is of the form $(\alpha - cg_0)^2 g_0^2 \delta^{-1}\overline{\sigma^{-1}}/4$, where $\overline{\sigma^{-1}}$ is the average $\sigma_j^{-1} = \beta_j^{-1}\kappa_j^{-2}$ in the population.[4]

Assume that there are enough consumers who are insensitive to contamination or who "underestimate" k to have $\sigma_j^{-1} < \overline{\sigma^{-1}}$. Incorporating the expected premium and compensation into the indirect utility function, it follows that the insurance adjusted indirect utility is

$$U_0 = \begin{cases} \frac{1}{4}(\alpha - cg_0)^2 g_0^2 \delta^{-1}(\sigma_j^{-1} - \overline{\sigma^{-1}}) + T_j & \text{if } \alpha/2c \leqslant g_0 < \alpha/c \\ T_j & \text{if } g_0 \geqslant \alpha/c. \end{cases} \quad (12.5)$$

Note that $g_0 = \alpha/2c$ minimizes U_0 if $\sigma_j^{-1} < \overline{\sigma^{-1}}$, i.e., the competitive equilibrium gives the worst value of g for the "pessimistic" consumer (Figure 12.1). The utility of this consumer is maximized for $g \geqslant \alpha/c$, in which case he consumes only gruel. This will be true even if a fixed cost of policing the ban is subtracted from T_j. As long as the policing cost is believed to be less than $(\alpha^4/64c^2)\delta^{-1}(\overline{\sigma^{-1}} - \sigma_j)$, the pessimists prefer restrictions on quality.

For "optimistic" consumers the market solution is best even considering the social cost since consumers with $\sigma_j^{-1} > \overline{\sigma^{-1}}$ receive a subsidy from the others (Figure 12.1). For these consumers the cost of policing any restrictions is a dead loss, but we have not included the cost of policing in the formal model.

In other words, a consumer who believes that many people are seriously underestimating the risk will prefer to give up sovereignty and let government force everyone, including himself, to avoid the risk. The argument is strength-

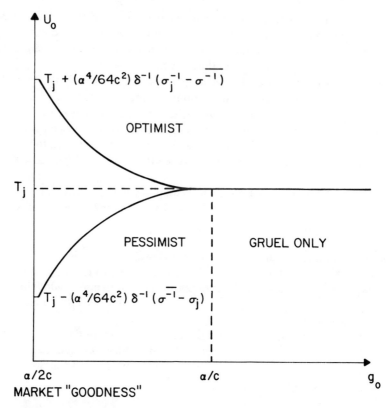

Figure 12.1. Indirect Utility Functions

ened if the consumer believes that there are individuals consuming lower quality ambrosia than he is, and as a consequence generating additional social costs.

MAJORITY-RULE CHOICE

Suppose that consumers are asked to vote for or against a referendum establishing a lower bound on the quality index $g = k^{-1}$, where the lower level g_0 is actually specified on the ballot.

In actual political life the mandate for regulation of free choice is determined by the legislative process and the specific restrictions are made by an agency of the executive. The political process is influenced by the industry to be regulated as well as agents of the regulatory bureaucracy and "citizen" groups. Nevertheless let us see what can be said for the simple majority rule social choice procedure.

The consumers who set $\sigma_j^{-1} < \overline{\sigma^{-1}}$ (pessimists) unanimously prefer setting $g_0 = \alpha/c$. If g is set at this level, all consumers abstain from ambrosia.

Any consumer in the group setting $\sigma_j^{-1} > \overline{\sigma^{-1}}$ (optimists) prefers the market solution $g = \alpha/2c$. If the number of pessimistic consumers is greater than the number of optimistic consumers, then a majority strictly prefers setting $g_0 = \alpha/c$ to the free market solution.

Suppose, however, that the level is not explicitly stated in the referendum. If pessimistic consumers expect the administered level will be high whereas the optimists expect it to be low, then a small minority of pessimists will be sufficient to push through the restrictions, especially if they are more politically active than the optimistic consumers who will be forced to substitute.

To be more specific, suppose that the political agents of the pessimists propose that the lower bound be set below the quality level in the market. Such a proposal will not generate opposition from the optimists unless they forecast what can follow. Once a lower bound is established in principle, future judicial or executive rulings can move up the level.

Rather than setting a lower level on g, suppose that it is proposed that the government provide quality information. Many people would prefer restrictions to governmental information dissemination because they believe that the government can police restrictions more effectively and efficiently than trying to get consumers to perceive the true quality of products, but for sake of argument assume that techniques can be devised wherein consumers set their subjective estimate of ambrosia contamination equal to the true rate k.

Recall, however, that there are two components of the $\sigma_j = \beta_j \kappa_j^2$ in the direct utility function. Setting $\kappa_j = 1$ for everyone will reduce the variance of the distribution of σ_j^{-1}, but for many σ_j^{-1} will still be set less than $\overline{\sigma^{-1}}$. If the pessimist believes that all consumers who underestimate k are sufficiently insensitive compared to him to have $\beta_j^{-1} < \overline{\beta^{-1}}$, then the increased information does not change his preference for g_0 limits. Moreover, if some of the optimists feel they are more sensitive than most, the increased knowledge will make them join the pessimists. Of course, the reverse can occur among the pessimists, but assume that individuals who overestimate k are more sensitive than the average and tend to reduce their k_j less than the increase in the k_j of those who underestimate k. Thus the readjustments in k_j do not result in a shift in preferences.

IMPLICATIONS OF A DECREASE IN THE MARGINAL COST ON POLITICAL PRESSURE

The model makes different implications for the effect of a decrease in the parameter c on the pressure to ban motivated by social cost reasons as compared with self-paternalistic motivations. Recall that the marginal cost has been assumed to be equal to cg for all firms, and as a result the market goodness of ambrosia is $\alpha/2c$. Suppose that a technological change results in a decrease in c. Then the market quality of ambrosia *increases*, which should lessen the pressure to ban from the self-paternalists.

If consumers behave according to the social cost model, then the pressure to ban *increases*. It is clear from Figure 12.1 that the difference in indirect utility for $g = \alpha/2c$ between optimists and pessimists increases as c decreases. The income redistribution through the insurance mechanism increases as the marginal cost decreases. The redistribution also increases as δ decreases, i.e., more of the total cost is compensated. In other words, as technology improves, product quality and social insurance become more widespread, and consumers who overestimate the risk or who are more sensitive to the risk than the average will have increased motivation to press for a total ban of the risky product.

NOTES

1. For an overview of federal safety regulation, see Cornell, Noll, and Weingast (1976).

2. Let us compare the competitive solution with a monopolist whose total cost function is cgQ, where Q is total demand, and who produces only one quality of ambrosia. The monopoly solution is found by maximizing the profit function $Q(p - cg)$. In the domain $p > a$ and $g > 0$, where it is clear from equation that demand Q is proportional to $(\alpha - p)g^2$ assuming that all consumers have the same α. The g which gives the maximum profit is $g = \alpha/2c$, the competitive solution. This result, assuming constant marginal cost, was derived from assumptions on the demand equation by Levhari and Peles (1973). The optimal price for the monopolist is $p = 3\alpha/4$ compared to $\alpha/2$ for the market.

3. The transmission of social cost through insurance is suggested by Calabresi (1970).

4. As δ, the fraction of the disutility which is not compensated by insurance, goes to zero, the premium goes to infinity. The premium is proportional to δ^{-1}. This is an extreme form of the moral hazard dilemma in insurance. As long as the psychic cost is not compensated, δ is not zero.

13 THE ENTRY PROBLEM IN A POLITICAL RACE

Steven J. Brams and Philip D. Straffin, Jr.

The two-party system has exhibited a remarkable stability in the United States and certain other countries. With the exception of recent work by William H. Riker (1976), however, no formal, rational-choice models have been developed to explain its persistence, or lack thereof.

Riker postulates two factors that may lead to the breakdown of a two-party system, given plurality voting in single-member constituencies. The first is *sophisticated voting*, under which supporters of a third party vote for the party that stands second in their preference order because they perceive their first choice, being the smallest party, cannot win. To try to prevent their least-preferred party from winning, they vote strategically for their second choice.

The second factor Riker postulates is *disillusioned voting*, under which some of the supporters of the largest party may vote for another party because their first choice is an oversized winning coalition. To maximize their individual gains in a zero-sum environment, they would prefer to be members of a smaller winning coalition.

Riker adduces several interesting conclusions about the rise and fall of third parties when both these factors are operative. In addition, he shows how these factors may have different consequences depending on the size of the party assumed to be in the middle of a postulated left–right ideological dimension along which three parties are arrayed.

Like Riker, we assume three—or more—parties (or candidates) can take positions on a left–right ideological dimension. Unlike Riker, however, we assume voting for parties/candidates is always *sincere*, by which we mean that citizens vote for the party/candidate whose position is closest to their most-preferred on this ideological dimension.

We shall henceforth speak only of candidates rather than parties since the subsequent analysis is at least as relevant to primary elections in which one's party is not a factor as to general elections in which it is. Among the conclusions we draw from the analysis is that if two candidates take positions on each side of the median of a left–right distribution of voters, and the number of voters between each and the median is the same but less than 1/6 of the electorate, there is *no position* on this dimension that a third candidate can take—whatever the distribution of voters is along the dimension—that ensures his victory. Quite the contrary: if plurality voting is used, one of the original two candidates will always win, though a third *and* fourth candidate could displace both the original candidates. Optimality calculations show that under certain conditions a third candidate can maximize his vote total by approaching his more moderate opponent, and win at the median if more than 2/3 of the electorate separate him from equidistant opponents on each side of the median. But probably the greatest barrier to his entry would be removed if approval voting—whereby a citizen can vote for as many candidates as he wishes—were adopted (Brams and Fishburn, 1978).

THE 1/3 SEPARATION OBSTACLE

In the basic model we assume the following:

1. There is a single left–right ideological dimension along which candidates take positions.
2. Each voter has a most-preferred position on this dimension.
3. Each voter has one vote and always casts it for the candidate whose position is closest to his most-preferred position.
4. The candidate with the most votes wins (plurality voting).

To begin the analysis, assume that there are two candidates, a liberal (L) and a conservative (C), whose positions on the left-right ideological dimension are known. Designate positions on this dimension by the real variable x, and assume voters are distributed over the interval $a \leqslant x \leqslant b$ according to continuous density function $f(x)$, where $f(x) > 0$ if $x \neq a$ and $x \neq b$.

Since $f(x)$ is assumed to be a continuous density function, $\int_a^b f(x)\,dx = 1$. Although we shall not give a probabilistic interpretation to $f(x)$, it is convenient to assume this kind of distribution of voters in order to be able to derive numerical results that indicate fractions of the total electorate falling between points on the left–right continuum.

Assume $x = M$ is the median of the distribution, $x = L$ is the position (as well as name) of the liberal candidate, where $a \leqslant L < M$, and $x = C$ is the position (as well as name) of the conservative candidate, where $M < C \leqslant b$. We shall now prove that if less than $1/3$ of the electorate lies between L and C—between each of whom and M there is the same (nonzero) number of voters—there is no position that a third candidate can take along the left-right dimension that is winning.

In other words, a third candidate cannot knock out *both* the original entrants and win the election if the original entrants straddle the median in such a way that less than $1/6$ of the electorate lies between each and the median. While we assume that the same number of voters (less than $1/6$) lie between M and L and between M and C, we assume nothing about the shape of the voter distribution except that $f(x)$ is always positive in the domain $a < x < b$. These results are summarized in

THEOREM 13.1: Let $x = L$ and $x = C$ be the positions of the liberal and conservative candidates, respectively, and let $x = M$ be the median of continuous density function $f(x) > 0$ that defines the distribution of voter positions over the interval $a < x < b$. If

$$0 < \int_L^M f(x)\,dx = \int_M^C f(x)\,dx \leqslant 1/6,$$

there is no position $x = X$ that some third candidate X can take that is winning.

Proof: For X to be winning, he must receive more votes than both L and C. There are four possible sets of positions he can take along the left–right continuum: (1) between a and L; (2) between L and C; (3) between C and b; (4) at L or C. Consider each in turn:

1. $a \leqslant X < L$: Clearly X maximizes his vote total by taking a position just to the left of L; any other position, closer to a, would mean that he would lose votes to L since some voters falling between them would be closer to L. But his vote total will always be less than C's because C will gain not only all the votes to his right (the same number as to the left of

L that X receives) but also some votes between L and C that X will not receive because L is just to his right.

2. $L < X < C$: Since the number of votes between L and C is less than $1/3$, L and C would receive more than $1/3$ of the vote and thereby both surpass the vote total of X.

3. $L < X \leqslant b$: Reasoning analogous to (1) above, but with left and right reversed.

4. $X = L$ or $X = C$: The candidate whose position X does *not* take would receive more than $1/3$ of the vote, whereas X and the candidate whose position he takes would split the remainder of the vote, each obtaining less than $1/3$.

Hence, there is no position $x = X$ that will ensure X more votes than one or both of the original entrants.   Q.E.D.

Note that X can always displace *either* L or C by taking a position just to his left or right, respectively. But in so doing, he always ensures the *other* original candidate some portion of the votes in the middle between L and C—in addition to those to his left or right—that makes the other candidate victorious.

Theorem 13.1 demonstrates that in a noncooperative three-person zero-sum game, a rational player may do worse by choosing a strategy after the other players, which is never true in two-person zero-sum games. In the particular spatial game we have described, the player choosing a position last will always lose, *vis-à-vis* at least one other player, if the conditions of the theorem are met.

It is easy to show that a relaxation of any of the conditions of the theorem could lead to a win for X. In particular:

1. If $\int_L^M f(x)\,dx = \int_M^L f(x)\,dx > 0$, i.e., if $L = M = C$, then X could take a position just to the left or right of the median and capture (essentially) $1/2$ of the vote, with L and M splitting the remaining $1/2$, or receiving $1/4$ each.

2. If $\int_L^M f(x)\,dx = \int_M^C f(x)\,dx > 1/6$, and the more than $1/3$ votes in the center between L and C were highly concentrated around a mode, X could capture (essentially) all of them by taking a position at the mode, with L and C receiving less than $1/3$ each.

3. If $\int_L^M f(x)\,dx \neq \int_M^C f(x)\,dx$, either the number of voters between a and L would be greater than the number between C and b or vice versa. Without loss of generality, assume the former is the case. Then by taking a position just to the left of L, X would receive more than $1/3$, and $L < 1/3$, of the vote. But X could also receive more votes than C, and hence win, if C captured too few votes in the center (e.g., because almost all voters in the center were closer to L than C) to augment the less than $1/3$ to his right.

Thus two candidates, equal numbers of voters distant from the median, cannot both be knocked out by a third candidate as long as they are separated by fewer than 1/3 of the electorate. The "1/3 separation obstacle," however, is no barrier to the displacement of both L and C should a fourth candidate Y also enter the race.

THEOREM 13.2:   Against two candidates L and C, there are always positions third and fourth candidates X and Y can take that ensure that either X or Y wins, unless L and C take positions such that the numbers of votes L or C gains to his left and right are exactly equal. In this case, X or Y can still at least tie L or C for the win.

Proof: Consider the positions of X and Y that are alongside L and C, respectively. Either X can gain more votes by being just to the left of L or just to his right, and similarly for Y with respect to C, unless the numbers of votes L or C gains to his left and right are exactly equal. Assume that X and Y choose such "straddling" positions to maximize their vote totals. (Since these straddling positions are essentially the positions of L and C, already known, maximization by X and Y is independent of the position the other new entrant takes, given that it is a straddling position.) Because these maximizing straddling positions result in X and Y candidates each receiving more votes than L and C, respectively, L and C will each be displaced by one of the two new entrants, one of whom necessarily wins.   Q.E.D.

Since it would obviously be extremely rare that L and C would occupy positions giving either an exactly equal number of votes to his left and right, Theorem 13.2 can be interpreted as saying that L and C can effectively be displaced by the entry of two new candidates. It might also be noted that even if the "exactly equal" condition were met, there may still be winning positions for X and Y. However, these winning positions will not necessarily be simple straddling positions.

In summary, we have shown that if two candidates' positions on each side of the median are separated from it by equal numbers of voters who together constitute less than 1/3 of the electorate, the candidates can collectively withstand the challenge of a third candidate but not the simultaneous challenge of a third and fourth candidate. These results are independent of the distribution of the voters on a left–right ideological dimension.

THE OPTIMAL POSITION OF A THIRD CANDIDATE

If a potential third candidate stands no chance of winning—as is the case under the conditions of Theorem 13.1—presumably he will not enter the race unless he desires to achieve goals other than winning. Given a new entrant's goal is to win, however, and his prospects for winning are not hopeless (i.e., one or more of the conditions of Theorem 13.1 is violated), where on the left–right continuum should he locate himself to maximize his vote total?

An example will illustrate the calculation the new entrant should make if he is rational with respect to the goal of winning. Assume voters are distributed according to the continuous density function $f(x) = 6(x - x^2)$, where $0 \leqslant x \leqslant 1$. This function, which is illustrated in Figure 13.1, defines the (unique) parabola, symmetric about a vertical axis, that passes through points $(0,0)$ and $(1,0)$ and whose area in the interval $0 \leqslant x \leqslant 1$ is $\int_0^1 6(x - x^2)\,dx = 1$.

As shown in Figure 13.1, assume $L = 0.2$ and $C = 0.7$. If X takes a position just to the left of L (for purposes of calculation, assume $X = 0.2$), his proportion of the total vote will be

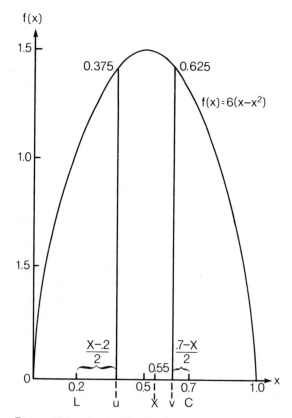

Figure 13.1. Voter Distribution

$$\int_0^{0.2} 6(x - x^2)\,dx = 6\left(\frac{x^2}{2} - \frac{x^3}{3}\right)\Bigg|_0^{0.2} = 0.104;$$

if he takes a position just to the right of C (for purposes of calculation, assume $X = 0.7$), his proportion of the total vote will be

$$\int_{0.7}^{1.0} 6(x - x^2)\,dx = 6\left(\frac{x^2}{2} - \frac{x^3}{3}\right)\Bigg|_{0.7}^{1.0} = 0.216.$$

To find the position in the middle between $L = 0.2$ and $C = 0.7$ that maximizes X's vote total, assume (as before) that citizens vote for the candidate whose position is closest to theirs. As can be seen from Figure 13.1, at any position between $x = 0.2$ and $x = 0.7$, citizens will vote for X in the interval $u \leqslant X \leqslant v$, where

$$u = 0.2 + \frac{X-0.2}{2} = \frac{X+0.2}{2}, \tag{13.1}$$

$$v = 0.7 - \frac{0.7-X}{2} = \frac{X+0.7}{2}. \tag{13.2}$$

The area under the curve in this interval is

$$A = \int_u^v f(x)\,dx,$$

which is at an extreme point when

$$\frac{dA}{dX} = f(v)\frac{dv}{dX} - f(u)\frac{du}{dX} = 0, \tag{13.3}$$

or

$$6\left[(v-v^2)\left(\frac{1}{2}\right) - (u-u^2)\left(\frac{1}{2}\right)\right] = 0,$$

$$3\left[(v-u) + (u^2-v^2)\right] = 0,$$

$$3(u-v)(u+v-1) = 0. \tag{13.4}$$

Substituting the expressions for u and v given by Equations (13.1) and (13.2) into Equation (13.4) yields

$$3(-0.25)\left(\frac{2X-1.1}{2}\right) = 0, \quad \text{or} \quad X = 0.55.$$

Since $d^2A/dX^2 = -3/4$, the extreme point is a maximum, and the number of voters is therefore maximized, when X's position is at $X = 0.55$.

Substituting this value into Equations (13.1) and (13.2), X wins all voters in the center of the distribution between $u = 0.375$ and $v = 0.625$. The proportion of the electorate in this interval is

$$\int_{0.375}^{0.625} 6(x - x^2)\,dx = 6\left(\frac{x^2}{2} - \frac{x^3}{3}\right)\bigg|_{0.375}^{0.625} = 0.3672.$$

Since L's proportion of the vote between 0 and 0.375 and C's proportion of the vote between 0.625 and 1 both equal 0.3164, X would win the election by taking a position at $X = 0.55$.

By comparison, we have seen that X would lose the election to C by taking a position to the left of L or by taking a position to the right of C. Hence, X's optimal (winning) position in the middle is at $X = 0.55$, where he captures approximately 37% of the vote.

This calculation can be generalized to yield the following result for a unimodal, symmetric distribution of voters:

THEOREM 13.3: Given a unimodal, symmetric distribution of voters, defined by density function $f(x)$, where $0 \leqslant x \leqslant 1$, X maximizes his vote total between L and C by taking a position on the same side of the median as his more "moderate" opponent (i.e., his opponent whose position is closer to the median $M = 0.5$).

Proof: From Equation (13.3), at an extreme point

$$f(v)\frac{dv}{dX} = f(u)\frac{du}{dX}.$$

But

$$\frac{du}{dX} = \frac{dv}{dX} = \frac{1}{2}$$

for any values of L and C in the equations that define u and v:

$$u = \frac{X+L}{2}; \quad v = \frac{X+C}{2}. \tag{13.5}$$

Hence,

$$f(u) = f(v)$$

at an extreme point, which is necessarily a maximum if the distribution is unimodal. Thus, X maximizes his vote total in the interval $L < X < C$ when $f(u) = f(v)$. Since the distribution is symmetric about the median $M = 0.5$,

$$0.5 - u = v - 0.5,$$

or, from Equations (13.5),

$$0.5 - \left(\frac{X+L}{2}\right) = \left(\frac{X+C}{2}\right) - 0.5,$$

$$X = 1 - \frac{C+L}{2}. \tag{13.6}$$

If L is more moderate than C, then $L > 1 - C$, or $L + C > 1$; from Equation (13.6), $X < 1/2$, so that X should locate on the same side of the median as L. If C is more moderate than L, then $L < 1 - C$, or $L + C < 1$; from Equation (13.6), $X > 1/2$, so that X should locate on the same side of the median as C. Thus, given a unimodal, symmetric distribution of voters, the optimal position of a candidate in the middle between L and C is on the same side of the median as the more moderate of L and C. Q.E.D.

Whereas Theorems 13.1 and 13.2 are essentially existence results that do not depend on the distribution of voters on a left–right ideological dimension, Theorem 13.3 is an optimality result that assumes a particular kind of voter distribution. In fact, for a unimodal, symmetric distribution, we know from Equation (13.6) that X maximizes his vote total between L and C when his position is at

$$X^* = 1 - \frac{C+L}{2}, \tag{13.7}$$

provided that C and L are such that $L < X^* < C$. Substituting X^* for X in Equation (13.5), we derive the following formulas for points on the 0–1 continuum between which voters who support maximizing candidate X fall:

$$u^* = \frac{1}{2} - \frac{C-L}{4}; \quad v^* = \frac{1}{2} + \frac{C-L}{4}. \tag{13.8}$$

We can describe geometrically the winning region for X in an L–C coordinate system. To do so, define the *left tertile* in terms of the area,

$$T = \int_0^t f(x)\, dx = \frac{1}{3},$$

that comprises the left 1/3 of the voter distribution given by density function

$f(x)$. In our previous example with the parabolic distribution, $t \approx 0.387$, or somewhat more than $1/3$ of the way along the 0-1 continuum.

Now X^* will be a winning position in the middle if

$$\int_{u*}^{v*} f(x)\, dx > \int_0^{u*} f(x)\, dx = \int_{v*}^1 f(x)\, dx;$$

this inequality will hold if $u^* < t$, or, from Equation (13.8),

$$\frac{1}{2} - \frac{C\text{-}L}{4} < t,$$

$$C - L > 2 - 4t. \qquad\qquad (13.9)$$

The conditions that X^* lie between L and C are $X^* < C$ or, from Equation (13.7),

$$1 - \frac{C\text{+}L}{2} < C,$$

$$2 - L < 3C; \qquad\qquad (13.10)$$

and $X^* > L$, or

$$1 - \frac{C\text{+}L}{2} > L,$$

$$2 - C > 3L. \qquad\qquad (13.11)$$

If either inequality (13.10) or (13.11) is violated, X^* is not between L and C. The optimal position for X between L and C would then be either just to the right of L or just to the left of C. Whether X would win there depends on the specific form of the distribution.

The region defined by these inequalities on the L-C coordinate system is shown by the shaded area in Figure 13.2. Note that the greater the value of t— that is, the more voters are concentrated in the middle—the closer the left boundary of this shaded area will be to the main diagonal, thereby expanding the region in which an optimal "middle" strategy by the third candidate will defeat L and C.

We previously showed (Theorem 13.1) that if L and C are separated from the median by equal numbers of voters who constitute less than $1/3$ of the electorate, there is no position a third candidate X can take that is winning, whatever the distribution of voters. We now turn this result around and ask how far apart L and C must be to *ensure* that X can always win in the middle. In general, the answer will depend on the distribution of voters, but for the case of a unimodal, symmetric distribution, there is a definite answer:

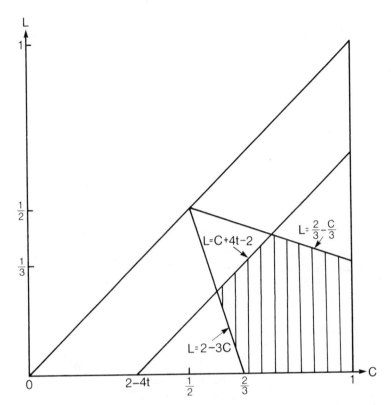

Figure 13.2.   Region in Which a Third Candidate, When between L and C, Can Win

THEOREM 13.4:   If $x = L$ and $x = C$ are the positions of the liberal and conservative candidates, and $f(x) > 0$ is a continuous, unimodal density function on $[a,b]$, symmetric about its median M, and

$$\int_{L}^{M} f(x)\,dx = \int_{M}^{C} f(x)\,dx \geqslant \frac{1}{3},$$

then a third candidate X can win at his optimal position $X^* = M$.

Proof: The symmetry assumption together with the assumption that $\int_{L}^{M} f(x)\,dx = \int_{M}^{C} f(x)\,dx$ imply that L and C are equidistant from M, so that $X^* = M$ is the optimal location for X. The unimodal assumption implies that the voter density is greatest at M and drops off to either side of M. Hence, the area under the curve between

$$u^* = \frac{X^*+L}{2} = \frac{M+L}{2}$$

and

$$v^* = \frac{X^*+C}{2} = \frac{M+C}{2}$$

is necessarily greater than one half the minimum area (2/3) assumed in the theorem to separate L and C:

$$\int_{(L+M)/2}^{(C+M)/2} f(x)\, dx > \frac{1}{2} \int_{L}^{C} f(x)\, dx \geqslant \left(\frac{1}{2}\right)\left(\frac{2}{3}\right) = \frac{1}{3}.$$

Consequently, X receives more than 1/3 of the total vote. Since L and C divide the remainder of the vote equally, each receives less than 1/3 and X wins. Q.E.D.

When the assumption of a unimodal, symmetric distribution is dropped, it is of course still possible to determine how a third candidate X should position himself in the center to maximize his vote total if the density function $f(x)$ is known. Yet, if $f(x)$ is not unimodal and symmetric, one cannot conclude that X should move closer to his more moderate opponent (Theorem 13.3), or that he can surely win if two thirds or more of the voters equally separate L and C from the median (Theorem 13.4).

With symmetry, unimodality, and L and C positioned equal distances from the extremes so as to include less than 1/6 of the voters, however, Theorem 13.4 tells us that X *can* be guaranteed a win at the median. In other words, the 1/3 separation *obstacle* of Theorem 13.1 turns into a 2/3 separation *opportunity* for the median candidate, given the symmetry and unimodality assumptions.

In the next section, we shall indicate some real-life implications of some of the theorems. In particular, Theorems 13.1 and 13.2 seem to suggest conditions under which two-party (or candidate) systems do and do not remain resistant to new entrants; Theorems 13.3 and 13.4 indicate how new entrants can best exploit the fixed positions of previously committed candidates. How the entry problem might change under approval voting will also be discussed.

IMPLICATIONS OF THE ANALYSIS

All the results in the paper assume that candidates take positions, defined by some ideological dimension, at points on the distribution of most-preferred voter positions. That there exists a single dimension underlying the most-preferred positions of citizens is, of course, a strong assumption, as is the assumption that citizens will vote sincerely for candidates whose position is closest to theirs. Nonetheless, certainly in some political races there is a single overriding issue, candidate positions on which determine the voting behavior of almost all citizens. In addition, though there is undoubtedly some sophisticated and disillusioned voting in most multicandidate races, in large electorates—as opposed, say, to legislatures or committees—sincere voting is probably much more common.

Given sincere voting in single-issue races, how likely is it that the conditions of Theorem 13.1 versus Theorem 13.4 are met? In presidential elections in the United States, the candidates of the two major parties usually take positions reasonably close to each other, the elections of 1964 and 1972 notwithstanding. Insofar as their positions from the median are separated by equal numbers of voters, then Theorem 13.1 says that a third candidate would have difficulty in positioning himself on the left–right dimension to capture a plurality of votes.

In fact, since 1900 only one third-party candidate (Theodore Roosevelt) has succeeded in defeating one of the two major-party candidates (William Howard Taft) in a presidential election, but Roosevelt lost decisively to the other major-party candidate (Woodrow Wilson). This occurred in the election of 1912; since then, only two third-party candidates (Robert La Follette in 1924 and George Wallace in 1968) have garnered more than 7% of the popular vote. Clearly, the national two-party system has been quite impervious to third-party challenges, though this fact may in part be attributable to the effects of the Electoral College, whose winner may not be the plurality winner. (Since 1900, however, the popular-vote and electoral-vote winners have been the same.)

Theorem 13.2 suggests the vulnerability of the two-party system to simultaneous challenges by third- and fourth-party candidates from both the left and right. In fact, such a two-pronged challenge occurred in the 1948 presidential election, when Henry Wallace's Progressive Party and Strom Thurmond's States' Rights Party each won 2.4% of the popular vote. However, since neither Wallace nor Thurmond mounted credible challenges to the two major-party candidates, they never seriously threatened the two-party system.

Presidential primaries, probably better than general elections, illustrate the optimal positioning of a third candidate in a political race (Brams, 1978). In the early 1976 Democratic primaries, for example, Morris Udall on the left and Henry Jackson on the right emerged as Jimmy Carter's most serious opposition. Although it is not clear that Carter, an early entrant in the 1976 race, anticipated such opposition, his positioning on a left–right dimension seems to have been nearly optimal in terms of the model. From the Massachusetts primary—in which Jackson finished first—onward, Carter probably stood closer to Jackson than Udall, who was generally perceived as his more ideological and less moderate opponent. By Theorem 13.3, this would enable Carter to capture most of the voters in the middle, which seems to have been exactly what he did. That his positioning did not meet the conditions of Theorem 13.4 in all primaries, however, is evidenced by the fact that he won pluralities in only 16 of the 27 primary states that had preference votes for delegates in 1976.

To be sure, the parameters of the model are not well defined in real campaigns. Our attempt here is only to suggest the plausibility of the results, not try to test them rigorously. Moreover, we want to stress that the model offers no explanation for the development of a competitive two-party system in the first place, which Riker's (1976) model—particularly his assumption about disillusioned voting—is useful in explaining. Rather, given two parties (or candidates), the model described here offers conditions for their persistence and breakdown in the face of possible challenges by new entrants who position themselves optimally on a left–right dimension.

As Theorem 13.1 demonstrates, there may be an entry problem for a candidate under plurality voting. By contrast, with approval voting, a third candidate can always position himself in the middle between the left and right candidates—however small the distance that separates them—and win by getting many

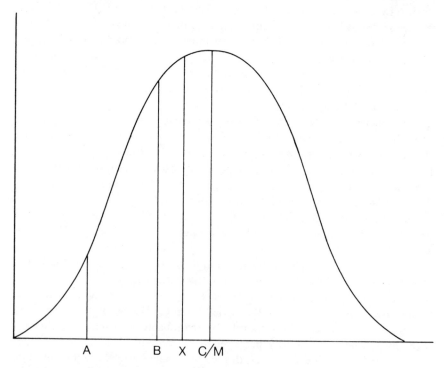

Figure 13.3. Multicandidate Race

second-place approval votes from most of their supporters. Thus, approval voting would seem to encourage the entry of new centrist candidates.

On the other hand, if there are already three or more candidates in a race—as is common in the early presidential primaries—the most centrist position may not be optimal, depending on how many candidates most voters approve of. For example, if voters support the two closest candidates, then given the positions of candidates A, B, and C (at the median M) in Figure 13.3, a fourth candidate X can maximize his approval-vote total by taking a position between B and C (as shown), picking up the support of all citizens whose first choice is C, and the support of most citizens whose first choice is B. This position is necessarily to the left of the median, where C is assumed located. By contrast, under plurality voting, X's optimal position would be just to C's right.

Clearly, if there are more than two candidates in a race, optimal positions of new entrants under plurality and approval voting require further investigation. The effects of these voting systems in encouraging centrist versus extremist candidates seem a particularly important aspect of these systems, given the long history of the two-party system in the United States and the fear expressed by some that approval voting would bring about its demise and possibly the election of extremist candidates. The model as developed so far suggests provisional support for the first contention but not for the second: approval voting would ease, if not eliminate, the entry problem of new candidates—and thereby perhaps weaken the two-party system—but the new candidates it would probably most help would be centrists.

REFERENCES

Aldrich, John H. (1980a). *Before the Convention: Strategies and Choices in Presidential Nomination Campaigns.* Chicago: University of Chicago Press.

—— (1980b). "A Dynamic Model of Presidential Nomination Campaigns." *American Political Science Review* 74 (forthcoming).

—— (1980c). "A Downsian Spatial Model with Party Activists." Working Paper No. 7, Michigan State University.

—— (1980d). "Do Parties Precipitate Electoral Realignments? Some Examples of Two-Dimensional Spatial Models with Party Activists." Mimeo, Michigan State University.

Aranson, Peter H. (1981). *American Government: Strategy and Choice.* Cambridge, Mass.: Winthrop.

Aranson, Peter H., and Peter C. Ordeshook (1972). "Spatial Strategies for Sequential Elections." In Richard G. Niemi and Herbert F. Weisberg (eds.), *Probability Models of Collective Decision Making.* Columbus: Charles E. Merrill, pp. 298–331.

—— (1977). "A Prolegomenon to a Theory of the Failure of Representative Democracy." In Richard D. Auster and Barbara Sears (eds.), *American Re-evolution: Papers and Proceedings.* Tucson: University of Arizona Department of Economics.

—— (1978). "The Political Bases of Public Sector Growth in a Representative

Democracy." Paper prepared for delivery at the annual convention of the American Political Science Association, Washington, D.C.

Arrow, Kenneth J. (1951). *Social Choice and Individual Values.* New York: Wiley.

—— (1963). *Social Choice and Individual Values,* 2nd ed. New Haven, Conn.: Yale University Press.

—— (1969). "Tullock and an Existence Theorem." *Public Choice 6:* 109–111.

Arrow, Kenneth J., and F.H. Hahn (1971). *General Competitive Analysis.* San Francisco: Holden-Day.

Aumann, Robert J. (1961). "The Core of a Cooperative Game without Side Payments." *Transactions of the American Mathematical Society* 98: 539–552.

—— (1967). "A Survey of Cooperative Games without Side Payments." In M. Shubik (ed.), *Essays in Mathematical Economics in Honor of Oskar Morgenstern.* Princeton, N.J.: Princeton University Press.

Aumann, Robert J., and B. Peleg (1974). "A Note on Gale's Example." *Journal of Mathematical Economics* 1: 209–211.

Beck, Paul Allen (1974). "A Socialization Theory of Partisan Realignment." In Richard G. Niemi et al., *The Politics of Future Citizens.* San Francisco: Jossey-Bass.

Bell, Colin E. (1978). "What Happens When Majority Rule Breaks Down? Some Probability Calculations." *Public Choice* 33: 121–127.

Bjurulf, Bo H., and Richard G. Niemi (1981). "Order-of-Voting Effects." In Manfred J. Holler (ed.), *Power, Voting, and Voting Power.* Wurzburg: Physica-Verlag.

Black, Duncan (1948). "On the Rationale of Group Decision Making." *Journal of Political Economy* 56: 23–34.

—— (1950). "The Unity of Political and Economic Science." *Economic Journal:* 506–514. (Reprinted in Martin Shubik [ed.], *Game Theory and Related Approaches to Social Behavior.* New York: John Wiley, pp. 110–120.)

—— (1958). *The Theory of Committees and Elections.* Cambridge: Cambridge University Press.

Black, Duncan, and R.A. Newing (1951). *Committee Decisions with Complementary Valuation.* Edinburgh: William Hodge.

Black's Law Dictionary, 5th ed. (1979). St. Paul: West.

Brams, Steven J. (1978). *The Presidential Election Game.* New Haven, Conn.: Yale University Press.

Brams, Steven J., and Morton D. Davis (1974). "The 3/2's Rule in Presidential Campaigning." *American Political Science Review* 68: 113–134.

—— (1975). "Comment." *American Political Science Review* 69: 155–161.

Brams, Steven J., Morton D. Davis, and Peter C. Fishburn (1978). "Approval Voting." *American Political Science Review* 72: 831–847.

Brown, D.J. (1973). "Acyclic Choice." Cowles Foundation, Yale University.

—— (1975). "Aggregation of Preferences." *Quarterly Journal of Economics* 89: 456–469.

Brown, D.J., and G. Heal (1979). "Equity, Efficiency and Increasing Returns." *Review of Economic Studies* 46: 571–585.

Buchanan, James, and Gordon Tullock (1962). *Calculus of Consent*. Ann Arbor: University of Michigan Press.

Calabresi, G. (1970). *The Costs of Accidents: A Legal and Economic Analysis*. New Haven, Conn.: Yale University Press.

Chambers, William Nisbet, and Walter Dean Burnham (1975). *The American Party Systems: Stages of Political Development*, 2nd ed. London: Oxford University Press.

Cohen, Linda (1979). "Cyclic Sets in Multidimensional Voting Models." *Journal of Economic Theory* 20: 1–12.

Cohen, Linda, and S. Matthews (1980). "Constrained Plott Equilibria, Directional Equilibria and Global Cyclic Sets." *Review of Economic Studies* 47: 975–986.

Colantoni, Claude S., Terrence J. Levesque, and Peter C. Ordeshook (1975a). "Campaign Resource Allocations under the Electoral College." *American Political Science Review* 69: 141–154.

—— (1975b). "Rejoinder." *American Political Science Review* 69: 155–161.

Condorcet, Marquis de (1785). *Essai sur l'application de l'analyse à la probabilité des decisions rendues a la pluralité des voix*. Paris: L'Imprimerie Royale.

Cornell, N., R. Noll, and B. Weingast (1976). "Safety Regulation." In C.E. Schultze (ed.), *Setting National Priorities*. Washington, D.C.: Brookings Institution.

Dahl, Robert (1956). *A Preface to Democratic Theory*. Chicago: University of Chicago Press.

Dasgupta, P., P. Hammond, and E. Maskin (1979). "The Implementation of Social Choice Rules: Some General Results on Incentive Compatibility." *Review of Economic Studies* 46: 185–216.

Dauer, Manning J., and Robert G. Kelsay (1955). "Unrepresentative States." *National Municipal Review* 44: 571–575.

David, Paul T., and Ralph Eisenberg (1961). *Devaluation of the Urban and Suburban Vote: A Statistical Investigation of Long-Term Trends in State Legislative Representation*. Charlottesville: Bureau of Public Administration, University of Virginia Press.

Davis, Otto, and Melvin Hinich (1966). "A Mathematical Model of Policy Formation in a Democratic Society." In J. Bernd (ed.), *Mathematical Applications in Political Science*. Dallas: Southern Methodist University Press.

Davis, Otto, Melvin Hinich, and Peter Ordeshook (1970). "An Expository Development of a Mathematical Model of the Electoral Process." *American Political Science Review* 64: 426–428.

Debreu, G. (1970). "Economies with a Finite Set of Equilibria." *Econometrica* 38: 387–392.

—— (1976). "The Application to Economics of Differential Topology and Global Analysis: Regular Differentiable Economics." *American Economic Review* 66: 280–287.

Demsetz, Harold (1965). "Minorities in the Market Place." *North Carolina Law Review* 43: 271–297.

Derge, David (1958). "Metropolitan and Outstate Alignments in the Illinois and

Missouri Legislative Delegations." *American Political Science Review* 53: 1051–1065.

Dodd, L.C. (1977). "Congress and the Quest for Power." In L.C. Dodd and B.I. Oppenheimer (eds.), *Congress Reconsidered.* New York: Praeger.

Downs, Anthony (1957). *An Economic Theory of Democracy.* New York: Harper.

Drèze, J., and D. de la Vallée Poussin (1971). "A Tâtonnement Process for Public Goods." *Review of Economic Studies* 38: 133–150.

Duignan, P., and A. Rabushka, eds. (1980). *The United States in the 1980's.* Stanford, Calif.: Hoover Institution.

Dutta, Bhaskar, and Prasanta K. Pattanaik (1978). "On Nicely Consistent Voting Systems." *Econometrica* 46: 163–170.

Dye, Thomas R. (1965). "Malapportionment and Public Policy in the States." *Journal of Politics* 27: 586–601.

Eliot, T.S. (1940). *The Idea of a Christian Society.* New York: Harcourt Brace.

Eulau, Heinz, et al. (1959). "The Role of the Representative: Some Empirical Observations on the Theory of Edmund Burke." *American Political Science Review* 53: 741–756.

Fama, Eugene F., and Merton H. Miller (1972). *The Theory of Finance.* Hinsdale, Ill.: Dryden.

Farquharson, R. (1969). *Theory of Voting.* New Haven, Conn.: Yale University Press.

Ferejohn, John A., and David M. Grether (1978). "Some New Impossibility Theorems." *Public Choice* 30: 35–42.

Ferejohn, John A., Morris P. Fiorina, and Edward W. Packel (1980). "Non-equilibrium Solutions for Legislative Systems." *Behavioral Science* 25: 140–148.

Fiorina, Morris P. (1977). *Congress: Keystone of the Washington Establishment.* New Haven, Conn.: Yale University Press.

Fiorina, Morris P., and Charles R. Plott (1978). "Committee Decisions under Majority Rule: An Experimental Study." *American Political Science Review* 72: 575–598.

Fishburn, Peter (1973). *The Theory of Social Choice.* Princeton, N.J.: Princeton University Press.

Frederickson, George H., and Yong Hyo Cho (1974). "Legislative Apportionment and Fiscal Policy in the American States." *Western Political Quarterly* 27: 5–37.

Frohlich, Norman, Joe A. Oppenheimer, and Oren R. Young (1971). *Political Leadership and Collective Goods.* Princeton, N.J.: Princeton University Press.

Fry, Brian R., and Richard F. Winters (1970). "The Politics of Redistribution." *American Political Science Review* 64: 508–522.

Gale, D. (1974). "Exchange Equilibrium and Coalitions: An Example." *Journal of Mathematical Economics* 1: 63–66.

Gibbard, Alan (1973). "Manipulation of Voting Schemes: A General Result." *Econometrica* 41: 587–601.

Gödel, K. (1962). *On Formally Undecidable Propositions.* New York: Basic Books. (Translated from "Über Formal Unentscheidbare Sätze der Principia Mathematica und Verwandter Systems, 1." *Monatshefte für Mathematik und Physik* 38: 173–198 [1931].)

Goldberg, Arthur S. (1968). "Political Science as Science." In Robert Dahl and Deane Neubauer (eds.), *Readings in Modern Political Analysis.* Englewood Cliffs, N.J.: Prentice-Hall, pp. 15–30.

Grandmont, J.-M. (1978). "Intermediate Preferences and the Majority Rule." *Econometrica* 46: 627–636.

Greenberg, J. (1979). "Consistent Majority Rules over Compact Sets of Alternatives." *Econometrica* 47: 627–636.

Groves, Theodore, and John Ledyard (1977). "Optimal Allocation of Public Goods: A Solution to the 'Free Rider' Problem." *Econometrica* 45: 783–809.

Guesnerie, R., and J.-J. Laffont (1978). "Advantageous Reallocations of Initial Resources." *Econometrica* 46: 835–841.

—— (1981). "On the Robustness of Strategy Proof Mechanisms." Mimeo, CEPREMAP, Toulouse.

Hanson, Roger A., and Robert E. Crew, Jr. (1973). "The Policy Impact of Reapportionment." *Law and Society Review* 69: 69–93.

Harsanyi, John C. (1978). "A Solution Theory for Noncooperative Games and Its Implications for Cooperative Games." In Peter C. Ordeshook (ed.), *Game Theory and Political Science.* New York: New York University Press, pp. 39–97.

Hart, H.L.A. (1979). "Between Utility and Rights." In Alan Ryan (ed.), *The Idea of Freedom.* Oxford: Oxford University Press.

Hibbs, Douglas A., Jr. (1977). "Political Parties and Macroeconomic Policy." *American Political Science Review* 71: 1467–1487.

—— (1979). "The Mass Public and Macroeconomic Performance: The Dynamics of Public Opinion toward Unemployment and Inflation." *American Journal of Political Science* 23: 705–731.

Hinich, Melvin J., and Peter C. Ordeshook (1974). "The Electoral College: A Spatial Analysis." *Political Methodology* (Summer): 1–29.

Hofferbert, Richard J. (1966). "The Relation between Public Policy and Some Structural and Environmental Variables in the American States." *American Political Science Review* 60: 73–82.

Hofstadter, Douglas R. (1979). *Gödel, Escher, Bach: An Eternal Golden Braid.* New York: Basic Books.

Hurwicz, Leonid (1972). "On Informationally Decentralized Systems." In R. Radner and C. McGuire (eds.), *Decision and Organization.* Amsterdam: North-Holland.

Jacob, Herbert (1964). "The Consequences of Malapportionment: A Note of Caution." *Social Forces* 43: 256–261.

Joyce, Ralph C. (1976). "Sophisticated Voting for Three Candidate Contests under the Plurality Rule." Unpublished doctoral dissertation, University of Rochester.

Kalai, E., A. Postlewaite, and J. Roberts (1979). "A Group Incentive Compatible Mechanism Yielding Core Allocations." *Journal of Economic Theory* 20: 13–22.

Kazman, Sam (1976). "The Economics of the 1974 Federal Election Campaign Act Amendments." *Buffalo Law Review* 25: 516–543.

Key, V. O., Jr. (1955). "A Theory of Critical Elections." *Journal of Politics* 17: 3–18.

Keynes, John Maynard (1936). *The General Theory of Employment, Interest and Money.* New York: Harcourt, Brace.

Kolakowski, Leszek (1968). "In Praise of Inconsistency." In Kolakowski, *Toward a Marxist Humanism.* New York: Grove Press.

Kolb, Klaus (1980). "Political Control of the West German Economy." Seniors honors thesis, Department of Political Science, Michigan State University.

Kornai, J. (1971). *Anti-equilibrium.* New York: Elsevier.

Kramer, G.H. (1972). "Sophisticated Voting over Multidimensional Choice Spaces." *Journal of Mathematical Sociology* 2: 165–181.

—— (1973). "On a Class of Equilibrium Conditions for Majority Rule." *Econometrica* 41: 285–297.

—— (1977). "A Dynamical Model of Political Equilibrium." *Journal of Economic Theory* 16: 310–334.

—— (1978). "Existence of Electoral Equilibrium." In Peter C. Ordeshook (ed.), *Game Theory and Political Science.* New York: New York University Press, pp. 375–391.

Kramer, G.H., and A.K. Klevorick (1974). "Existence of a 'Local' Cooperative Equilibrium in a Class of Voting Games." *Review of Economic Studies* 41: 539–547.

Laing, J.D., and S. Olmstead (1978). "An Experimental and Game-Theoretic Study of Committees." In Peter C. Ordeshook (ed.), *Game Theory and Political Science.* New York: New York University Press.

Leffler, Keith B. (1978). "Minimum Wages, Welfare, and Transfer Payments to the Poor." *Journal of Law and Economics* 21: 345–358.

Leijonhufvud, A. (1968). *On Keynesian Economics and the Economics of Keynes.* New York: Oxford University Press.

Levhari, D., and Y. Peles (1973). "Market Structure, Quality and Durability." *Bell Journal of Economics and Management Science* 4: 235–248.

Lockard, Duane (1963). *The Politics of State and Local Government.* New York: Macmillan.

Lucas, J.R. (1961). "Minds, Machines and Gödel." In A.R. Anderson (ed.), *Minds and Machines.* Englewood Cliffs, N.J.: Prentice-Hall, pp. 43–59.

Lucas, William F. (1969). "The Proof That a Game May Not Have a Solution." *Transactions of the American Mathematical Society* 137: 219–230.

Luce, R. Duncan, and Howard Raiffa (1957). *Games and Decisions.* New York: John Wiley.

McCracken, P. (1977). *Towards Full Employment and Price Stability.* Paris: OECD.

MacCrae, C. Duncan (1977). "A Political Model of Business Cycles." *Journal of Political Economy* 85: 239–63.

McKelvey, Richard D. (1976). "Intransitivities in Multidimensional Voting Models and Some Implications for Agenda Control." *Journal of Economic Theory* 12: 472–482.

—— (1977). "Constructing Majority Paths between Arbitrary Points: A Solution to the Agenda Design Problem for Quadratic Preferences." Paper presented at the annual meeting of the American Economic Association, New York.

—— (1978). "A Theory of Optimal Agenda Design." Paper presented at the Conference on Political Science and the Study of Public Policy, Hickory Corners, Mich.

—— (1979). "General Conditions for Global Intransitivities in Formal Voting Models." *Econometrica* 47: 1085–1111.

McKelvey, Richard D., and Peter C. Ordeshook (1976). "Symmetric Spatial Games without Majority Rule Equilibrium." *American Political Science Review* 70: 1171–1184.

McKelvey, Richard D., and Richard G. Niemi (1978). "A Multistage Game Representation of Sophisticated Voting for Binary Procedures." *Journal of Economic Theory* 18: 1–22.

Manley, John F. (1973). "The Conservative Coalition in Congress." *American Behavioral Scientist* 17: 233–247.

Marx, Karl (1906). *Capital,* Vol. 1. New York: Modern Library.

Maskin, E. (1978). "Implementation and Strong Nash Equilibrium." Mimeo, Massachusetts Institute of Technology.

Matthews, S. (1977). "Undominated Directions in Simple Dynamic Games." Social Science Working Paper No. 169, California Institute of Technology.

—— (1978). "Pairwise Symmetry Conditions for Voting Equilibria." Social Science Working Paper No. 202, California Institute of Technology. (Forthcoming in *International Journal of Game Theory.*)

—— (1980). "Local Simple Games." Northwestern University.

Mayhew, David (1974). *Congress: The Electoral Connection.* New Haven, Conn.: Yale University Press.

Mill, John Stuart (1849). *On Liberty.* New York: New American Library.

Miller, Nicholas R. (1977). "Graph-Theoretical Approaches to the Theory of Voting." *American Journal of Political Science* 21: 769–803.

Mills, C. Wright (1951). *The Power Elite.* New York: Oxford University Press.

Nakamura, K. (1978). "The Vetoers in a Simple Game with Ordinal Preferences." *International Journal of Game Theory* 8: 55–61.

Nash, John F. (1951). "Non-cooperative Games." *Annals of Mathematics* 54: 286–295.

Newcomer, Kathryn E., and Richard J. Hardy (1980). "Analyzing Political Impact: Selection of a Linear Trend Model." *Policy Studies Journal* 8: 928–941.

Niemi, Richard G., and John Deegan, Jr. (1978). "A Theory of Political Districting." *American Political Science Review* 72: 1302–1323.

Nikaido, Hukukane (1968). *Convex Structures and Economic Theory.* New York: Academic Press.

Nordhaus, William D. (1975). "The Political Business Cycle." *Review of Economic Statistics* 42: 169–190.

Olson, Mancur, Jr. (1971). *The Logic of Collective Action: Public Goods and the Theory of Groups,* rev. ed. New York: Schocken.

Ordeshook, Peter C. (1980). "Political Disequilibrium and Scientific Inquiry." *American Political Science Review* 74: 447–450. (Reprinted in this volume.)

Ornstein, Norman, and David Rohde (1974). "The Strategy of Reform: Recorded Teller Voting in the U.S. House of Representatives." Paper presented at the annual meeting of the Midwest Political Science Association, Chicago.

—— (1975). "Senority and Future Power in Congress." In Norman Ornstein (ed.), *Congress in Change.* New York: Praeger, pp. 72–87.

—— (1977). "Shifting Forces, Changing Rules and Political Outcomes: The Impact of Congressional Change on Four House Committees." In Robert Peabody and Nelson Polsby (eds.), *New Perspectives on the House of Representatives,* 3rd ed. Chicago: Rand McNally, pp. 186–269.

Orosel, G.O. (1974). "A Paradox of the Market Mechanism." *Journal of Political Economy* 82: 202–209.

Page, Benjamin I. (1978). *Choices and Echoes in Presidential Elections.* Chicago: University of Chicago Press.

Paine, Thomas (1953). "Dissertation on First Principles of Government." In *Paine.* Indianapolis: Bobbs-Merrill.

Pareto, Vilfredo (1971). *Manual of Political Economy.* Translated by Ann S. Schwier. New York: Augustus M. Kelley.

Peleg, Bezalel (1978). "Consistent Voting Systems." *Econometrica* 46: 153–161.

Plamenatz, John (1973). *Democracy and Illusion.* London: Longman Group.

Plott, Charles R. (1967). "A Notion of Equilibrium and Its Possibility under Majority Rule." *American Economic Review* 67: 787–806.

—— (1976). "Axiomatic Social Choice Theory: An Overview and Interpretation." *American Journal of Political Science* 20: 511–596.

Plott, Charles R., and Michael E. Levine (1978). "A Model of Agenda Influence on Committee Decisions." *American Economic Review* 68: 146–160.

Posner, Richard A. (1977). *Economic Analysis of Law,* 2nd ed. Boston: Little, Brown.

Prigogine, I. (1980). *From Being to Becoming: Time and Complexity in the Physical Sciences.* San Francisco: W.H. Freeman.

Pulsipher, Allan G., and Jack Weatherby, Jr. (1968). "Malapportionment, Party Competition, and the Functional Distribution of Government Expenditures." *American Political Science Review* 62: 1207–1219.

Radner, R. (1968). "Competitive Equilibrium under Uncertainty." *Econometrica* 36: 31–58

Rae, Douglas (1975). "Limits of Consensual Decision." *American Political Science Review* 69: 1270–1294.

—— (1980). "An Altimeter for Mr. Escher's Stairway." *American Political Science Review* 74: 451–455. (Reprinted in this volume.)

Riker, William H. (1961). "Voting and the Summation of Preferences." *American Political Science Review* 55: 900–911.

—— (1962). *The Theory of Political Coalitions.* New Haven, Conn.: Yale University Press.

—— (1965a). *Democracy in the United States,* 2nd ed. New York: Macmillan.

—— (1965b). "Some Ambiguities in the Notion of Power." *American Political Science Review* 57: 341–349.

—— (1976). "The Number of Political Parties: A Reexamination of Duverger's Law." *Comparative Politics* 9: 93–106.

—— (1977). "The Future of a Science in Politics." *American Behavioral Scientist* 21: 11–38.

—— (1978). "A Confrontation between the Theory of Democracy and the Theory of Social Choice." Paper presented at the annual meeting of the American Political Science Association, New York.

—— (1980a). "Implications from the Disequilibrium of Majority Rule for the Study of Institutions." *American Political Science Review* 74: 432–446. (Reprinted in this volume.)

—— (1980b). *Liberalism against Populism.* San Francisco: W.H. Freeman.

Riker, William H., and P.C. Ordeshook (1973). *An Introduction to Positive Political Theory.* Englewood Cliffs, N.J.: Prentice-Hall.

Robertson, Dennis (1976). *A Theory of Party Competition.* New York: John Wiley.

Rubinstein, Ariel (1979). "A Note about the 'Nowhere Denseness' of Societies Having an Equilibrium under Majority Rule." *Econometrica* 47: 511–514.

Salisbury, Robert H. (1969). "An Exchange Theory of Interest Groups." *Midwest Journal of Political Science* 13: 1–32.

Samuelson, Paul A. (1954). "The Pure Theory of Public Expenditure." *Review of Economics and Statistics* 36: 387–389.

—— (1965). "Proof That Properly Anticipated Prices Fluctuate Randomly." *Industrial Management Review* 6: 41–49.

—— (1967). "Arrow's Mathematical Politics." In Sidney Hook (ed.), *Human Values and Economic Policy.* New York: New York University Press, pp. 41–53.

—— (1973). "Proof That Properly Discounted Present Values of Assets Vibrate Randomly." *Bell Journal of Economics and Management Science* 4: 369–374.

Satterthwaite, Mark A. (1975). "Strategy-Proofness and Arrow's Conditions: Existence and Correspondence Theorems for Voting Procedures and Social Welfare Functions." *Journal of Economic Theory* 10: 187–217.

Satterthwaite, Mark A., and H. Sonnenschein (1979). "Strategy-Proof Allocation Mechanism." Mimeo, Northwestern University.

Scarf, Herbert (1960). "Some Examples of Global Instability of the Competitive Equilibrium." *International Economic Review* 1: 157–172.

—— (1971). "On the Existence of a Cooperative Solution for a General Class of N-Person Games." *Journal of Economic Theory* 3: 169–181.

Schattschneider, E.E. (1963). *Politics, Pressures, and the Tariff: A Study of Free Private Enterprise in Pressure Politics, as Shown in the 1929-1930 Revision of the Tariff.* Hamden, Conn.: Archon.

Schofield, Norman (1977a). "Transitivity of Preferences on a Smooth Manifold." *Journal of Economic Theory* 14: 148–172.
—— (1977b). "Dynamic Games of Collective Action." *Public Choice* 30: 77–104.
—— (1978). "Instability of Simple Dynamic Games." *The Review of Economic Studies* 45: 575–594.
—— (1980a). "Generic Properties of Simple Bergson-Samuelson Welfare Functions." *Journal of Mathematical Economics* 7: 175–192.
—— (1980b). "Catastrophe Theory and Dynamic Games." *Quality and Quantity* 14: 519–545.
—— (1980c). "Equilibrium in a Political Economy." In P. Whiteley (ed.), *Models of Political Economy*. London: Sage.
—— (1981a). "Equilibria in Simple Dynamic Games." In M. Salles and P. Pattanaik (eds.), *Social Choice and Welfare*. Amsterdam: North-Holland.
—— (1981b). "Equilibrium and Cycles in Voting on Compacta: On the Relevance of the General Impossibility Theorem." Economics Discussion Paper No. 173, University of Essex.
—— (1981c). "Generic Instability of Simple Majority Rule." Economics Discussion Paper No. 174, University of Essex.
—— (1981d). "Political and Economic Equilibrium on a Manifold." Economics Discussion Paper No. 177, University of Essex.
—— (1981e). "Social Choice and Democracy." Mimeo, University of Essex.
Schubert, Glendon, and Charles Press (1964a). "Malapportionment Remeasured." *American Political Science Review* 57: 578–580.
—— (1964b). "Measuring Malapportionment." *American Political Science Review* 57: 302–327.
Selten, R. (1975). "Reexamination of the Perfectness Concept for Equilibrium Points in Extensive Games." *International Journal of Game Theory* 4: 25–55.
Sen, Amartya K. (1966). "A Possibility Theorem on Majority Decisions." *Econometrica* 34: 491–499.
—— (1970). *Collective Choice and Social Welfare*. San Francisco: Holden-Day.
Sen, Amartya K., and P.K. Pattanaik (1969). "Necessary and Sufficient Conditions for Rational Choice and Majority Decision." *Journal of Economic Theory* 1: 178–202.
Shafer, W., and H. Sonnenschein (1975). "Equilibrium in Abstract Economies without Ordered Preferences." *Journal of Mathematical Economics* 2: 345–348.
Shapley, Lloyd S. (1953). "A Value for N-Person Games." In H.W. Kuhn and A.W. Tucker (eds.), *Contributions to the Theory of Games*. Princeton, N.J.: Princeton University Press. (Annals of Mathematics Studies, No. 28.)
Shapley, Lloyd S., and Martin Shubik (1954). "A Method for Evaluating the Distribution of Power in a Committee System." *American Political Science Review* 48: 787–792.
Shepsle, Kenneth A. (1978). "Institutional Structure and Policy Choice: Some Comparative Statics of Amendment Control Procedures." Paper presented at the Conference on Political Science and the Study of Public Policy, Hickory

Corners, Mich., and at the annual meeting of the American Political Science Association, New York.

—— (1979a). "Institutional Arrangements and Equilibrium in Multidimensional Voting Models." *American Journal of Political Science* 23: 27–60.

—— (1979b). "The Role of Institutional Structure in the Creation of Policy Equilibrium." In Douglas W. Rae and Theodore J. Eismeier (eds.), *Public Policy and Public Choice*. Beverly Hills, Calif.: Sage, pp. 249–281.

Sloss, Judith (1971). *Stable Points of Directional Preference Relations*. Technical Report No. 71-7, Stanford University.

—— (1973). "Stable Outcomes in Majority Voting Games. *Public Choice* 15: 19–48.

Slutsky, S.A. (1977). "A Voting Model for the Allocation of Public Goods: Existence of an Equilibrium." *Journal of Economic Theory* 14: 299–325.

—— (1979). "Restricted Voting Equilibria in Multidimensional Spaces." Department of Economics, Cornell University.

Stone, Bernell K. (1975). "The Conformity of Stock Values Based on Discounted Dividends to a Fair-Return Process." *Bell Journal of Economics* 6: 698–702.

Student Note (1972). "Equalization of Municipal Services: The Economics of Serrano and Shaw." *Yale Law Journal* 82: 89–124.

Sundquist, James L. (1973). *Dynamics of Party Systems*. Washington, D.C.: Brookings Institution.

Tiebout, Charles M. (1956). "A Pure Theory of Local Expenditures." *Journal of Political Economy* 64: 416–424.

Tufte, Edward R. (1978). *Political Control of the Economy*. Princeton, N.J.: Princeton University Press.

Tullock, Gordon (1967). "The General Irrelevance of the General Impossibility Theorem." In Tullock, *Towards a Mathematics of Politics*. Ann Arbor: University of Michigan Press, Chap. 3.

—— (1975). "The Transitional Gains Trap." *Bell Journal of Economics* 6: 671–678.

Turnovsky, Stephen J. (1977). *Macroeconomic Analysis and Stabilization Policy*. Cambridge: Cambridge University Press.

Wagner, Richard E. (1969). "Pressure Groups and Political Entrepreneurs: A Review Article." *Papers on Non-market Decision Making* 1: 151–170.

Weber, Max (1950). *Natural Right and History*. Chicago: University of Chicago Press.

Weingast, Barry R., Kenneth A. Shepsle, and Christopher Johnson (1981). "The Political Economy of Benefits and Costs: A Neoclassical Approach to the Politics of Distribution." *Journal of Political Economy* 89: 642–665.

Weintraub, E. Roy (1979). *Microfoundations: The Compatibility of Microeconomics and Macroeconomics*. Cambridge: Cambridge University Press.

LIST OF CONTRIBUTORS

JOHN H. ALDRICH, Professor of Political Science, University of Minnesota

PETER H. ARANSON, Professor of Economics and Research Associate of the Law and Economics Center, Emory University

STEVEN J. BRAMS, Professor of Politics, New York University

JOHN A. FEREJOHN, Professor of Political Science, California Institute of Technology

MORRIS P. FIORINA, Professor of Political Science, California Institute of Technology

ARTHUR Q. FRANK, Assistant Professor of Political Science, University of Rochester

DAVID M. GRETHER, Professor of Economics, California Institute of Technology

MELVIN J. HINICH, Professor of Economics, Virginia Polytechnic Institute and State University

209

RICHARD D. MCKELVEY, Professor of Political Science, California Institute of Technology

RICHARD G. NIEMI, Professor of Political Science, University of Rochester

PETER C. ORDESHOOK, Professor of Political Science, Carnegie-Mellon University

DOUGLAS RAE, Professor of Political Science, Yale University

WILLIAM H. RIKER, Professor of Political Science, University of Rochester

DAVID W. ROHDE, Professor of Political Science, Michigan State University

NORMAN SCHOFIELD, Reader in Economics, University of Essex

KENNETH A. SHEPSLE, Professor of Political Science and Research Associate of the Center for the Study of American Business, Washington University

PHILIP D. STRAFFIN, Jr., Associate Professor of Mathematics, Beloit College